BEHAVIOR AND PSYCHOLOGICAL
MAN

BEHAVIOR AND PSYCHOLOGICAL MAN

Essays in Motivation and Learning

BY EDWARD CHACE TOLMAN

UNIVERSITY OF CALIFORNIA PRESS

Berkeley and Los Angeles · 1966

University of California Press
Berkeley and Los Angeles
California

Cambridge University Press
London, England

Originally published as
Collected Papers in Psychology
by Edward Chace Tolman

Fourth printing, 1966

Printed in the United States of America

FOREWORD

[This foreword was prepared from suggestions and comments of several of Professor Tolman's colleagues and students. It is hoped that what it lacks in coherent style because of this mongrel parentage is compensated for by the variety and vitality of its understanding and appreciation.]

THIS COLLECTION of papers by Edward Chace Tolman, sponsored by a group of his former students and present colleagues, is not only an appropriate commemoration of his more than thirty years at the University of California but an important psychological document which shows the development of his systematic theory from its early neonatal stirrings to its later more consolidated but still-maturing phases. The development of a system has more than historical interest. It throws light on the very processes by which knowledge is expanded, integrated, and given meaning.

Tolman's complete bibliography contains over eighty items. The problem of selection was therefore a considerable one. Since it was felt, however, that he himself was in the best position to make the most meaningful and useful selection, he was persuaded to pick out the articles which to him meant steps in the development of his theoretical system. The result can best be characterized as a "Progress Report." Tolman is a system builder who not only theorizes, but also experiments. This means that his work is never done. He is constantly accumulating new data in his own laboratories and studying the data of other workers. He is continually adding and subtracting concepts, revising propositions, reorganizing ideas, and manipulating them creatively to see what new gestalten they might form. Tolman's now classical *Purposive Behavior in Animals and Men* was published in 1932. But that book was a milestone, not a capstone, for he has continued to expand, revise, and reformulate his system; and these papers, which include several systematic articles written before the book's publication, should enable the reader to glimpse, with Tolman, the nature of the changes which take place in a systematic purposive behaviorism as it is modified to encompass the data of an expanding field.

This collection of papers is not only as a significant scientific publication, but also a revealing human document. Tolman is one of those rare beings among system builders who has a sense of humor about himself and his theorizing. System building for him is not a grim business. It is a happy, gay, creative activity, and his papers express all of this to the full. No matter what the subject, how abstract the treatment, his wit, humor, magnanimity, and tolerance are written into each analysis. He is constitutionally incapable of writing dogmatically or of publishing a polemic. The papers in the present book not only trace explicitly the history of significant ideas but also portray a person with grace.

Tolman's system is characterized by two major attributes: the first of these is the breadth and all-inclusiveness of his psychology. Above all else, he has insisted that behavior is multidetermined and that an adequate system must encompass *all* psychological data. He believes that a theorist's job is to try to describe and account for the entire field which lies within his discipline, and not to restrict it arbitrarily to the more amenable areas. Tolman has never been interested in writing a "small scientific theoretical system"— he has always sought the complete formulation. This has meant the witting rejection of attempting finalistic formulation at this stage of the science, and the characteristically cheerful acceptance of a programmatic role.

The second major characteristic of Tolman's system building—his use of intervening variables and other hypothetical constructs—has been decisive in forcing theorizing in psychology out of peripheralism and into centralism. The genius of his theorizing lies in his clear understanding that attempts to deal with correlations between stimulus field and resulting behavior can be understood only in terms of postulated intervening variables, hypothetical constructs, dynamic central processes. The problem of science, for him, is not that of seeking correlations but of seeking the systematic meaning of the observed correlations.

The papers in this volume testify to Tolman's respect for the multifaceted data of psychology. Some give the impression that Tolman is primarily a learning theorist; others, that he is primarily concerned with the problems of motivation; still others, with the problem of perception, or clinical experience, or with social psychological problems. If these papers are analyzed in terms of theoretical approaches rather than in terms of problems, a similar breadth is seen, for in some of them are overtones of Gestalttheorie; in others, of behaviorism, or of operationalism, or of purposivism, or of Freudianism. And yet, when all the papers have been read, one cannot leave this collection without a feeling of closure, of having read through a carefully thought-out, consistent, provocative, and original integration of concepts—in other words, a scientific system.

Although Tolman is a psychologist who is interested in all behavior and all psychological problems, his experimental work has been confined primarily to the rat; so it is perhaps appropriate to add here a parenthetical note about him as a "rat psychologist." His use of rats for the experimental mediation of theoretical problems in part reflects the era in which he developed as a psychologist; in part, it represents his own strong belief that the concept which cannot be studied by natural-science methods and demonstrated in lower animals is not a useful or valid concept for a basic science of behavior. And like the anthropologist who establishes his basic principles through the study of relatively simple primitive societies, the psychologist finds simple organisms to be useful tools. In humorous appreciation, Tolman flaunts his rodent orientation by dedicating his major work, *Purposive Behavior in Animals and Men,* to *Mus norgegicus albinus.* The rank and file of contemporary American psychologists, mainly interested in the applied fields and the complexities of man's environment, have tended to regard theory-oriented experimentation with rats as "rat experiments" with little of human relevance. They have failed to appreciate, until recently, when the need for systematization to integrate the mass of empirical data forced it upon them, the difference between the phenotypic nature of data and its genotypic meanings in the hands of a creative theorist. Tolman, the "rat psychologist," can truly say with Terence, *"Homo sum: humani nihil a me alienum puto."*

That nothing human or psychological is foreign to Tolman is very clearly illustrated by the following historical note which was prepared by one of his students.

In noting Tolman's theoretical experimental work on "universal" or "normative" psychological laws, one should not forget that he was among the first animal psychologists to make extensive use of the methods of differential analysis. The importance of differential psychology is now accepted so much as a matter of course that one is likely to forget that around 1920 the really dignified and important psychology was experimental, of which animal psychology was really a psychobiological offshoot, and that anyone working with tests and measurements, statistics, clinical psychology, or personality carried the taint of being an "applied" psychologist or worse, and, if a statistician, was regarded as a sort of glorified clerk.

Those who then worked in this field can attest to Tolman's active support of study in these areas. He supported it because, as always with Tolman, everything that happens has to be accounted for—in fact, he *had* to get these facts, viewpoints, approaches, into his system. He was one of the first, if not the first, to study hereditary differences among rats in maze ability, and substantial studies of heredity by his students spring from this interest. He was one of the first to make a statistical study of the reliability of individual differences among rats in learning ability.

His systematic thinking in this area at this time came to a head in the final section of his book, *Purposive Behavior in Animals and Men,* where he attempted an integration of differential and normal psychology, one of the few such systematic integrations in psychological literature. His active sponsorship of quantitative methodology contributed to the University of California's early development of a balanced emphasis on measurement in its curriculum and research laboratories.

Clinical psychology and personality psychology are today in the ascendance. But twenty-five years ago, under the dominance of experimental psychology, clinical psychology was generally considered as a rather disreputable field—something with which psychology unfortunately had to suffer because of practical and social pressures. Tolman never shared with other respectable psychologists these experimento-centric prejudices. One has but to read his earlier papers oriented around the nature of motivation to note that he long ago considered the problems of the clinician and personologist to be *necessarily* a part of the field of psychology, and he has given active and understanding support to the development of this field.

As for Freud and Freudian concepts, this was for years an area of downright taboo. Yet students and associates have never heard Tolman offer disparagements of Freud and psychoanalysis. His questions have always been: How must we fit into a systematic body of psychological thought the dynamic mechanisms these people are concerned with, disregarding the rather colorful language they use to describe them? How can we, specifically, frame critical experiments better to study and describe them? An examination of the writings of Tolman and of the many experiments by him and by his students show plainly the early influence of these then-tabooed types of thinking and work.

Tolman's early acceptance and support of the thinking and work in these *verboten* aspects of the field of individual differences, clinical psychology, Freudian theory, etc., is not mentioned here in order to reveal magnanimity, tolerance, permissiveness, and intellectual courage—though, these attributes he possesses in high degree. A measure of his stature is that he grasped at once the essential relevance of these subject matters, and was soon busily at work eagerly absorbing them into a broad, systematic treatment of psychology because they simply *had* to belong.

Seen from the point of view of his appreciation of various theoretical approaches rather than from that of his responsiveness to all kinds of data, Tolman's theorizing is the first major systematic effort based on a clear recognition of the compatibility of the "Gestalt," "depth," and "behavioristic" approaches. This contrasts most sharply with the traditional cleavages in psychological theorizing—cleavages which still exist for many. He was quick to make use of the many significant contributions of all three major systematic efforts in the construction of his own original and provocative system. A brief comparison of Tolman's approach with the other three illustrates this convincingly.

The intuitionists, or "understanding" psychologists, have agreed that, although the natural-science approach may be adequate for the study of lower sensory functions, it most certainly could not do for the study of higher mental processes, such as insightful thinking, or of personality. Tolman refused to accept such a dichotomy and has demonstrated the fruitfulness of attacking the higher mental processes experimentally and in a natural-science manner. Although such groups as the various denominations of the Gestalt persuasion have not explicitly subscribed to the cleavage of the "understanding" psychologists, and although they too have applied themselves to experimentation, quantification, and law finding in the higher mental processes, they have tended to shy away from the study of these processes through analysis of behavior. They have to a considerable extent remained introspectionists or phenomenologists in principle. Tolman has accepted many of their molar and field concepts, but, experimentally, remains a behaviorist rather than a phenomenologist. Because Tolman is so convinced of the multiplicity of variables which determine behavior, his theory, unlike that of the more orthodox Gestaltists, is just as concerned with motivation, personality, and learning as it is with cognitive and perceptual factors. Thus, in lieu of the concept of Gestalt, he has invented the more functional concept of sign-gestalt.

Tolman is much more given to psychological constructs in his system building than to physiological ones. In this, he is much closer to the depth psychologists than to the Gestaltists. Unlike the Gestalt psychologists and like the depth psychologists, Tolman does attempt to deal with genetic problems, but unlike the depth psychologists, he does so without falling back upon purely historical answers to systematic questions. He seems to have accepted many of the dynamisms of the depth psychologists but has balked at their constructs such as "ego," "ego-ideal," etc. More parsimonious in listing and classifying needs than they, and less concerned with layers of personality, he has addressed himself more directly and more clearly to the conceptual representation of the differences between enduring and momentary structures. And in this he again departs both from Kurt Lewin and the more orthodox Gestalt psychologists with their heavy emphasis upon situationalism.

In elaborating his system, Tolman has, of course, found it necessary to refashion behaviorism. As a behaviorist and as a "rat psychologist," it is Tolman's paradoxical contribution that he has returned man to psychology by insisting upon molar behaviorism, purposively organized, as the unit of psychological analysis. He gave back to psychology its mind, lost through the mischief of a naïve behaviorism, by inventing a method for inferring mental factors from behavioral events which has both scientific respectability and philosophic sophistication. And finally, it must be noted that his concept of the sign-gestalt—a concept which is basic to his whole system—is one of the major theoretical forerunners of the current dynamic perceptual school.

This eclecticism of Tolman's approach to psychological data and theoretical orientations is made possible primarily by the second major characteristic of his system—his free and creative use of inter-vening variables or hypothetical constructs. At several points in his publications—most clearly in his American Psychological Association presidential address which is reprinted in the present volume—Tolman has demonstrated that psychological science must proceed by stating and manipulating a system of independent variables of which behavior is a function, and that basic to an understanding of the functions of these independent variables are hypothetical constructs which intervene between stimulus field and behavior. But, reflecting his behavioristic orientation, he has always insisted on seeking for an operational definition of these constructs. Tied in with both an independent variable and a construct is the neces-sity of citing the defining experiment in which the independent manipulation is made and which justifies the hypothetical construct. It is only because of his faith in the centralist approach that the courage for an operational redefinition of higher-function terms can be mustered. And Tolman and his students have succeeded, in experiment after experiment, in redefining such terms as "purpose," "insight," "hypotheses," "expectations," etc. It should, however, also be pointed out that his search for an operational definition does not enslave him to operationalism and does not lead him to the sterility of the extreme operationalist who would see in a construct nothing but a set of pointer readings.

One very important aspect of Tolman's stress on generality and centralism is seen in his treatment of the learning problem. As a colleague points out:

> In the special field of animal maze learning, Watson's classical be-haviorism of the 1910's and the 1920's with its search for "the" locus of learning—thought to be sensory or motor, but in any event periph-erally channeled and focused—has given way to a recognition of the generality, and thus of the central character, of the learning mechanism. This progress was carried by Lashley and his group, and by the "molar" behaviorism of Tolman and his collaborators.

To point up the nature of Tolman's contributions to learning theory and to clarify what is meant by his generality and his cen-tralist approach to learning (so important for educational psy-chology as antidotes for Thorndike's specificity), it is necessary to examine, briefly, his reasons for rejecting the two theories of learning which were dominant at the time he wrote *Purposive Behavior in Animals and Men*—the conditioned-reflex theories of Pavlov, and the connectionist theories of Thorndike and others. Tolman, in discussing the conditioned-reflex theories, points out that one of the basic difficulties with such theories lies in the fact that the learned response is practically never the same as that made to the unconditioned stimulus. He has never let anyone ignore the fact that the learned response varies appropriately with the situation. His emphasis on the adaptive and changing character of the learned response distinguishes his viewpoint from that of all the stimulus-response psychologists. Of the latter he might say that they seem so absorbed in computing habit strengths, momentary effective reaction potentials, and the like, that they fail to notice the qualitative changes that occur during the learning process.

Tolman's criticism of the connectionist theories is based primarily upon experimental data on latent learning. Numerous experiments, he asserts, suggest that learning is not a matter of direct and immediate connections between stimuli and responses, but that the organism, instead, learns "what leads to what." Tolman's interest in the adjustive, changing, and generalized character of the learned response, together with his demonstration that what is learned is only partly revealed in the performance of the organism, form the basic tenets of his theory of learning. Experimental data made it necessary for him to seek for the answer in such hypothetical constructs as "expectations," "hypotheses," "sign-gestalten," "cognitive maps."

Tolman's viewpoint has produced a profound change in our way of thinking about learning theory. Before we can proceed to formulate any quantitative laws of learning, we must first make sure that we know the character of the learned performance, unearthing the central processes which determine the changes in the character of the learned response. In the study of human problem solving and thinking such an understanding of the cognitive structures underlying the observed behavior is essential, if we are to gain any insight into the nature of human thought. The recognition and insistence that it is this problem which comes first, and the invention and experimental use of techniques for solving this problem, constitute perhaps Tolman's greatest contribution to contemporary learning theory.

The ingenious use of hypothetical constructs has not been limited by Tolman to learning problems. He has applied this technique to problems of motivation, to social problems, to personality problems. His "intervening variable" has become one of psychology's most powerful conceptual tools and has made it possible to make a fresh approach to all of psychology's problems and to think more clearly about those mediational processes which are involved in man's commerce with the world about him.

◇   ◇   ◇   ◇   ◇

No assessment of Tolman the scientist would be complete without at least a brief note on Tolman as a teacher. It is in that capacity that most of us have known him best, and it is in that role that we have seen him display so clearly those attributes of character and mind which can be seen in the papers in this collection. From a colleague who has watched his ways with students over the years comes this statement about him and his teaching: "His scientific and personal flexibility, his youthful zest and energy for ideas, for work, for friendships have created students who, while devoted to him, are not devotees. Instead, they have largely gone into fields far removed from rat experimentation, and most of them have developed theoretical organizations of their own somewhat different from his. He has not been a 'master' with followers, but as a New England liberal mellowed in the West he has inspired students to become independent psychologists and to carry on in their own ways with the open-minded and zestful spirit which he helped them discover and develop in themselves." Those of us who have had the benefit of having been in close contact with Professor Tolman have all had the feeling, at one time or another, that we have contributed to great creations. He has done this for us because he does not over-teach. His lectures cannot be described as smoothly finished, carefully prepared expositions, but as galvanizers to creative thinking by his students. His classes (which frequently evolve into loud free-for-alls in which student and teacher cannot be differentiated) reveal the searchings and fumblings of the creative scientific mind rather than a digest of conclusions already reached, organized, and neatly filed away. Nothing has ever been authoritarian, static, or finished either in his systematic psychology or in his personal relations. For Tolman, as for so many artists, the fun of the game is in the act of creation. This leads to the sharing of his ideas with his students so fully and so consistently that he has frequently given credit to students for ideas which he actually evolved himself. The picture many of us have of Tolman is that of a man who with high, good fun plays with constructs and models to his delight, to the inspiration of his students, and to the profit of psychology.

I feel impelled to apologize. The above, far too flattering foreword I first saw only after it was in page proof. I basked and I preened. I wished that a mere half of the kind things said had been true.—E.C.T.

CONTENTS

1

A NEW FORMULA FOR BEHAVIORISM

[*Psychological Review,* JANUARY, 1922]

THE IDEA OF BEHAVIORISM is abroad. In the most diverse quarters its lingo, if not its substance, is spreading like wildfire. Why?

In the first place, it is to be observed that ever since the days of Ebbinghaus's experiments on memory the inadequacy of the merely introspective method as such has been becoming more and more obvious. And the recent work in mental tests and animal psychology has strengthened this conviction. In the second place, there has always been a formal logical difficulty about the introspective method which has troubled certain minds. That is, the definition of psychology as the examination and analysis of private conscious contents has been something of a logical sticker. For how *can* one build up a science upon elements which by very definition are said to be private and noncommunicable? And, thirdly, the introspective method is practically arduous and seemingly barren of results. It is these three features, then, which seem to have been primarily responsible for the spread and catching of behavioristic categories.

What, now, does the behaviorist offer as a substitute? We turn to the archbehaviorist, Watson. Behaviorism, he says, will be the study of stimulus and response such that given the stimulus we can predict the response, and given the response we can predict the stimulus. Very good! But how does he define stimulus and response? He defines them, he says, in the terms in which physiology defines them; that is, stimuli are such things as "rays of light of different wave lengths, sound waves differing in amplitude, length, phase and combination, gaseous particles given off in such small diameters that they affect the membrane of the nose," etc., and responses are such things as "muscle contractions and gland secretions."[1] We turn, however, to a later chapter[2] and read with astonishment, in a footnote, that "it is perfectly possible for a student of behavior entirely ignorant of the sympathetic nervous system and of the glands and smooth muscles or even of the central nervous system as a whole, to write a thoroughly comprehensive and accurate study of the emotions." But how can this be, we ask, if, by very definition, behavior is a matter of "muscle contractions" and "gland secretions"? How, on the basis of this definition, can a person "ignorant of glands and muscles" write a behavioristic account of anything? That he can write such an account we would admit. The only difference between our point of view and Watson's would be that we should insist that such an account would be the only truly *behavior* account, and that an account in terms of muscle contraction and gland secretion, as such, would not be behaviorism at all but a mere physiology.

It should be noted that the possibility of a behaviorism which shall be not a mere physiology but something different has apparently already occurred to a number of writers. Thus, for example, Holt says that "the phenomena evinced by the integrated organism are no longer merely the excitation of nerve or the twitching of muscle, nor yet the play merely of reflexes touched off by stimuli. These are all present and essential to the phenomena in question, but they are merely the components now—the biological sciences have long recognized this *new and further thing and called it 'behavior.'* "[3] Mrs. de Laguna also explicitly states that what we want is a behaviorism which is not mere physiology. "In order to understand behavior we must resolve it into a system of interrelated *functions,* just as in order to understand the physiological workings of the human body we must envisage the complex of chemical and mechanical processes as falling into such fundamental groups as digestion, circulation, etc., constitutive of the physiological economy. Now just as there is a physiological economy, so there is a larger vital economy in closest union with, yet distinguishable from it. This is the system of behavior, by means of which the being, animal or human, maintains his relations with the environment and forms a factor in its transformation. The science of behavior has the task of tracing the lineaments of this larger economy."[4]

[1] John B. Watson, *Psychology from the standpoint of a behaviorist,* Philadelphia, Lippincott, 1919, p. 10.
[2] *Ibid.,* chapter vi, "Hereditary modes of response: emotions," p. 195.
[3] E. B. Holt, *J. of Phil., Psychol. & Sci. Methods,* 12 (1915), 366.
[4] Grace A. de Laguna, "Emotion and perception from the behaviorist standpoint,"

A. P. Weiss also seems, to some slight extent at any rate, to lean towards this same view of the desirability of a nonphysiological behaviorism. For example, the following: "The investigation of the internal neural conditions forms part of the behavioristic programme, of course, but the inability to trace the ramification of any given nervous excitation through the nervous system is no more a restriction on the study of effective stimuli and reactions in the educational, industrial or social phases of life than is the physicist's inability to determine just what is going on in the electrolyte of a battery while a current is passing, a limitation that makes research in electricity impossible."[5]

The two essential theses which we wish to maintain in this paper are, first, that such a true nonphysiological behaviorism is really possible; and, second, that when it is worked out[6] this new behaviorism will be found capable of covering not merely the results of mental tests, objective measurements of memory, and animal psychology as such, but also all that was valid in the results of the older introspective psychology. And this new formula for behaviorism which we would propose is intended as a formula for *all* of psychology—a formula to bring formal peace, not merely to the animal worker, but also to the addict of imagery and feeling tone.

But how can this be done? By what single common set of concepts can we possibly take care both of the facts of gross behavior and of those of consciousness and imagery?

Psychol. Rev., 26 (1919), 410–411. See also other articles by the same author. "Dualism in animal psychology," *J. of Phil., Psychol. & Sci. Methods* 15 (1918), 617–627; "Dualism and animal psychology: a rejoinder," *J. of Phil., Psychol. & Sci. Methods*, 16 (1919), 296–300, and "Empirical correlations of mental and bodily phenomena," *J. of Phil., Psychol. & Sci. Methods*, 15 (1918), 533–541.

[5] "The relation between physiological psychology and behavior psychology," *J. of Phil., Psychol. & Sci. Methods*, 16 (1919), 626.

[6] Attention should be drawn to two other very significant attempts to begin a detailed "working out" of such a behaviorism in addition to Mrs. de Laguna's in the article on "Emotion and perception from the behaviorist standpoint" already quoted from. These are to be found in a series of articles by J. R. Kantor: "A functional interpretation of human instincts," *Psychol. Rev.*, 27 (1920), 50–72; "Suggestions toward a scientific interpretation of perception," *Psychol. Rev.* 27 (1920), 197–216; "An attempt towards a naturalistic description of emotions," *Psychol. Rev.*, 28 (1921), 19–42, and 120–140; "A tentative analysis of the primary data of psychology," *J. of Phil.*, 18 (1921), 253–269. And in a series of articles by R. B. Perry, "A behavioristic view of purpose," *J. of Phil.*, 18 (1921), 85–105; "The independent universality of purpose and belief," *J. of Phil.*, 18 (1921), 169–180; "The cognitive interest and its refinements," *J. of Phil.*, 18 (1921), 365–375. It must be pointed out, however, that whereas both these authors are giving yeoman strokes in the direction of just such a nonphysiological behaviorism as the writer is contending for, neither of them seems himself to be wholly self-conscious of this essential difference between such a true behaviorism and a mere physiology.

Before attempting to suggest such a set of concepts, let us indulge in a preliminary epistemological skirmish. Let us start from the usual dualistic hypothesis implicit in traditional psychological thinking. Suppose, that is, we assume that consciousness is (for the purposes of psychology at any rate if not for those of an ultimate metaphysics) a new kind of something or other which is added to certain behavior situations but not to others. Introspective psychology claims the study and analysis of this new something or other as its own peculiar field. Consciousness is assumed by it to be something private to each individual which he alone can analyze and report upon. And the introspective account purports to be such an analysis and report. What now can our behaviorism answer to this? Our behaviorism will reply that whether or not there is such a private something or other present in the conscious behavior situation and lacking in the unconscious one, this private something or other never "gets across," as such, from one individual to another. All the things that do "get across" are merely *behavior* phenomena or the objective possibilities of such phenonema. Suppose, for example, that I introspect concerning my consciousness of colors. All you can ever really learn from such introspection is whether or not I shall behave towards those colors in the same ways that you do. You never can learn what the colors really "feel" like to me. It is indeed conceivable that just as immediate "feels" (if there are any such things) the colors may be something quite different for me from what they are for you, and yet if I agree with you in behaving to them, i.e., in my namings of and pointings to the colors, no amount of introspection will ever discover to you this fact of their uniqueness to each of us as immediate "feels." You will only discover what the colors are for me as behavior possibilities.

Let us now turn to some of the actual concepts which seem to me to be required by such a point of view. We will confine ourselves to four: *stimulating agency, behavior cue, behavior object,* and *behavior act.* They may be thought of as very loosely analogous to the physiologist's concepts of external stimulus, receptor process, conductor process, and effector process.

The *stimulating agency* may be defined in any standardized terms, those of physics, of physiology, or of common sense, and it constitutes the independent, initiating cause of the whole behavior phenomena. Thus on different occasions it may consist variously in, and be describable as, a sense-organ stimulation (in the case of perceptual behavior), as the administering of a particular drug, e.g., hasheeh (in the case of hallucinatory behavior), or as the neurological end result of a preceding activity (in the case of a behavior based upon memory or recall).

The nature of the *behavior cue* will be understood most readily from a consideration of the dialectic which underlies the experimental work on sensory discrimination in animals. In such work the results, when strictly interpreted, are found to tell us nothing but the possibility of differences of behavior as a result of different stimulating agencies. If, for example, we find that a mouse can learn to behave differently as a result of blue and yellow stimuli but not as a result of a red and green stimuli, we do not conclude anything as regards the animal's consciousness of these colors, as such, but merely something as regards the behavior cues which these colors are capable of evoking in him. That is, blue and yellow wavelengths are capable of producing in him two different behavior cues, whereas red and green wavelengths are capable of producing in him only one. In other words, where the older psychology talked about sense qualities our new behaviorism will talk about behavior cues.

The new concept is identifiable with the older one in so far, but only in so far, as the latter explained the possibility or lack of possibility of differences *of behavior*. The new concept departs utterly from the old in so far as the latter implied something concerning "immediate feels" as such. By applying different stimulating agencies to our organism we discover the number and range of his possible behavior cues. We learn which stimulating agencies he can use as a basis for differences of behavior and which he can not use as cues for different behaviors. And we learn something concerning the degrees of difference between these different behavior cues. For example, we learn that, in a human of normal color vision, although the stimulating agencies designated as orange and red wavelengths produce behavior cues which are different from one another, still these behavior cues are more similar to one another (in that, on occasion, they are more likely to lead to an identical behavior) than are the two behavior cues produced by the stimulating agencies known as red and green wavelengths—and so on. In other words the sum of the behavior cues possible for any given organism constitutes a total system which is to be defined not merely in terms of its relation to the stimulating agencies which evoke its members, but also in terms of the interrelations of similarity and difference between those members. We do not learn, however, anything about sensation qualities, as such, either when we observe the gross behavior of another organism or when we ask the latter to *introspect*. We learn the nature of his behavior cues. We do not learn the nature of his "immediate feels."

Let us turn now to a consideration of the next of our four concepts, that of the *behavior object*. Just as the concept of the behavior cue was

found to bear a certain relation to a concept of the older psychology
(viz., that of sense quality) so the concept of the behavior object bears
an analogous relation to another concept of the older psychology; viz.,
that of the perceived or apperceived *meaning*. A behavior object results
from a behavior cue or a group of behavior cues which, because of a
particular behavior situation, possesses for the organism in question
a specific behavior meaning. For example, we present an ordinary western European with a chair, it produces in him, because of the structure
of his sense organs and as a result of its color, shape, etc., certain specific
behavior cues. In addition, however, because of his particular training
and past experience and state of behavior readiness at the moment such
behavior cues resulting from these shapes, colors, etc., arouse in him a
very specific group of behavior tendencies; e.g., those of sitting upon,
getting up from, kneeling on, moving up to the table, etc. This group
of aroused tendencies defines his behavior object. That is, they constitute on that particular occasion the behavior meaning of the colors,
shapes, etc.

To use the terminology of the older psychology we would say that
the behavior cues in question are here apperceived as the behavior-
object chair. On another occasion, however, this same group of behavior
cues might be apperceived not as a chair, but as a very different sort
of behavior object. If we were drunk, it might be apperceived, not as a
thing to sit on, to kneel on, but as a thing to run away from, to scream
at, etc. Thus, the behavior object is to be defined in the last analysis
simply in terms of the group of behaviors to which it may lead. And it
is to be emphasized that it, no more than the behavior cue, can be defined in terms of "immediate conscious feels." For no one of us ever
knows for certain what another organism's "conscious feels" may be.
We know only the behavior implications of those conscious feels.

We turn now to the last of our four concepts—that of the *behavior
act*. The behavior act is simply the name to be given to the final bits of
behavior as such. The behavior act together with the stimulating agencies constitute the fundamentals upon which the rest of the system is
based. They are such entities as to "sniff," to "sit," to "scratch," to
"walk," to "gallop," to "talk." They are directly correlated with the
action system of the given organism. They vary and increase in number
with the growth and development of the organism. But it is they alone
which, at any given stage in this growth and development, tell us all
that we know of such an organism's "mentality" (even when that organism is another human being who can "introspect"[7]). Used as a means

---

[7] Such introspection is itself but one of these behavior acts.

of comparing different stimulating agencies on the basis simply of the relative discriminability and nondiscriminability of the latter, the behavior acts provide us with our definition of behavior cues (i.e., sensation and image qualities). And used to discover the totality of different alternative behaviors which may result from a given collection of behavior cues, the behavior acts provide us with our definition of behavior objects (i.e., perceptions and ideations).

If, now, we sum up the situation it will appear that the problems for our behavioristic science must fall into three groups: those of (1), given the stimulating agency, determining the behavior cues, (2), given the behavior cues, determining the behavior object, and (3), given the behavior object, determining the behavior act. The first of these problems is the well-known one of the older physiological psychology of determining the relations between sensory and image qualities and their underlying physiological conditions. The second problem, that of the relation of behavior object to behavior cue, is the old one of perception and apperception. Our rewording of it will not, I think, make it any the less easy of final solution. Finally, the problem of the relation of behavior act to behavior object is the extremely important problem of *motive*. It is the problem of desire, emotion, instinct, habit, determining set. It is a problem which the older analytical formulation tended to obscure and make almost impossible. If our behavioristic formulation has any practical value at all—if, that is, it has any value in addition to that of unifying under a single rubric all the different types of method which psychology employs, then that practical value will be, I believe, in the more successful treatment which it will allow and suggest for this matter of motive, determining set, and the like.

What, finally, are we to say about those difficult, and to the opponents of behaviorism, seemingly insuperable problems of imagery, feeling tone, language, introspection? An adequate discussion would cover many pages. I can here merely throw out a suggestion or two. In the first place I would suggest that consciousness as such, i.e., conscious behavior as opposed to merely unconscious behavior, is to be thought of simply as the case in which a *number* of behavior acts are being made or tending to be made simultaneously. If I am *conscious* of the chairness of a chair, it is because I tend not only to sit, but to stand up, to kneel, etc., simultaneously. If, in addition, I am conscious of the color and shape of the chair as such, I tend (am set) not merely to behave in these appropriate ways toward chairs but also to discriminate by all other possible behaviors its particular color and shape from all other colors and shapes.

Images and ideas would be simply a particular case where behavior object and behavior cue have different space and time implications from those holding in the case of presented objects and qualities. And feelings and emotions would be treated as combining both behavior objects and behavior cues in that they involve both discriminable qualities and specific unvarying types of behavior (for example, approach, avoidance, and the like). Finally, language in general and introspection in particular are simply themselves behavior acts which in the last analysis indicate to the observer the very same behavior cues and behavior objects which might be indicated by the mere gross forms of behavior for which they are substitutes.

In closing this very brief and inadequate sketch it may be remarked that its excuse is to be found in the hope that it may have suggestive and propaganda value, if nothing else. The five points I should wish to emphasize are:

1. There are obvious formal inconsistencies in the subjectivistic formula as such.

2. The possibilities of a new nonphysiological behaviorism have already found expression on the part of a number of writers.

3. Such a nonphysiological behaviorism seems to be capable of covering not only behaviorism proper but introspectionism as well. For, if there are any such things as private mental "feels" they are never revealed to us (even in introspection). All that is revealed are potentialities for behavior.

4. As a first step in working out such a nonphysiological behaviorism I suggest the concepts of stimulating agency, behavior cue, behavior object, and behavior act.

5. The value of the new formation will be in part theoretical, in that it will bring under a single rubric all the apparently different and contradictory methods of actual psychology; but in part, also, practical, in that it will allow for a more ready and adequate treatment of the problems of motive, purpose, determining tendency, and the like, than was made easy by the older subjectivistic formulation.

2

CAN INSTINCTS BE GIVEN UP IN PSYCHOLOGY?

[*Journal of Abnormal Psychology and Social Psychology*, JULY–SEPTEMBER, 1922]

MR. KUO'S RECENT most stimulating article, "Giving up Instincts in Psychology,"[1] implies two theses: (1) that our current definitions of instinct are self-contradictory and arbitrary, and (2) that a more careful analysis and observation would indicate that there are no instincts (in the sense of inherited tendencies) but that what we have been wont to call instincts in the past are really only habits.

Of the first of these theses I shall have nothing further to say. I am in the heartiest sympathy with it. It seems, in fact, to judge from the tenor of recent articles, to be rapidly gaining a widespread acceptance. Nor am I temperamentally, and before the fact, opposed to the second thesis. For it may very well be that further observation and study of just what does take place in the early days and years of the organism's development—such a further observation and study as that for which Mr. Kuo himself makes a plea—will substantiate his doctrine of the completely acquisitional character of instinct. I do wish, however, to outline what seem to me to be the alternative possibilities. For I think the outlining of such alternatives will help to make the issue clearer until such time as actual observation shall have come to the rescue and decided it.

I shall begin first by briefly summing up Mr. Kuo's theory in my own terms. It seems to me to have two parts: (1) the assertion that even in the case of the "units of reaction"[2] the connections between response

[1] *J. of Phil.*, 18 (1921), 645–664.
[2] *Ibid.*, p. 658.

and stimulus are acquired and not innate; and (2) the further hypothesis that, in the case of those more complicated forms of behavior, built up out of these "units of reaction" (which in the past we have been wont to call instincts), the form and pattern of the combination are also not innate but acquired. In a word, the doctrine seems to be summed up by saying that it implies that in the unlearned organism the nervous system is, as far as any innate sensory-motor connections are concerned, a completely uncharted sea.[3]

Let us now, however, note certain further implications. How, we ask, if all actions both simple and complex are acquired, does it happen that much the same types of action get built up in all the different individuals of one and the same species? The answer of Mr. Kuo to this would seem to be threefold: (1) The different individuals of the same species all have the same sense organs and hence must all be innately responsive to the same general types of stimulus. (2) They all have the same action systems (response organs) and hence their responses must necessarily fall into the same general kinds, and (3) they are all subject to much the same essential environment and hence are necessarily driven to similar types of complex behavior.[4] As regards 1 and 2 I have no criticism and I think Mr. Kuo has done us a great service in indicating their importance. Undoubtedly part of that which is distinctive of each species, and which we have been wont to attribute to the possession of special instincts (i.e., innate sensory-motor connections) is really the outcome merely of the possession of the specific sense organs and response organs peculiar to the species in question. But as regards 3; how, I would ask, if as Mr. Kuo's fundamental assertion states, there are no original connections of response to stimulus, can the presence of either the same environment or of different environments in any way determine the type of behavior the organism shall develop? To assume that the environment "demands" or calls out particular types of behavior[5] is to assume some fixed connection between type of stimulus and type of response. But the original presence of any such connections has been denied. This

---

[3] This perhaps would be asserted by Mr. Kuo only as regards those "units of reaction" which get combined into "instincts" or habits. For he does seem to admit the functioning of certain independent elementary acts (*ibid.*, p. 664, i.e., relatively fixed reflexes) which are not of a sort to get integrated into more complicated reaction systems and to which he perhaps would allow a certain amount of innate givenness of the original sensory-motor connections.

[4] *Ibid.*, pp. 653, 661, 662.

[5] "Our daily acts are organized as a result of environmental demands." *Ibid.*, p. 661. "The fact that the nature of environment determines the organization of reaction systems accounts for both social solidarity and individual differences in occupations and in types of behavior." *Ibid.*, p. 662.

is a difficulty which as far as I can discover is nowhere resolved in Mr. Kuo's article. Fortunately, however, for the real understanding of the problem in question, the writer has had the advantage of personal conversations with Mr. Kuo, and, as a result of such conversations, he concludes that the latter really holds an additional hypothesis not stated in the article. This hypothesis maintains that although all responses *are* originally random, there is an operative factor which determines that certain ones of them shall soon get learned (i.e., attached to specific stimuli). This operative factor is the simple one that, if a random response succeeds in separating the organism from the exciting stimulus, the response gets learned; otherwise not. This explains trial and error learning.[6] Having once accepted this further principle Mr. Kuo can go on to assume that when a unit response has once thus been learned it thereafter constitutes a specific connection of response to stimulus which can serve as the foundation stone in the building up (by the principle of the conditioned reflex) of more complicated adjustments. Accepting this principle as an addition to Mr. Kuo's thesis, we can sum up his entire doctrine by the following four points: (1) All the original unit acts are random (i.e., completely unattached to specific stimuli). (2) They do, however, soon get specifically attached to stimuli as a result of trial and error learning (i.e., if they are successful in separating the organism from the exciting stimulus). (3) When they have once got attached they are used in the building up, by the principle of the conditioned reflex, of those more complicated forms of behavior which we are wont to call "instincts" and habits. And (4) as the complement of 3 it is assumed that these more complicated forms of behavior themselves are acquired and never innate.

Let us turn now to the presentation of what, before further empirical observation shall have decided the issue, seem to me the possible alternative theories.

FIRST ALTERNATIVE

The first theory I would suggest would be one diametrically opposed to Mr. Kuo's. It would assume (1) that in the case of the original unit acts the connections between stimulus and response are fixed, and (2) that this also holds in the case of the more complex forms of behavior. As regards instincts, then, everything would be given and nothing learned. This, obviously, is the "inherited-reflex-pattern" type of theory. And we need not dwell upon it further. Although it is still an a priori possibility the evidence seems to be fast accumulating against it even for

---

[6] *Ibid.*, 659. "The process of the integration always involves selection and elimination."

the lower animals. See, for example, the work of Swindel[7] on nest building; of Craig[8] and Whitman[9] on the sexual anomalies of pigeons; of Hamilton[10] on the sexual anomalies of monkeys; of Scott[11] on the largely acquired character of bird songs. (To some of these Mr. Kuo has already referred.)[12] All this work shows a surprising ununiformity and variability in the instincts even of the lower animals.

SECOND ALTERNATIVE

The next possible type of theory which occurs to me is one, which, while it would admit the nonoriginal character of the more complicated forms of behavior, would posit fixed innate stimulus-response connections for some at least of the "units of reaction." The complicated forms of response would then be built up, in the form of habits, out of and upon these simpler units.

Such a view may perhaps be identified with a certain feature in McDougall's well-known doctrine. In so far, that is, as he defines his primary instincts chiefly in terms of certain original simple stimulus-response sequences as, for example: running from, in the case of fright; striking at, in the case of anger; etc., and assumes, further, that it is upon the basis of these simple sequences, as such, that the later more complicated forms of behavior get built up; such would certainly seem to be his view.

It must be pointed out, on the other hand, however, that in so far as he emphasizes not these original simple stimulus-response sequences but rather the emotions as the permanent and central things and as constituting the cores for the later more complicated responses, his theory would be of a different type—of a type, it may be noted in passing, which, when translated into our language would be related to, if not identical with, the third alternative, to be presented below.

Another writer, whose theory sometimes at least seems to fall under this second alternative, is Kantor. In his article "How Do We Acquire Our Basic Reactions?"[13] we find him speaking of "basic forms of actions as infant behavior (e.g., vocalization whether considered as random acts or *instincts*) which soon become integrated into more complex re-

[7] E. P. Swindel, *Amer. J. of Psychol.*, 30 (1919), 180.

[8] W. Craig, *J. of Animal Behav.*, 4 (1914), 121–133.

[9] C. O. Whitman, *The behavior of pigeons*, Carnegie Inst. Washington Publ., no. 257, (1919), p. 28 f.

[10] G. V. Hamilton, *J. of Animal Behav.*, 4 (1914), 295–318.

[11] W. E. D. Scott, *Science*, 14 (1901), 522; 15 (1902), 178; 19 (1904), 154; 19 (1904), 551.

[12] *Op. cit.*, p. 657.

[13] *Psychol. Rev.*, 28 (1921), 328–355.

sponses."[14] Now, in so far as he accepts the latter of his two alternatives and assumes that the "basic forms of actions" are *instincts;* i.e., involve innate stimulus-response connections, his theory seems to fall into the type we are here considering. It should be observed, however, that in so far, on the other hand, as he accepts the former of the alternatives and assumes that the "basic forms of actions" are "random" his theory becomes, on the contrary, identical with Mr. Kuo's. And it has to be admitted that in by far the larger portion of this particular article he does seem to be accepting this former alternative. For example, in his conclusion we find him asserting that "the number and kind of reaction systems we acquire depends entirely upon the kind and frequency of stimuli with which we are in contact, plus the reaction systems previously *acquired.*"[15] On the other hand, it is to be pointed out, finally, that in other articles, both earlier and later, he leans pretty decidedly toward the view here presented of the innate nonacquired character of the instinct elements.[16]

Lastly, as a third possible representative of this second alternative let me suggest Thorndike. For it will be remembered what great emphasis he lays upon the simplicity of all that we may be supposed to possess in the way of innate responses.[17] He lists some forty-two simple innate connections between stimulus and response. And anything more complicated he apparently would assume to be built up upon the basis of these.

Third Alternative

One remaining type of theory suggests itself to me. It would differ from Mr. Kuo's primarily in two features: (1) while it would also admit that the original "units of reaction" are random, it would deny that they are completely random, but assert rather that their randomness is *usually* restricted within certain fairly definite and discoverable limits. Thus, when an organism is presented with a new stimulus for which no response has as yet been learned this theory would suppose, not as does Mr. Kuo's that the animal will respond with *all* the acts of which

[14] *Ibid.,* p. 328 (Italics mine).

[15] *Ibid.,* p. 354 (Italics mine). It is to be observed that in so far as he adopts this other theory he is equally lacking, as was Mr. Kuo, in any expressed statement of an underlying principle whereby changes in the "kind and frequency of stimuli" (*ibid.,* p. 331) can come to effect the building up of fixed responses out of initially random ones.

[16] Cf. "A functional interpretation of human instincts," *Psychol. Rev.* 27 (1920), 50–72, especially 56 ff. And "The psychology of reflex action," *Amer. J. of Psychol.* 33 (1922), 19–42, especially 38 ff.

[17] *Educational psychology,* vol. 2. New York, Teachers College, Columbia University, 1913.

it is capable, but rather that it will ring the changes upon only a relatively small and definite number of such random acts. When, for example, a young infant is suddenly dropped from a slight height the
theory does not suppose, as would Mr. Kuo's, that the child will coo
and smile and make sucking movements *as well as* cry and draw in its
breath, but merely that it will tend primarily to do the latter two.[18]
The theory would not necessarily deny that there might be occasions
where, if the stimulus were strong enough and "relief" was not achieved
by any of the first set of random acts, the child might eventually do *all*
the things of which he was capable. It would merely assert that for any
ordinary strength of stimulus only a certain somewhat restricted number of random acts tends to occur. (2) The second feature in which the
theory would differ from Mr. Kuo's consists in the fact that instead of
assuming merely one ultimate type of success (viz., the simple removal
of the organism from the given exciting stimulus) it would assume a
number of different types of success. It would assume, further, that the
nature of these successes would be in each case related to the underlying
factor which also explains which particular set of random acts tends to
occur on that occasion. The explanation of the mechanism of this underlying factor depends upon the assumption of what we will call "driving
adjustments." These are to be conceived as internal behavior sets originally and innately set off by particular types of stimulus. These adjustments tend to release particular groups of random acts, which ordinarily
ring the changes upon each other in a purely haphazard fashion until
some one finally occurs which presents the organism with some new
stimulus or condition which automatically leads to the disappearance
of the driving adjustment itself. Thus, for example, suppose the driving
adjustment is that condition which on its introspective side we call
hunger. This driving adjustment releases a series of random acts—not
ordinarily all the random acts of which the organism is capable, but
only a certain discoverable set—seeking movements of head, face and
lips, etc. These continue in random fashion until some one or combination of them occurs which achieves food so that the driving adjustment itself thereby becomes removed. This act or set of acts constitutes
success and tends to be learned; i.e., to become specifically attached to
the whole situation (to the hunger adjustment itself and to the type of
external stimulus then present). It is to be seen, therefore, that it is the
nature of the driving adjustment which determines both which acts shall
be released and which one or ones shall constitute success. And when

---

[18] Cf. J. B. Watson, *Psychol. Rev.*, 26 (1919), 165–196.

once these simple specific stimulus-response connections have been formed then the building up of more complicated forms of behavior in terms of habit can be easily accounted for.

To sum up, then, the theory as so far expressed; it assumes (1) that, whereas there are no innate connections of external response to external stimulus, there are innate connections of specific types of driving adjustments to particular types of stimuli, external or internal; (2) that these driving adjustments tend to release particular sets of random acts, and (3) that that random act or set of acts get learned; i.e., specifically attached to the external situation and the driving adjustment in question, which leads to the removal of said driving adjustment.

But there is another important feature of the theory yet to be emphasized; to wit, that these driving adjustments while they are to be assumed as ultimately explainable in terms of underlying physiological sets, are nevertheless, primarily identifiable and describable, not in physiological, but in behavior terms.[19] And when thus described they are found to be stated primarily in terms of the abstract natures of the successes which they respectively predicate. Let us, for example, for purposes merely of illustration, list tentatively the following as possible original types of driving adjustment: flight, pugnacity, repulsion, curiosity, parental instinct, self-assertion, self-abasement, hunger, and sex.[20] The list is for illustrative purposes only and does not claim special validity or exhaustiveness. Let us, now, examine it. It is to be observed that in each case an identifying description can be made simply in terms of the abstract type of success predicated quite irrespective of the specific object responded to and the specific detailed nature of the response. Flight equals getting away from an object; pugnacity—attacking an object; repulsion—avoiding an object; curiosity—manipulating an object; parental instinct—caressing an object; self-assertion—determining the behavior of an object; hunger—eating an object; and sex—arousing activities of the sexual organs by means of the presence of an object. The particular objects fled from, fought, avoided, etc., will depend upon the chances of the first arousal plus learning, and, similarly, the detailed nature of the response itself, whether it consist of running, walking, hiding, etc., in the case of flight; striking, kicking, biting, etc., in the case of fighting; pushing, turning up nose, turning away face, etc., in the case of repulsion, will likewise be a matter of the chances of the first arousal plus subsequent learning; and so on. But the nature of these

[19] Indeed we usually do not know what the underlying physiology is.
[20] It may be noted in passing that I have simply taken McDougall's seven primary instincts and added hunger and sex.

different responses will always be reducible to the same abstract terms in which the underlying driving adjustments themselves are to be defined.

Another feature about the doctrine which thus appears is that, as thus behavioristically defined, these adjustments are found to be stated in purposive terms. They are defined in terms of the ends they achieve. This means, not that those ends are necessarily before the organism itself, but rather that they are before us the observers. They are the conceptual pegs upon which *we*, for convenience, hang *our* descriptions. When we observe an organism time and again running, hiding, flying, walking from objects, we descry a similar element in each of these behaviors which for descriptive convenience we may identify in the teleological terms of "getting away from an object." It is to be observed, however, that this need of teleological language by no means implies that all such behavior cannot be explained physiologically in a purely causal fashion.

Finally, one more feature of the theory must be noted: viz., that just as Mr. Kuo's does, it also avoids the assumption of any mysterious degree of "preëstablished harmony" between the specific nature of the environment which the young organism is to be born into and the specific nature of the responses which he is to make to it. It does suppose, however, that the driving adjustments are *innately* set off by particular types of exciting stimulating conditions; and it does suppose, further, that they are innately neutralized by certain other particular types of relaxing stimulating conditions. So that it does assume enough preestablished harmony such that, if the organism's driving adjustments are to achieve success, the given exciting stimulating conditions will usually, and in the main, be connected with somewhere nearly the "right" driving adjustments, and such that somewhere near the "right" driving environmental rearrangements will produce the requisite relaxing stimulating conditions. For example, it does have to assume (i.e., if the organism is to survive) that the original innate exciting stimulating condition for the driving adjustment of flight shall not innately be attached to such environmental conditions as the protective presence of the parent, but rather to such environmental conditions as those of loud sudden disturbances; and similarly, it does have to assume that the original and innate relaxing stimulating condition for this same adjustment of flight shall not innately arise from the nearer presence of the original frightening object, but rather from a decreased intensity of it; and so on. But whether the original frightening object shall be gun, loud voice, or what not, or just in what mode of locomotion successful getting away shall prove to consist, is not preëstablished but is a matter dependent upon the chances of experience. Finally, the amount of pre-established harmony which is thus assumed seems to be no more than can easily be accounted for on the basis of evolution.

We may now, then, once more sum up the features of this third type of theory. (1) Whereas there are no innate connections of external response to original stimulating condition, there are innate connections of specific driving adjustments to original external or internal stimulating conditions. (2) These driving adjustments tend to release particular sets of random acts. (3) They also set a particular goal for the random acts in that these acts tend to continue until some one occurs which provides a stimulating condition which *innately* relaxes the driving adjustment itself. (4) These driving adjustments are definable in terms of the purely abstract types of success which they predicate. (5) As so defined they necessarily involve a teleological use of language. (6) The theory predicates no mysterious degree of preëstablished harmony between the nature of the environment and the nature of the organism. This theory, it seems to me, is in all essentials the one advocated by Woodworth.[21] And to him, I believe, belongs the credit for having first suggested it. It must be observed, however, that his discussions of what we have been calling the driving adjustments are almost entirely in terms of the physiology underlying them. This restriction to physiology has prevented him from realizing the possibility and importance of their purely behavioristic definition and that they can be so defined even when their underlying physiology is not known.[22] It is to be noted, further, that Perry also, in a series of extremely original and stimulating behavioristic studies of purpose and knowledge, has evolved a doctrine which, when worked out in its psychological (as distance from its epistemological or value) details, would seem to imply much this same theory of instinct.[23] It is to be pointed out, however, that in these articles Professor Perry was not interested in the problem of instinct as such (i.e., the problem

---

[21] See particularly his book, *Psychology: A study of mental life,* New York, Holt, 1921. The theory is also presented in less developed form in his earlier series of lectures, "Dynamic Psychology."

[22] As a matter of fact his actual method of identifying individual adjustments would seem to be in introspective terms, which may be very well in the case of human adults, but certainly fails in the case of the lower animals and infants.

[23] R. B. Perry, "Docility and purposiveness," *Psychol. Rev.,* 25 (1918), 1–21; "A behavioristic view of purpose," *J. of Phil.,* 18 (1921), 85–105; "The independent variability of purpose and belief," *J. of Phil.,* 18 (1921), 169–180; "The cognitive interest and its refinements," *J. of Phil.,* 18 (1921), 365–375; "The appeal to reason," *Philos. Rev.,* 30 (1921), 131–169.

of innate connections) and hence his discussions imply a theory of instinct rather than state one.[24] The present theory has also been previously urged by the present writer,[25] although at that time its implications were not worked out in such detail.

Lastly, it is to be noted that in its essential features the theory is closely related to one of the most important aspects of McDougall's doctrine. What is it, in the last analysis, which gives the latter its overwhelming appeal? The significant points about it which do this, it seems to me are two; first, the positing of a specific type of central tendency or disposition (the emotion) which remains constant no matter what the varying circumstances of actual stimulus and actual response; and, second, the positing of a special type of abstract response originally given for and appropriate to each such central set or tendency (i.e., running away, in the case of fear; striking out, in the case of anger, etc.). But it is these two features which are the significant points about our theory. And our theory seems to me preferable, first, in that it gives a behavioristic rather than a merely mentalistic (i.e., the emotion) account of these central sets; and, second, in that it emphasizes more clearly the nonspecific nature of the type of response; for example, not a running away, or walking away, or flying away, but merely as getting away, irrespective of the particular type of locomotion employed.

Finally, before concluding, it may not be amiss if, merely for purposes of rhetoric, we attempt to give the theory a little more concreteness by indicating a possible, though not necessarily correct, physiological substructure for it. I find the possibility of such a substructure in the very suggestive though no doubt still somewhat chaotic notion of Kempf's[26] of the autonomic and projicient apparatuses. He supposes that the autonomic nervous system, together with the unstriped muscles and glands which it innervates, constitute a single independent and relatively autonomous mechanism. It is this autonomic apparatus which is to be conceived of as the prime mover of the organism—as that which controls and sets the goals for the projicient apparatus; i.e., the cerebrospinal nervous system plus its terminal organs. When a stimulus external or internal excites the autonomic apparatus it causes some adjustment of viscera or of postural tension. This adjustment results in the arousal of a series of sensory impulses in the organs affected which flow into the

---

[24] His "Determining Tendency," in other words, cannot be directly identified with what we are here calling driving adjustment. It would be something based upon this driving adjustment but would seem capable of involving acquired factors as well.

[25] E. C. Tolman, "Instinct and purpose," *Psychol. Rev.*, 27 (1920), 230.

[26] E. J. Kempf, *The automatic functions and the personality*, Nervous and Mental Diseases Monograph Series, no. 28 (1918).

cerebrospinal system and there constitute what he calls an affective stream or "itch" (i.e., that of hunger or sex) which innervates this system, i.e., the projicient apparatus. This affective stream keeps the organism restless and moving until it eventually achieves a new stimulus which produces an opposing or neutralizing adjustment.[27] All we need to do is to explain our driving adjustments in terms of Kempf's adjustments of the autonomic apparatus and our "random movements" in terms of his movements of the projicient apparatus and we will have the requisite substructure.

The fact that the random units of reaction on any given occasion fall within a certain relatively restricted limit of possibilities would be explained by supposing that the affective sensory stream resulting from the given autonomic adjustment, the given driving adjustment, is of such a nature as to excite innately only certain of the projicient activities. Thus, for example, when the infant is stimulated by having its limbs restrained, one sort of autonomic adjustment may be assumed to take place such that it goes through one set of random movements (the strugglings and cryings of anger). When stimulated by a loud sudden noise, another adjustment takes place and it goes through a second somewhat, though not entirely, different set of activities. Finally when stimulated by stroking or patting still a third adjustment takes place, and a third set of projicient activities; those of reaching out, smiling, cooing, etc.[28]

The feature of our theory which assumes that the same mechanism explains the *success* of a random act is provided for by supposing, as is assumed by Kempf, that success consists in any act which succeeds in providing a new stimulus which automatically and innately produces an opposing or neutralizing autonomic adjustment. Certain difficulties about the picture no doubt remain. It is not, for example, altogether clear just what would be the relative functions of the internal sensory stream coming from the driving adjustment, and of the sensory impulses coming from the external stimuli as such. When Thorndike's kitten,[29] for example, is shut up in the puzzle box and goes through its random acts of scratching, clawing, biting, etc., these acts are certainly controlled and guided not merely by some internal sensory stream but also by the sensory stimuli coming from the outside; viz., the parts of the

[27] Part of the plausibility of Kempf's doctrine depends upon his thesis that the skeletal muscles contain unstriped as well as striped components, and that it is the unstriped components which control postural tension and that these are part of the automatic system.

[28] J. B. Watson, *op. cit.*

[29] E. L. Thorndike, *Animal intelligence,* New York, Macmillian, 1911, p. 38.

cage scratched at, clawed at, and bitten. What may be assumed to be the relative functions of these two sets of sensory stimuli? Let us consider the case of the absolutely unlearned organism. In the case of such an organism it is presumably the internal stimuli which alone function. Such an organism's acts are *really and truly* random. It will go through a whole set of random hittings, strikings-out, etc., quite independently of the true nature of the surrounding objects. And we may suppose that as a result of the contacts, i.e., as a result of the new stimuli which these contacts furnish, the organism will acquire attachments of its activities to these objects. This attachment to external stimuli is to be conceived as the first instance of that whole process the nature of which we are explaining. We assume, in short, that those random strikings-out which "score hits"; that is, which come into succcessful contact with surrounding objects, are more pleasing to the organism in that they lead to stimuli producing a more successful reëstablishment of autonomic equilibrium than is the case of the nonscoring strikings-out. Hence it is the former which tend to get learned—attached to the external stimuli in question. To return, now, to Thorndike's kitten: we must assume that at an early age; i.e., long before it was first confronted with the puzzle-box situation, its purely random acts had become developed and modified to the extent of becoming attached to definite external stimuli, so that when put in the box its desire for escape (i.e., its controlling autonomic adjustment) led for the most part to bitings, scratchings, and clawings of the actual cage and not to mere mid-air activities.

The answer, then, to our original question as to the relative functions of the internal and external stimuli in the production of random acts would seem to be the following: Originally it is the internal autonomic-adjustment-produced stimuli which alone function. They produce *really* random acts; i.e., acts which have no dependence upon or necessary relevance to the external stimuli actually present. Soon, however, these really random acts tend to lose their pure character and to acquire specific attachments to external stimuli.[30] And whenever thereafter an autonomic adjustment gives rise to a series of random acts these acts are for the most part no longer purely random, but acts which are already modified; i.e., selected and attached to specific external stimuli. In this latter stage we may perhaps sum it up by saying that the internal stimuli release the acts and determine the type, but that the external stimuli

---

[30] The most obvious case of this type of process would seem to be the acquiring of spatial adjustments; that is, the acquiring by the young organism of the ability to strike, claw, etc., at the actual space points from which visual stimuli excite it. The latter may develop perhaps in part *in utero*.

provide the specifying control and regulation. For example, the internal stimuli would determine which of Watson's three sets of random responses[31] anger, fear, or love, should be released, but the external stimuli would guide and regulate the particular cryings, hittings, reachings out, head turnings, etc.

A second detail about the hypothesis which also remains to be discussed concerns, of course, the matter of the exact mechanism of learning. We have supposed that acts get learned; i.e., reënforced and attached to external stimuli, in so far as they result in new stimuli which innately (or as a result of acquired connections) lead to an opposing neutralizing sort of autonomic adjustment. Now, obviously, this is a pretty large assumption and we must admit our present complete inability to give an adequate explanation for it. But we can at least show as much justification for it as for any of the other current assumptions, including Mr. Kuo's that learning depends upon the removal of the exciting stimulus itself. This whole matter of the underlying mechanism of the fixation of arcs in trial and error learning[32] is, of course, one of the dark chapters of psychology. On the one hand we have Watson and his followers emphasizing the mechanical efficiency of mere frequency and recency, and on the other we have Thorndike, while admitting the efficiency of recency and frequency in his "Law of Exercise," also emphasizing the importance of resultant pleasure and pain (or of their concomitant physiological effects) in his "Law of Effect."[33] Now, it may be noted that the assumption we have made above could, if necessary, be brought under either head. The reëstablishment of autonomic equilibrium could be declared to be the physiological basis for pleasure and the lack of such reëstablishment the physiological basis for pain. Or, on the other hand, it could be declared that the reason that the act leading to the autonomic readjustment was learned was primarily because it had the advantage of frequency and recency, because, by hypothesis, it necessarily terminates any series of acts and, therefore, must always occur at least once in each trial, and must also be the most recent at the beginning of each new trial.[34] Our doctrine, therefore, would seem to have as good a chance as any other.

---

[31] *Op. cit.*

[32] Cf. J. B. Watson, *Behavior: An introduction to comparative psychology*, New York, Holt, 1914, chap. vii.

[33] E. L. Thorndike, *op. cit.* A long list of further theories, but all more or less modifications of one or the other of the above two, could be made out. For an illuminating discussion of this whole matter see Z. Y. Kuo, "The nature of unsuccessful acts and their order of elimination in animal learning," *J. of Comp. Psychol.*, 2 (1922).

[34] In this connection cf. J. B. Watson, *Behavior*, p. 259 ff.

So much for a sketchy suggestion as to how Kempf's doctrine might perhaps be used as a physiological basis for this third type of alternative theory. But quite apart from the correctness or incorrectness of this or any other physiological picture, the behavior implications of the theory, its doctrines of driving adjustments and of random acts, do seem to us valid.

In conclusion, let us again draw attention to Mr. Kuo's own theory and to each of the three alternatives which, a priori, all seem to be possible views until further empirical observations shall have been made. But let us also confess our own faith that *instincts cannot be given up in psychology,* but rather that they must be retained, and retained under some such conception as that of the driving adjustment of this third alternative theory.

3

A BEHAVIORISTIC ACCOUNT OF THE EMOTIONS

[*Psychological Review*, MAY, 1923]

THE EMOTIONS are now being investigated in new places. Interest is no longer centered exclusively upon adult normal humans, but is turning to subadults, subnormals, and subhumans. But these suborganisms cannot introspect. This sets a problem. How does one identify the emotions in these suborganisms? If one is studying anger and fear in infants and imbeciles, how does one decide when it is anger and when fear? It would seem that some explicit statement and agreement concerning such difficulties might well have preceded actual experiments. Perhaps fortunately, however, men (including psychologists) are not over nice in their logic so that, as a matter of actual practice, they have proceeded gaily with their experiments, leaving the purely methodological analysis of their procedure for post facto dissection. It is such a post facto dissection that the present paper wishes to undertake.

Our task is to discover by what criterion, implicit or explicit, one does actually recognize and label the emotions in the nonintrospecting organisms. It seems obvious that this criterion, whatever it may be, is to be found somewhere in the *externals* of the situation. Either, that is, one recognizes and labels the emotions by virtue of the sorts of *stimuli* which evoke them, or by virtue of the sorts of *responses* in which they eventuate, or lastly, perhaps, by virtue of something about *both* stimuli and responses. The aim of this paper is to discover which of these criteria it may be.

Before proceeding to the task, however, let us put the question in a wider setting. Suppose that, instead of being concerned with the emotions of the nonintrospecting organisms, we think ourselves back into the good old days when we were concerned with the emotions of the introspecting organisms. How, *then,* did we distinguish between anger and fear? The answer, of course, is that we induced introspection.[1] We asked the organism to tell us whether he was angry or whether he was afraid. But how do we know what the words "angry" and "afraid" mean? There is no mystical connection between the emotional states, as such, and these particular words. A Frenchman will say not "angry" but "en colère," and a German, "zornig." The connection between the particular words and the particular emotional states must be acquired. But how?

Suppose we turn to the young child learning to talk. He hears the words "anger" or "angry" in certain situations. I behave angrily and he is told that I am "angry." The child cannot get inside me nor directly experience my anger. The one thing therefore which can ultimately identify the word for him and give it its meaning, must be something about my behavior or the situation which produces it, or both. Or, again, he exhibits anger in his behavior and is told that he is "angry." Again the word must get its identification and meaning from something about the behavior situation and from that only. But, perhaps you will say that since in this second case the child does directly experience his own conscious emotion, as such, this time the meaning of the word will get directly attached by him to the conscious state as such. Very good. But, be it noted, this conscious state when you tell him that he is angry no more gets directly into you than did your conscious state, when you are angry, get directly into him. It was only because he was *behaving* in such and such a way that you knew that he was angry and told him so. You could not see his anger any more than he could see yours. In both cases it was only what may perhaps be called the *behavior analogue* of the emotion which was the common term mediating between you. Hence, ultimately it seems to be this behavior analogue which defines, if not your meanings for, at any rate your uses of, the word. When an introspecting organism reports that he is angry, what you thereby know and identify is not his conscious state as such (which never gets into you) but rather that he is in a condition which makes him likely to behave in a certain way. You know that he is probably going to behave in the way which determined your and his original acquisition of the word. Introspection, no more than any other type of behavior, can display directly to you the "private contents" of the other person's mind.

The situation involves a second point which needs emphasis. It is not the actually exhibited behavior, as such, which constitutes, be-

[1] Of the "Kundgabe" variety.

havioristically speaking, the emotion, but rather the *readiness* or *drive* for such a behavior—a readiness or drive which, as a result of acquired habits, may come to vent itself sometimes in quite other than the original, and initially defining behavior.[2] But it is only through tracing these other behaviors back to this initial and defining behavior that we know what emotion they express.

It appears that the study of emotions in the introspecting organisms is ultimately in much the same status that it is in the study of the non-introspecting organisms. The animal and abnormal psychologists have in reality been no more hasty than, and indeed perhaps not as hasty as, were the good old introspectionists themselves. The latter no less than the former proceeded without first making clear to themselves the nature of their methodological assumptions. The introspective study of emotions no more than any other study of them gets directly at private mental contents. For both types of study the emotion is in the last analysis defined, characterized, and identified in terms of a *behavior* situation.

If the above be true, it is indeed high time we sought to discover the nature of these ultimate and defining behavior-situations. As a step in this direction, let us turn to Watson's now classical study on the emotions of infants.[3] There, if anywhere, it would seem as if we might get light upon our problem. But even there, it appears, we shall have difficulty. For, strangely enough, Watson himself seems to have been almost as serenely and naïvely unconscious of the real theoretical crux of the situation as the most dyed-in-the-wool introspectionist. Note, for example, the naïvete of the following: "What stimulus," he asks, "apart from all training will call out fear responses; what are these responses, and how early may they be called out?"[4] In the first part of his question he defines fear in terms of its responses and asks what are its stimuli, and then in the second part he immediately turns round and asks what are its responses. In other words, he knows *neither* the stimuli *nor* the responses which define fear and yet he knows fear. Here he might perhaps reply that he knows fear as he knows all emotions, by means of its internal responses. "An emotion is an hereditary 'pattern reaction' involving profound changes of the bodily mechanism as a whole, but particularly of the visceral and glandular systems."[5] But it is to be pointed out that in the particular case in question no knowledge of the

---

[2] The introspective speech reaction constitutes one of the most common of these acquired behaviors.

[3] J. B. Watson, *Psychology from the standpoint of a behaviorist.* Philadelphia, Lippincott, 1919, chapter vi.

[4] *Ibid.*, p. 199.

[5] *Ibid.*, p. 195.

internal responses in fear was, as a matter of fact, obtained by Watson, or even suggested in his account.

Truly, our subjectivistic friends are not to be blamed for suspecting an inconsistency in the Watsonian logic. Unfortunately for them, however, his inconsistency does not lie as they seem to suppose, in any secret reliance by him upon an immediate intuitive knowledge of the private mental contents of other organisms, including infants. Rather it is that he possesses an immediate, though unexpressed, recognition of the external *behavior* characteristics which define emotions.

Let us turn now to the record of his actual observations and see if we cannot discover for ourselves what these defining behavior characteristics were, not only for fear, but for each of his three emotions. We may tabulate the observations, as follows:

FEAR

Stimuli	*Responses*
Suddenly removing all means of support (dropped from the hands to be caught by an assistant).	Sudden catching of breath.
	Clutching (grasping reflex).
	Blinking of eyelids.
Loud sound.	Puckering of lips.
Sudden push or slight shake (when just falling asleep or just waking up).	Crying.
	In older children, possibly flight or hiding (not yet observed by Watson as original reactions).
Sudden pulling of supporting blanket (when just going to sleep).	

Any or all of the responses can apparently appear for any one of the stimuli (the account is perhaps not altogether clear upon this point). The grasping reflex, however, invariably appears when the child is dropped.

RAGE

Stimuli	*Responses*
Hampering the infant's movements, i.e., holding of face or head; or holding arms tightly to sides. This "is the factor which apart from all training brings out the movements characterized as rage."	Crying.
	Screaming.
	Body stiffening.
	Fairly well coördinated slashing or striking movements of the hands and arms.
	Feet and legs drawn up and down.
	Holding breath.
	In older children, kicking, slapping, pushing.

LOVE

Stimuli	*Responses*
Stroking or manipulation of an erogenous zone.	If the infant is crying, crying ceases.
	A smile appears.
Tickling.	Attempts at gurgling and cooing.
Shaking.	In slightly older children, the extension of the arms.
Gentle rocking.	
Patting.	
Turning on stomach across attendant's knee.	

Surveying the above lists, I think we are ready to agree that these really were cases of fear, rage, and love, respectively. But why do we agree? The distinguishing characteristics hardly seem to lie in the individual stimuli as such. It would be no outrage, to my conception of fear, at least, if none of the listed stimuli had actually happened to evoke fear, or indeed, if other quite different stimuli had evoked it. If the dropping of the child had caused not fear but anger, I should have felt no particular surprise. Indeed the same may be said for any of the other stimuli. It can hardly then be the stimuli as such that defined the emotions. But neither does it seem to have been the responses, *merely as such,* that defined them. Sudden catching of the breath, random clutching (i.e., the grasping reflex), blinking of eyelids, puckering of the lips, crying, flight and hiding, these, just as such and such muscle contractions, do not define fear. Catching of the breath, merely, as catching of the breath, grasping, merely as grasping, blinking, merely as blinking, puckering, merely as puckering, crying, merely as crying, running away, merely as running away, and hiding, merely as hiding, might severally occur in any one of numerous *non*-fear situations. When, however, we take them all altogether and evaluate them not merely as involving such and such muscle contractions, but rather as obviously calculated to produce, to be appropriate for, such and such a reaction back upon the stimuli which produced them, then they *do* indicate fear.

It is not a response, *as such,* nor a stimulus situation, *as such,* that constitutes the behavior definition of an emotion, but rather the response as affecting or calculated to affect the stimulus situation. The responses of catching breath, clutching, blinking, puckering of lips, crying, running, and hiding seem all, with the possible exception of the first, to be of a nature to *protect* the organisms from exciting stimuli of one sort or another. Clutching protects against dropping, blinking against light, puckering of lips against things shoved into the mouth, and crying, running away, and hiding, against all kinds of stimuli either by bringing help or by totally removing the organism. They are all *protection* responses. And it is in this character that they alone identify the instance as one of fear.

Turning now to anger. Again it is obvious that it is neither hampering stimuli, as such, nor slashing, striking, crying, stiffening responses, as such, that identify the case as anger, but rather, the fact that slashing, striking, crying, stiffening are all responses calculated to produce, to be appropriate for, another type of back action upon the exciting stimulus, viz: the destruction of the latter. Anger is a destruction-of-the-stimulus response. Fear and anger are alike in that they both cause the removal of the stimulus, but they are different in that whereas the behavior situation which defines fear is one in which the organism is merely protected against, the behavior situation which defines anger is primarily one in which the stimulus is destroyed. The one operates by leading away from, the other by leading towards and destroying.

Consider now, finally, his case of "love." The responses here seem all appropriate for the further continuation of the stimulus. The stopping of crying, smiling, cooing, gurgling, the stretching out of the arms are one and all, given a social environment, responses calculated either to leave the stimulating condition undisturbed or actually to reach out and get more of it. Human organisms have evolved in a social environment and, given this fact, the early postnatal appearance of smiling, cooing, gurgling, stretching out of the arms can easily be explained as having evolved as appropriate for "getting more of the given stimulus."

It must be observed that all response tendencies would apparently fall into one or the other of the two classes of "tending to remove" or of "tending to continue and get more of" the stimulus. Anger and fear go in the first group and love in the second. We have not as yet, however, distinguished between love and other possible innate "getting more of" tendencies. Watson mentions no other innate tendencies under emotion. He does, however, mention others under "instinct," for example, "manipulation" or "curiosity." Manipulation or curiosity, assuming that there is such an innate propensity, would seem to be another original "to get more of" tendency. How are we to distinguish between it and love? The answer seems to be that whereas love is a "to get more of" by encouraging or enticing; curiosity is a "to get more of" by examining, or exercising one's sense organs upon.

To sum up, now, our three emotions. In the case of each it appears that the thing which is characteristic and which defines it for us as an instance of such and such an emotion is not the nature of the individual stimuli, as such, nor the nature of the individual responses, as such, but rather the gross *behavior result,* i.e., the nature of the back-action of the responses upon the stimuli. And these gross behavior results, be it noted, are not privately and subjectively defined but are perfectly objective characteristics about the behavior-situations which even those who run may read. The human infant (*albeit in a blind haphazard fashion*) innately tends to protect itself from certain stimuli, to destroy certain others, and to encourage or entice still others, and we can observe him doing it. These are the sorts of facts about total behavior situations which we learned as children to designate as fear, rage, and love, respectively. They are facts not of stimulus alone nor of response alone but of *response-as-back-acting-upon-stimulus.*

Certain other features about the situation must also be considered. In the first place, it should be emphasized that those behavior tendencies which define the emotions are probably always of a relatively blind and chaotic nature. A *precise and accurate* getting away from or a *precise and accurate* destruction of the stimulus would seem to be hardly the behavior analogues of emotions but of relatively cold mental states. Certainly, intense fear and intense anger as well as intense love would seem to exhibit a certain convulsiveness in their behavior analogues.[6]

Finally, and this is a most crucial point, it may perhaps be objected that as yet we have really offered behavior analogues for one phase of emotions[7] only, viz. their purely impulsive phase, and that emotions are not merely impulsions but rather and more significantly, unique types of more or less passive mental presentations. Very good, but when so characterized do they not reduce to organic sensations? (No one yet seems to have been able to avoid the James-Lange theory.) But as sensations, they are again susceptible to (and indeed can find none other than) a further behavioristic definition. In a previous article I have already shown (or if you prefer *attempted* to show) that sensations also can, in the last analysis, be defined in behavioristic terms only.[8] We may sum up the gist of the argument there presented as follows:

Every experimental study of the sensation qualities of another organism, including the introspective examination of those of a normal, adult human, can be seen to reduce in the last analysis to the principle of the Yerkes-Watson discrimination box. In the use of the latter, a pair of stimuli are presented and the animal is forced, if he can, to discriminate between them. In this way, a single stimulus may be paired with as many others as desired. And the observer learns which of these other stimuli can be discriminated from the given one and which can not. Indeed, he can learn all the *degrees* of similarity and difference of any one stimulus to all other stimuli. But this is just what, and no less than, he can discover from human introspection. The words with which one introspects upon one's sensation qualites acquired their meaning in terms of the standard stimulus situations, to which as children we heard them ap-

---

[6] See in this connection Kantor's contention that an emotion corresponds to an actual breakdown of behavior. J. R. Kantor, "An attempt toward a naturalistic description of the emotions," *Psychol. Rev.* 28 (1921), 19–42, 120–140.

[7] A phase which, indeed, we would be perfectly willing to designate as instinct rather than as emotion, if that should seem more consonant with desirable usage.

[8] E. C. Tolman, "Concerning the sensation quality: A behavioristic account," *Psychol. Rev.,* 29 (1922), 140–145.

plied, and in terms of the similarites and differences of these standard situations. The word "red" as used in interhuman communication means simply a certain standard stimulus or stimuli plus the similarities and differences of this given stimulus to such and such other stimuli. Its meaning is a *classification* of the given stimulus, a classification which is read off from purely behavior observations. What "red" may be as a private "feel" for you, I do not know. I only know it as a something produced in you by such and such ether waves, and which appears to you as thus and thus similar to, or different from, that which is produced by such and such other ether waves.

Applying these conclusions to the emotions, it means that the passive, substantive, mental-presentation, side of an emotion is defined in terms of the stimulus or stimuli which produce it and in terms of the similarities and differences (for the purposes of behavior discrimination) of this stimulus or these stimuli to such and such other stimuli. Further, the stimuli in question are primarily internal organic ones (i.e., accepting the James-Lange theory) and they are presumably produced by the organic and muscular changes which result from or accompany the impulsive phase of the emotion. It must be observed, however, that an experimental determination of these internal stimuli and of their similarities and differences to other stimuli is very diffcult, if not impossible, in the case of the nonintrospecting organisms. Much the same, however, can be said for the case of the introspecting organisms. With both types it seems very difficult to arrange it so that the organisms will react discriminatively to the resultant internal stimuli, as such, rather than to the external stimuli which by calling out the emotional attitude are producing these internal stimuli. We know, that is, very little as regards the similarities and differences between the substantive presentation sides of fear and anger in either men or animals. Though we are, to be sure, beginning, through the work of Cannon and others, to learn as a first step, something about the probable stimuli which produce them.

These practical difficulties, however, are of less importance since as a matter of practical value it seems to be the impulse sides of the emotions which are of more importance. It matters little that we cannot yet describe fear, anger, or love as mental presentations, i.e., as groups of sensations, as long as we can and do describe them as types of *impulse*.

We may sum up the main points of the argument and the conclusions as follows:

1. The recent change of direction in the study of the emotions from the introspecting to the nonintrospecting organisms raises the theoretical question as to the ultimate definition of the emotion.

2. A careful examination of the implications of actual procedure seems to indicate that for *both introspecting* and *nonintrospecting* organisms the definitions are ultimately *behavioristic*.

3. Further analysis shows that such behavioristic definitions have two parts: (*a*) the definition of the impulse side of the emotion as a *drive* or *tendency* toward a particular type of behavior result, of *response-as-affecting-stimulus;* e.g., in the case of fear, protection from stimulus, in the case of anger, destruction of stimulus, and in the case of love, encouragement or enticement of stimulus; and (*b*) the definition of the substantive, presentation, side of the emotion as a particular group of internal sensations, which sensations themselves are ultimately also to be defined in purely behavioristic terms, i.e., in terms of stimuli and of their relations of similarity and difference to other stimuli.

4. It seems, however, to be the impulse phase of the emotion that is of more practical interest and importance, and this is apparently the phase which is the more easily identified and defined.

5. Finally, we would conclude that further attempts at behavioristic identification and definition may well precede or accompany future programs for empirical research.

4

BEHAVIORISM AND PURPOSE

[*The Journal of Philosophy*, JANUARY 15, 1925]

EARLY IN THE HISTORY of philosophic and theologic thought there appeared a distinction between mechanism and purpose. And at the beginning of "modern" philosophy this dichotomy became embodied, as we all know, in metaphysical systems which were avowedly dualistic—systems which postulated spirit and matter as two fundamentally different types of substance. Today, although metaphysical dualisms are no longer fashionable, a similar distinction still remains in the form of a working postulate of psychology. Orthodox "mentalistic" psychology assumes, that is, that as descriptive fields, mind and body are two distinct types of entity; and it sees in 'purpose" a character which belongs to the former field only. For, even though mind be ultimately, metaphysically, reducible to body (or *vice versa* in case one is an idealist), still orthodox psychology maintains that from the point of view of immediate description mind exhibits "purpose," whereas body does not. Purpose is held to be essentially a mentalistic category.

Such being the general background and point of view of modern psychology, it is natural that it should look with suspicion upon behaviorism. For "behavior" to the ordinary psychologist is a phenomenon belonging to the body side of the dualism. And, though it may in itself be an interesting and important subject for study, it must, by hypothesis, be incapable of covering the whole subject matter for investigation. It must be incapable of dealing with "purpose."

Now it will be the thesis of the present paper that a behaviorism (if it be of the proper sort)[1] finds it just as easy and just as necessary to

---

[1] I.e., not a mere Muscle Twitchism of the Watsonian variety. See E. C. Tolman, "A new formula for behaviorism," *Psychol. Rev.*, 29 (1922), 44–53.

include the descriptive phenomena of "purpose" as does a mentalism. Purpose, adequately conceived, it will be held, is itself but an objective aspect of behavior. When an animal is learning a maze, or escaping from a puzzle box, or merely going about his daily business of eating, nest building, sleeping, and the like, it will be noted that in all such performances a certain *persistence until* character is to be found. Now it is just this *persistence until* character which we will define as purpose.

It may be noted in passing that Professor McDougall[2] has drawn attention to a similar character in behavior. Thus he finds the following six descriptive marks: (1) "a certain spontaneity of movement"; (2) "the persistence of activity independent of the continuance of the impression which may have initiated it"; (3) "variation of direction of persistent movements"; (4) "the coming to an end of the animal's movements as soon as they have brought a particular kind of change in its situation"; (5) "preparation for the new situation toward the production of which the action contributes"; (6) "some degree of improvement in the effectiveness of behavior, when it is repeated by the animal under similar circumstances." And he declares, much as we should, that the first five of them correspond to purpose. But the fundamental difference between him and us arises in that he, being a "mentalist," merely *infers* purpose from these aspects of behavior; whereas we, being behaviorists, *identify* purpose with such aspects. When one observes an animal performing, one knows nothing concerning possible "contents" in the latter's "mind" and to assume such contents seems to us to add nothing to one's description. One does, however, see certain aspects of the behavior itself which are important and for which the term "purpose" seems a good name. And there is no additional explanatory value, we should contend, in making the further assumption that such responses are accompanied by a mentalistic something, also to be known as "purpose."

It is, then, the argument of this paper that wherever the purely objective description of either a simple or complex behavior discovers a *persistence until* character there we have what behaviorism defines as purpose. And upon further analysis, we discover that such a description appears whenever in order merely to *identify* the given behavior a reference to some "end object" or "situation" is found necessary. Then, when a rat is running a maze and is exhibiting trial and error, such trials and errors, we discover, are not wholly identifiable in terms of specific muscle contraction A, followed by specific muscle contraction,

---

[2] *Outline of psychology*, Scribners, 1923, chapter ii. See also "Purposive or mechanical psychology," *Psychol. Rev.*, 30 (1923), 273–288.

B, etc. They are only completely describable as responses which persist until a specific "end object," food, is reached. An identification of these trial-and-error explorations has to include, in short, a statement of the end-situation (i.e., the presence of food) toward which they eventuate. Such a behavior is, therefore, in our terminology a case of purpose. Let us illustrate by other examples.

The Peckhams,[3] in describing the nest-provisioning behavior of the solitary wasp, Bembex, reports as follows: "Sometimes she drops the fly behind her, and then turning around, pulls it in with her mandibles. In other cases, where a longer portion of tunnel has been filled with earth, the fly is left lying on the ground while the wasp clears the way. The dirt that is kicked out sometimes covers it so that when the way is clear the careless proprietor must search it out and clean it off before she can store it away. In one instance, in which we had been opening a nest close by, the tunnel was entirely blocked by the loose earth which we had disturbed, and the wasp worked for ten minutes before she cleared a way to her nest." In short, this behavior of the wasp, containing, as it does, all these possible variations, has for its one constant and identifying characteristic the fact that it always ends in "getting the fly in the burrow." It is a case of purpose. Again the struggles of Thorndike's kitten[4] are struggles to "get out." That is, the complete descriptive identification of its behavior requires the inclusion of this to "get-out" character. The behavior exhibits purpose. Also the behavior of Köhler's chickens, dogs, and apes[5] in "rounding" obstacles (i.e., taking *Umwege*) in order to reach food has, in each instance, to be described with reference to the relative position of the goal object. These behaviors, therefore, also exhibit the purpose aspect. Finally, the behaviors of a man escaping from a burning hotel,[6] of a child withdrawing from a hot stove, of a college student crossing the street to escape an unwelcome acquaintance, and of a chick[7] rejecting the nasty caterpillar, again one and all require for their descriptive identification the statement of their respective *a quo* characters. They are completely identifiable only if we include *what* it is and *where* it is *from* which the escape is being made.

To sum up, then, whenever, in merely describing a behavior, it is found necessary to include a statement of something either *toward which* or *from which* the behavior is directed, there we have purpose. But we

---

[3] *Wasps, social and solitary*, Boston, Houghton, Mifflin, 1905, p. 123.

[4] *Animal intelligence*, New York, Macmillan, 1911, p. 35.

[5] Wolfgang Köhler, *Intelligenz Prüfungen an Menschenaffen*, 2te Auflage. Berlin, Springer, 1921, p. 8–17.

[6] E. C. Tolman, "Instinct and purpose," *Psychol. Rev.* 27 (1920), 217–233.

[7] S. J. Holmes, *Studies in animal behavior*, Boston, Badger, 1916, p. 131.

may analyze further. Just when is it we find a statement of a "toward whichness" or of a "from whichness" thus necessary? We find it necessary, whenever, by modifying the various attendant circumstances, we discover that the same goal is still there and still identifying the given response. Thus, when we make minor changes in the position or nature of the *intervening objects* and the behavior readjusts so as to again come to the same end object, the case is one of purpose. Or finally, when we remove the goal object entirely and behavior thereupon ceases, purpose must again have been a descriptive feature. In short, purpose is present, descriptively, whenever a statement of the goal object is necessary to indicate (1) constancy of goal object in spite of variations in adjustment to intervening obstacles, or (2) variations in final direction corresponding to differing positions of the goal object, or (3) cessation of activity when a given goal object is entirely removed.

But here, perhaps, our "mentalist" friends will wish to intervene. They will agree with us, no doubt, that these aspects of behavior lead naturally enough to the use of the word "purpose," but they will deny that such "purpose" is a mere aspect of the behavior itself. And perhaps, in support of this denial, they will point out that such changes in behavior, as we have been suggesting, require "memory." The organism has to note and "remember" the changes in the position or character of the goal object, if his behavior is to be thus affected. If a rat readjusts his behavior to changes in the position of the food box or to changes in the intervening route, he can do so only by virtue of *remembering* the old or new position of the food box. Hence they will declare that, even if purpose itself were not an ultimately "mentalistic" phenomenom, the actual working of it must be based on *memory,* and memory at any rate is a mentalistic phenomenom. But we shall also deny this latter assumption.

Memory, like purpose itself, may be conceived, we would hold, as a purely empirical aspect of the behavior. To say that an animal remembers "such and such" is merely another way of saying that his present behavior can be shown to be causally dependent upon "such and such." The animal's going-to-or-from an object, not immediately present, does, to be sure, imply that his behavior is then and there a function of a now absent object. But this tempero-functional dependence of behavior is a purely objective fact and all that need be meant by memory. But such memory, like the "purpose" itself, is but another objective aspect of the behavior.

We conclude, then, that whenever in order to describe a behavior our description has to include that it is a function of an object toward or from which the animal is going, there we have *purpose*. And whenever, at the same time, this object is nonpresent to sense, there we also have memory.

It should be noted that to Professor Perry is due the credit for having first pointed out the possibility of such a purely objective and behavior-istic definition of purpose. In his article "Docility and Purposiveness"[8] he has discovered purpose to be objectively inherent in every behavior involving learning. But it appears, therefore, that for him it is not the mere direction of the behavior with "reference to the goal object" which defines purpose, but rather the fact of *learning, per se*. Thorndike's kitten, in escaping from the puzzle box, exhibited purpose according to him, because it improved in getting out on succeeding trials.

Now, it is obvious that what one calls purpose, and what one calls less than purpose are, of course, in the last analysis merely matters of convenience in the use of terminology. If, therefore, Professor Perry feels that he wants to reserve the word "purpose" for those cases only in which learning is involved, he is not to be convicted of bad logic. But, to the present writer, it seems more desirable and less confusing to apply the term to all behavior which can be seen to be a function of an end situation, irrespective of whether learning does or does not super-vene. Professor Perry would reserve the term "purpose" for a description of such behavior as that of Thorndike's kitten, in which the end is reached sooner on succeeding trials. The present writer, on the contrary, would apply it *also* to behavior in which, even though no improvement appears, the animal on each trial may be seen to persist until a given end is reached. Thus stentor's behavior[9] in bending away from the drop-ning carmine, then of reversing cilia and then of shrinking, and finally of doing this latter so hard as to pull up roots and swim away to a new location, would be, for the present writer, a case of purpose, even if on a later trial there were no sooner appearance of the final shrinking response. For the complete descriptive account of even this first behavior requires a reference to an end situation; *viz.*, the end of avoiding the carmine. For it is found that the behavior keeps up *only until* this latter is accomplished. And if, for example, as a result of the first bending, the animal is allowed to reach "success" the activity stops. The avoidance of the carmine, in short, is a real descriptive feature of the behavior. The responses, even on the first occasion and before learning has had a chance, continue only until such avoidance is consummated.

---

[8] *Psychol. Rev.*, 25 (1918), 1–20. See also *J. of Phil.*, 17 (1921), 85–105, 169–180, 365–375; *Phil. Rev.*, 30 (1921), 131–169.

[9] Jennings, *The behavior of the lower organisms*, New York, Macmillan, 1906, p. 174.

The fact of learning, on the other hand, which appears in the higher organisms (and perhaps even in stentor itself) would seem to us to be something different. It is, of course, in itself an interesting and important phenomenon. But it seems to be something superimposed upon purpose, rather than identical with purpose. Docility results from purpose and will not occur without purpose, but it is something more than the latter. We cannot hold, therefore, with Professor Perry in his defining of docility and purposiveness as coextensive. The latter appears, wherever an end is involved, irrespective of whether or not the animal improves in reaching that end. And it may now be recalled that Professor McDougall presented actually six marks of behavior and that his sixth was that of learning. But he found purpose implied by his first five characteristics only. Here, then, we agree with him.

In conclusion, although we agree with Professor McDougall in finding his first five marks of behavior characteristic of purpose, we disagree with him in supposing such "purpose" to be something added on to the mere objective description of the behavior itself. In this matter, we would follow rather Professor Perry. Purpose seems to us, as it does to him, a purely objective aspect of the behavior itself. We disagree with Professor Perry, however, in that we would not restrict this objective "purpose" aspect to the fact of learning. Purpose is a more extensive and more fundamental phenomenon than learning. Purpose, we should assert, is that aspect of behavior which is present wherever merely to describe the behavior it is necessary to include a reference to the position or nature of the goal-object, as such.

5

PURPOSE AND COGNITION: THE DETERMINERS OF ANIMAL LEARNING

[*Psychological Review,* JULY, 1925]

THE PRESENT PAPER will offer a new set of concepts for describing and interpreting the facts of animal learning. These new concepts will differ from the usual ones in not being restricted to the customary physiological notions of stimulus, neural excitation, synaptic resistance, and muscle contraction (or gland secretion). They will rather include such immediate and common sense notions as *purpose* and *cognition.* These latter, however, will be defined objectively and behavioristically, not "mentalistically."

More specifically, the reader is to be asked to envisage the facts of animal learning (and, indeed, of human learning as well) in terms of (I) a *goal seeking* (purpose), (II) a set of innate or acquired *initial exploratory impulses* (initial cognitive "hunches"), and (III) the acquisition of a set of *final object adjustments* (final cognitions). And, in order to indicate the real fruitfulness of such concepts, they will be concretely and severally discussed for the particular case of maze learning in rats. The necessary material for this discussion will be drawn from the published literature, from a description of experiments already performed at California, but not yet published, and from a description of experiments which ought to be performed. We begin with the matter of goal seeking.

GOAL SEEKING (PURPOSE)

When a rat runs a maze, it is to be observed that his running and searching activities *persist until food is reached.* And it appears that his persistence is the result of the physiological condition of hunger. We do not know whether the rat, in so "persisting" is "conscious"; we do not know whether he "feels a purpose" (to use the terminology of the mentalists); but we do know that, given (1) the physiological condition of hunger and given (2) the objective conditions of the maze, the rat thus *persists until the food is reached*. It is this purely *objective* fact of persistence until a certain specific type of goal object is reached that we define as a *goal seeking*. And as thus defined, a goal seeking is a wholly objective and a wholly behavioristic phenomenon. There is nothing "mentalistic" about it.

The one important experiment already in the literature directly oriented toward this question is that of Dr. Simmons on *The Relative Effectiveness of Certain Incentives in Animal Learning*.[1] In this experiment, she found that the rate of maze learning may be varied by using different types of goal objects. She found, for example, that bread and milk as food caused a more rapid learning than sunflower seed. She found also that complete satisfaction of hunger immediately at the end of the run is more effective than merely partial satisfaction (followed by delayed feeding an hour later). Such findings indicate gross facts concerning the importance of goal seeking. They indicate that the nature and strength of this goal seeking and its satisfaction have important effects upon the learning rate. They do not indicate, however, in just what qualitative ways the different goals produce their different effects. She did not, for example, devise her experiments so as to discover whether the different effects are a matter of calling out more and better initial exploratory impulses or rather of a more rapid "stamping in." Nor do her results indicate whether the one type of food was better than the other because the one food was less lasting and hence the animal was more *hungry* at the beginning of each new trial, or whether it was rather a matter of the greater satisfactoriness (pleasantness) of one food as such. These are all important points left as problems for further investigation.

Under the head of such further investigations we might suggest the following. First, we might, perhaps, test the "satisfactoriness" of the goal object *per se*. Suppose a maze were so constructed that the living cage of the animal were directly connected with the food box. Our experiment would then attempt to use the desire to get back home (i.e., to the living cage *per se*) as a *standard* against which to measure strengths of the food desire. We might, perhaps, measure the time spent in the food box as against the time spent in the living cage in any fixed period

---

[1] Comp. Psychol. Monog., 2 (1924), Serial no. 7.

allowed for eating, or in some similar way measure the relative strengths of the food-box-getting-to tendency as over against the home-going tendency. Having such a method of measurement, we could then discover to what extent this food-getting-to tendency *per se* varied in terms of the home-going tendency with different sorts of foods and at different stages of learning. What, for example, would be the results, given the same physiologically defined degree of hunger, for bread and milk and for sunflower seed? What those as regards the initial and the final stages of learning? Etc., etc.?

It is obvious that after gathering such data together we would have infinitely more information for explaining and describing a maze learning curve than we have at present.

A second line of investigation might be directed toward discovering the nature of the goal features. What features of a given goal object is it which make the latter a goal object? Experimentally, that is, we would want, by varying the stimuli which a given food presents, to discover just what are its essential and defining goal features. Is it, for example, its color, its taste, its smell or its what, which determines its acceptance as a goal? And does this necessary feature perhaps vary with the different stages of learning,

Finally, a third sort of investigation suggests itself. For it appears that goal seeking must be defined not only as a tendency to *persist* in more or less random fashion *until food is reached* but also as a tendency to *select* within limits the *shorter* (and probably also the easier and pleasanter) of two or more alternative ways. This appeared first in De Camp's classical experiment.[2] For it will be remembered that he found that a rat will, within certain limits, discriminate between and prefer the *spatially* shorter of two alternative routes to food.

At California we have now done a further experiment from which it has been discovered that a rat will also select, other things being equal, the *temporally* shorter of two routes. Mr. Sams, in an experiment to be soon published, found that a rat, when given the choice between two ways to food, one temporally longer and the other temporally shorter, will, within limits, select the latter. The apparatus was simple. At the exit from a starting box the animal could go either to the right or to the left. Both the right and the left alleys would lead him in symmetrical fashion and by spatially equal distances to one and the same food box. Correspondingly placed down each of these alleys were "confinement spaces"; each with a door in front and a door behind. When the rat reached one of these spaces he found the door in front closed and as

---

[2] J. E. De Camp, *Psychobiology*, 2 (1921), 245–253.

soon as he got there the door was closed behind him. He then had to wait between the two doors for a certain predetermined length of time, after which the door in front of him was opened and he was allowed to pass on toward food. After a few experiments the rat settled down to the necessities of the situation and took the enforced waiting calmly. The essential experimental procedure consisted in making him wait longer on one side than the other. As yet, the experiment has not been performed with a great many animals nor have the limens been determined with accuracy. But with the three animals tested it was definitely discovered that a wait of one minute would be discriminated and selected as against a wait of six minutes. And when the sides for these long and short waits were interchanged, the animal readjusted and went to the new side.

Summing up, then, from De Camp's experiment and from this experiment of Mr. Sams' we conclude that the goal seekings (purposes) which govern a rat's maze learning include not only the tendency toward such and such a goal object as such but also a further selective tendency to get to this goal object by the shortest route both (a) spatially and (b) temporally.

Finally, it appears probable that in addition to these spatial and temporal preferences, further investigations might indicate that a rat will also prefer a "physiologically easier" route when spatial and temporal distances are rendered constant.

INITIAL EXPLORATORY IMPULSES (INITIAL COGNITIVE HUNCHES)

Given the tendency to persist *until* the food box is reached and given the further tendency eventually to select both the spatially and temporally shorter route, what sorts of exploratory impulses are initially called into play?

The one important investigation bearing upon this point is Hamilton's.[3] Hamilton investigated with a four-box "multiple choice" apparatus what he called "Trial and Error," or "Perseverance Reactions." He presented his animals with a series of settings in which the only essential feature was that the correct door in any given setting was never the same as it had been in the just preceding setting. When confronted with this series of practically insolvable problems, he found that the responses of his animals grouped themselves into certain very definite types:

1. Responses which indicated an appreciation of the experimenter's rule that no alley is the right for two successive trials.

---

[3] G. V. Hamilton, *J. Animal Behavior*, 1 (1911), 33–66; *Behavior Monog.*, 3 (1916), 65.

2. Responses which indicated an appreciation that it is useless to try an alley more than once during a given trial; all four alleys tried and in an irregular order.

3. An effort to escape by trying the alleys one by one in succession, beginning at the extreme left and working to the right or beginning at the extreme right and working to the left.

4. More than one separate effort to escape by a given alley during the same trial but with an interruption of such efforts by an interval of effort to escape by one or more of the other alleys.

5. During a given trial the subject enters an alley which does not afford escape, leaves it and reënters it one or more times without having tried another alley; or, having tried a group of two or three alleys in a certain order, he reënters all alleys of the group in the same order one or more times.

Reviewing these five types of responses from our present point of view, we see that to a large extent they are nothing more or less than descriptions of the nature of the exploratory impulses (or initial cognitions), which appeared in his different animals.

The tendency to try all doors (but each one not more than once), the tendency to work in regular fashion from left to right or from right to left, the tendency to try the same door several times, either with or without intervening attempts at other alleys, and finally, the tendency to persist at some small group of doors over and over again are pretty evidently *objective* descriptions of the innate nature, extent, and flexibility of the animals' initial exploratory tendencies (initial cognitive "hunches" of how to get there). The animal that persists at the same door over and over again obviously has an inferior set of exploratory tendencies (cognitive "hunches") to the one that tries other doors in between.

And it is of course clear how important information of such an order will be if we are to be prepared wholly to understand and explain maze learning. How fast and in what manner a rat "learns" will be conditioned among other things by the range, methodicalness, and flexibility of his exploratory impulses.

Another bit of experimental evidence bearing upon this matter of exploratory impulses is to be found in some, as yet unpublished, experiments performed at California. In these experiments a simple T maze was used. And it was arranged so that the animal could get back to the food box in identical fashion whether he chose the left or the right angle of the T. Either route met with success. The interesting point which came out and which is of prime importance to us here is that, although some animals acquired a consistent preference for one side rather than for the other, this preference often appeared relatively late and in some animals not at all and as long as such a preference was absent there was instead a very pronounced tendency toward continuous and regular alternation—left, right, left, right, or right, left, right, left. That is, not only did the animals tend to average five times to the right and five times to the left, out of the total of ten trials on any day, but the percentages of immediate alternations from left to right and from right to left were much greater than would have resulted from mere chance. It appeared, in short, that even where either side was equally "satisfactory" there was in our rats a positive tendency left over toward variation of responses. But, if this is so, it indicates that trial and error does not result merely because of failure, but that it is a positive tendency in and of itself.

Finally, there is still a third bit of experimental evidence concerning the initial exploratory tendencies, evidence concerning immanent orientation factors which may be found to run through them. For Dashiell[4] found that the proportion of animals, who on the initial trial entered any given alley or blind, varied with the relative direction of this alley or blind. An opening straight ahead, for example, was entered much more frequently than one to the side, and on coming out of a blind, retracings were less frequent than goings-in.

So much for such experimental evidence as is now on hand. It is only a beginning. The questions concerning the causal determiners of these initial exploratory propensities is still unanswered. How much are they due to experience? How much are they conditioned by the particular type of goal and the particular type of physiological need back of that goal? Do, for example, fear and sex call out different initial exploratory tendencies from hunger and from one another, and so on? And how much, finally, do they vary in kind or extensity with the mere urgency and intensity of the need? Would we find that the more intense the motive, the more restricted the exploratory readiness, and the less intense the motive, the more leisurely and widespread the sallies? Etc., etc.?

FINAL OBJECT ADJUSTMENTS (FINAL COGNITIONS)

What are the defining elements of, and the causal factors determining, the acquisition of the final object adjustments (cognitions)? We must note, in the first place, that such final object adjustments seem to be made up of two phases or aspects: (1) what we may call their intent or noëtic aspects, and (2) what we may call their sensory cue or sensory aspects. We shall consider these separately.

---

[4] J. S. Dashiell, *Psychobiology*, 2 (1920), 181–186.

1. The intent or noëtic aspect of an object adjustment we will define as the object structure (i.e., that behavior possibility) which the animal's behavior can be observed quite definitely to *impute* (whether correctly or incorrectly) to such and such a particular part of the maze. Thus, for example, the behavior of the rat who runs straight into the end of the shortened maze blind may be said quite objectively to impute an object structure (a behavior possibility) to this part of the maze which the latter does not possess. It imputes, that is, a greater length to the alley than it has. Or, again, when a rat, at a given stage of learning, tends to enter alleys pointing in the general direction of the food box more often than those pointing in the opposite direction, such a predominance of entrances obviously states, exhibits, an imputation that the food box lies in the general direction of such alleys. Given, in short, that the animal is dominated by the food-seeking impulse, his various behaviors in the successive parts of the maze can be said, at any stage of learning, quite objectively to express his thereunto acquired object adjustments (cognitions) with respect to the "getting-on-toward-food" possibilities of such maze parts. It must be emphasized that these object adjustments to the maze structure have meaning only with reference to the task of *getting to the food and getting there as quickly, both spatially and temporally, as possible.* What the animal's behavior exhibits in the way of object adjustments to (cognitions of) the maze structure are not, of course, comparable to what the physicist would tell us about the maze, but are merely (cognitions of) adjustments to the maze from the one point of view of getting to the food box.

So much for an indication of the intent or noëtic aspect of the animal's object adjustments.

2. It appears, however, that learning consists not merely in the acquisition and improvement of these intent or noëtic aspects of the animal's adjustment to the maze, but it involves also the attachment of such intents to the *right stimulus cues.* The functioning of any given object adjustment requires the presence of stimuli. The rat imputes a behavior possibility to a particular part of the maze as a result of particular stimuli presented by that maze part. And the phenomenon of learning consists in large part in the attaching of the object adjustment intents to these stimuli.

We may now turn to the experimental evidence on these points.

1. We may begin by recalling De Camp's and Sams' experiments. For these really give evidence not only about facts of "purpose" but also about facts of "cognition." They indicated not merely that rats will *prefer,* other things being equal, the spatially and temporally shorter

of two paths, but that they can also within certain limits *adjust* to (*impute*) the ones which are the spatially and temporally shorter. As a result of such experiments we may conclude therefore that the first important features of behavior structure to which the rat acquires a cognition intent are just these of relative spatial and temporal extents. Whenever a given alley presents too great a distance or too great a time, it comes to be rejected for one which is shorter.

But are the above the only adjusted-to features which maze learning involves? What about blind alleys? Are they also merely a matter of excess distance or excess time? And is the reason for their elimination merely the fact that the going in and out of them is adjusted to (cognized) as involving this excess distance and this excess time? That distance factors do play a part in their elimination is evident from certain experiments which have been tried out at California. Thus Mr. White and myself[5] found that, given two blinds (both relatively deep and both presenting the same sort of initial straightaway) the longer of these two was eliminated first. In other words, that which causes a blind to be eliminated *is*, in part at least, its excess distance. For the greater the excess distance which a blind presents, the sooner it will be eliminated.[6] But this is not all. We have been performing another experiment at California. In this further experiment the animal was presented with a blind, with a true path, and with a roundabout route symmetrically placed as compared with the blind. Further, the blind was of a length such that the going in to it and the coming out again, plus the then taking of the true path, was of exactly the same length as going all the way by the roundabout route. Our results, as far as we have gathered them, indicate that in such a situation the blind is eliminated a *little before* the roundabout route involving the same total distance. Or, in other words, it appears that a blind, as such, *does* allow some additional type of object adjustment (cognition) over and above that of its mere excess distance. The question next arises, of course, as to what this further feature is. Two possibilities suggest themselves. The first would be that the essence of this further feature of the behavior structure of a blind is that it brings the animal back to its starting point. The other would be that its essence is to be found in the fact that the blind end

---

[5] E. C. Tolman and A. E. White, *J. Comp. Psychol.*, 3 (1923), 327–331.

[6] It will be recalled that Peterson found that the shorter of two blind alleys was eliminated first. But both his blinds were, absolutely speaking, short and it seems probable that his animals were responding directly to immediate cues which would be more prominent in his shorter blinds than in his longer ones. His results, in short, probably indicated facts about perception rather than facts about learning. Joseph Peterson, *Behavior Monog.*, 3 (1915).

brings the animal up "on its haunches." Which of these it is must be tested out. An experiment to do so would be quite simple. All that would be needed would be to present the animal with a blind and with an excess distance of the same length which went around in a circle and therefore, like the blind, brought the animal back to the starting point. If, then, the blind were eliminated before this roundabout route, we could conclude that the distinctive thing about the to-be-cognized behavior structure presented by a blind was something more than its bringing the animal back to the entrance, and presumably something about its bringing the animal to a stop and forcing retracing *per se*.

2. We turn now to the other point—the nature of the stimulus cues and of the laws governing the attachment of the cognition intents to them. Initially and before experience an animal cannot know (except in the case of relatively short blinds—i.e., the case of immediate perception) what the behavior structure of a given alley is to be.

He must enter and find out whether it is long or short, or whether it is of the nature of a blind or of an unobstructed passage. And learning consists in attaching such resulting cognition intents (object adjustments) to whatever distinctive stimulus cues may be discoverable at the entrances. The more capable animal will be the one who can thus attach the cognition intent to earlier and earlier sensory cues and make such adjustments quickly.

The immediate problem subdivides therefore into (a) a discussion of what distinctive stimulus cues the particular organism is capable of attaching its cognition intents (object adjustments) to; and (b) what are the governing circumstances for the acquisition of such attachments.

As regards (a) the literature is relatively extensive. The well-known work of Watson[7] on the apparent ability of animals to learn mazes with all but the kinesthetic cues eliminated falls under this head, as does also that of Miss Vincent[8] in showing that on occasion the animals nevertheless can be made to depend upon visual, olfactory, or tactual cues, when these are emphasized.

As regards (b) discussion is still rife. Are the mere frequency and recency with which given stimulus cues are followed by given behavior structures the only factors determining the formation of associative connections from the former to the latter, or are other influences of an instinctive or emotional character also involved? Is, in short, the "law of exercise" enough, or is the "law of effect" also necessary? The evidence is still obscure and largely so, I believe, because the sort of analysis of

---

[7] J. B. Watson, Psychol. Monog., Serial no. 33.

[8] S. B. Vincent, *J. Animal Behavior*, 5 (1915), 1–24, 140–157, 175–184, 367–374.

the situation which we are here recommending has not ordinarily been made. Previous work, for example, has made no distinction between an animal's mere *knowledge* of the behavior possibilities which will get him to food and his *desire* for those behavior possibilities. Whether an animal actually enters a given alley or not is probably a function, not merely of the growth of his *knowledge* about the nature of that alley but also of the state of his desires as we indicated in Section I. And experimental work must be done on tearing these two factors apart, before we can be certain to what extent the acquisition of mere knowledge, as such, is a function of mere frequency and recency or how much it depends also upon the satisfactoriness or unsatisfactoriness of the result.

CONCLUSION

First, it is to be emphasized that the primary object of this paper has been to demonstrate the *fruitfulness* of some sort of purposive (goal seeking) and cognitive (object adjustment) categories applied to learning. It has not been to insist that the particular purpose and cognition categories here suggested are necessarily the best that could be found.

Second, we wish to point out that in adopting such purpose and cognition categories as a substitute for the usual stock, physiological ones of synaptic resistance and conditioned reflex, we are not denying that the physiological concepts will ultimately prove the more comprehensive and accurate. Eventually we will undoubtedly have to reduce and explain our more immediate categories of goal seeking and object adjustment in terms of physiological categories. But the date at which this last will be possible is far distant. And, practically, it seems that the current tendency to talk and think primarily in terms of such inadequate and premature physiological concepts as are now on hand is in part responsible for some of the barrenness of our present animal research.

Finally, it is to be pointed out that the above discussion, in spite of its use of the terms *purpose* and *cognition,* is *behavioristic*. For in no place in using these concepts have we defined them "mentalistically." We have not in some mysterious fashion "looked within" and so discovered them. Rather have we looked without at the rat in the maze and merely proceeded to describe the behavior which we saw. And the animal's cognitions (object adjustments) and his purposes (goal seekings) as we have observed them have been described and *defined* in purely *objective* terms; in terms, that is, of (a) the objective maze situation itself, and of (b) purely objective and descriptive aspects of the rat's behavior in the presence of that situation.

6

A BEHAVIORISTIC THEORY OF IDEAS

[*Psychological Review,* SEPTEMBER, 1926]

IN THE COURSE OF writing this paper[1] I have become more and more aghast at the number of separate items I have tried to pack into it. Far too many for clearness. And yet I don't know how I could have done otherwise. I wanted to introduce you to a new way of viewing things. And I felt that for my argument to have cogency, I must suggest my whole system and not limit myself to merely one feature about ideas, a feature such as might properly be encompassed in a single paper. The result, as you will see, is the following overstuffed boa constrictor of an affair with contents not wholly digested, and perhaps you will say by very nature indigestible. Anyway, so much for plea and for apology.

Turning, now, to the paper itself. In the first place, it is to be made clear that the theory of ideas I am going to present is merely a scientific or methodological hypothesis. I, as nought but a scientist, neither can, nor hope, nor, indeed, would want to attempt anything like a fundamental philosophical doctrine. For it is obvious that questions such as that of the final epistemological and metaphysical significance of ideas must be left to thinkers with wider foundations and a wider interest. As a mere psychologist, I am under compulsion to discuss ideas only from the one point of view of attempting to reduce them to a workable causal scheme. My only justification for speaking to you philosophers on such a matter at all is the presumption that you, whatever else the basis of your larger considerations, will also want to take cognizance of what we, the scientists of the moment, happen to be saying. It is, then,

---

[1] Read before the Philosophical Union of the University of California, April 2, 1926.

merely as one such scientist of the moment that I am proposing to you the following considerations.

The orthodox psychologist, whom I shall oppose and whom we may call for convenience the "mentalist," conceives ideas as lying in, or as bits of, a unique type of conscious stuff. Ideas are described by him in their character as states or processes in this stuff. Overt behavior intrigues him only in so far as he believes he can infer conscious-stuff happenings from it.

Turn, now, to the behaviorists. We behaviorists, whatever else our divergences, are agreed in viewing overt behavior as the primary datum for psychology. It is from a study of such overt behavior and its environmental settings that we believe we will obtain our causal understanding both of the grosser activities of the lower animals, and of the higher conscious activities of human beings. Consciousness is for us but some moment or aspect in overt behavior.

But consider, now, more specifically the brand of behaviorism I shall present in this paper. For in order to understand my doctrine of ideas, you must first understand my notions of behavior simply as such. Behavior for me is not as it is for many, probably most, behaviorists primarily a matter of mere muscle contraction and gland secretion, of mere "motions," that is, described as motions. I conceive behavior rather as presenting a new and unique set of descriptive properties all its own,— new properties which, as such, can be described and known, irrespective of whatever muscular or glandular activities underly them. This new set of properties of behavior *qua* behavior is, of course, correlated with and probably completely dependent upon physiological motions, but descriptively and *per se* it is different from those motions.

"A rat running a maze; a cat getting out of a puzzle box; a man riding home to dinner; a beast of prey stalking its quarry; a child hiding from a stranger; a woman doing her washing or gossiping over the phone; a pupil marking a mental test sheet; a psychologist reciting a list of nonsense syllables; myself and my friend telling one another our thoughts and feelings." These are *behaviors*. And it is to be noted that in mentioning no one of them have I referred to, or, I blush to confess it, for the most part even known, what were the exact muscles and glands, sensory nerves and motor nerves involved. For these responses somehow had other sufficiently identifying properties of their own. And it is these other properties in which, as a behaviorist, I am interested.

But what now, more specifically, are these other distinctive properties? Well, to begin with, we may note two important features which seem to run through and be found in all instances of behavior. They are *trial and error,* and *learning.* Any case of behavior, if not a product of past trial and error and learning, is, if unwonted obstructions be introduced, capable of new trial and error and new learning. The activities of the rat running the maze, those of the man riding home to dinner, and the rest, are peculiarly susceptible to such trials and error and such learning. Indeed, it is just because they are thus susceptible that they seem to differentiate themselves in our minds from activities such as the beating of the heart, the expansion and contraction of the lungs, and the other "mere reflexes" of physiology. Let us consider these two features, then, in more detail.

First, *trial and error.* Thorndike's kitten in the puzzle box went through a series of random "trial and error" acts—clawing, biting, squeezing,—*until* by a chance clawing at the loop of string connected with the catch it got out. The author's own description was as follows:

> When put into the box the cat would show evident signs of discomfort and of an impulse to escape from confinement. It tries to squeeze through any opening; it claws and bites at the bars or wire; it thrusts its paws out through any opening and claws at everything it reaches; it continues its efforts when it strikes anything loose and shaky; it may claw at things within the box. It does not pay very much attention to the food outside, but seems simply to strive instinctively to escape from confinement. The vigor with which it struggles is extraordinary. For eight or ten minutes it will claw and bite and squeeze incessantly.[2]

Similarly, the rat in a maze exhibits the trials of turning here, there, and yonder, *until* it gets to the food box. The man coming home for dinner goes through the trials of examining this street car, that street car, and the other, *until* he gets to the car that will take him home. And the child tries hiding behind this chair, that chair, and the other, *until* he gets *from* the sight of the stranger. In each case the trials (and errors) *keep on until* some particular and objectively discoverable end object or situation is got to or from. But this is tantamount to saying that each such series of trials and errors exhibits a purpose to get thus to or from. The cat's trials are quite objectively exhibiting the purpose to *get to* the outside of the cage; the rat's runnings-about that to get *to* the food box; the man's examining of successive cars that to get *to* house and dinner; the child's hidings that to get *from* the stranger. These purposes to get to or from are part of the very descriptive texture of the act.[3]

But here a "mentalist" may perhaps protest. "Very true," he may say, "trial and error *do* exhibit purpose. But purpose is a mental phe-

---

[2] E. L. Thorndike, *Animal intelligence,* New York, Macmillan, 1911, p. 35.

[3] See also, E. C. Tolman, "Behaviorism and purpose," *J. Phil.,* 22 (1925), 36–41. (Reprinted in this volume, pp. 32–37.)

nomenon, and if you admit it, you are ceasing to be a behaviorist." "Not at all," I must reply. "The purposes we have here observed, these purposes which exhibit themselves in trial and error, these *persistences until*, are not mentalistically defined entities at all, but behavioristically defined ones." To a mentalist, a purpose, if he sticks to his fundamental postulates, must be essentially an introspectively get-at-able affair. The purpose he means must be, in the last analysis, a "content," "process" or "function" which is found introspectively within his or somebody else's *consciousness*. The purposes we have been pointing to, on the other hand, are different. They are discovered by looking *at* another organism. One observes that the latter *persists* through trials and errors *until* a given *end* is *got to* or *from*. Such a purpose is quite an objective and purely behavioristic affair. It is a descriptive feature immanent in the character of the behavior *qua* behavior. It is not a mentalistic entity supposed to exist parallel to, and to run along side of, the behavior. It is *out there in* the behavior; of its descriptive warp and woof.

Turn, now, to the second feature, *learning*. Not only do organisms vary and persist in their responses until they finally get to or from, but they also upon successive occasions repeat more readily those particular responses which have proved to lead most easily or most quickly to or from. That is, they learn. For example, white rats can learn to select, up to a certain measurable difference, the shorter of two alleys leading to food. But such a fact indicates not only that they have the purpose to get to food, but that they also do, within limits, cognize the shorter versus the longer way. Behavior *qua* behavior exhibits not only purposes, but also *cognitive postulations* as to the nature of the environment for mediating and supporting the purposes.

We have, then, these two conclusions: (1) Behavior expresses immanent purposes,—purposes which exhibit themselves as persistences through trial and error to get to or from. And (2) it expresses, as is indicated by the facts of learning, immanent cognitions,—cognitions as to the nature of the environment for mediating such gettings to or from. It is these cognitions which are of chief interest to us tonight. They are *ideas*, at least in some sense of that word. And our remaining task is simply that of working them out more clearly.

As our first step, we may note their transcending, reaching out, or, as Professor Adams has called it, "setting up of a claim" character. For the very essence of these "in-behavior" ideas is to make postulations or claims as to the environment. For example, consider a rat which has completely learned a maze, so that when put in at the entrance, he dashes through like a shot, turning here, there, and yonder, entering no blinds and arriving at the food box in only some four or five seconds from the start. Suppose, now, one of the alleys be considerably shortened between trials. What happens? On the trial after, the animal runs ker-plunk into the new end of the alley. In short, he acts as if the old length of alley were going to be still present. His behavior postulates, expects, makes a claim for that old length. It must be noted, however, that our evaluation of his claim involves a knowledge also of his purpose. It is only because we know (or assume) that the rat does not want to bump his head, that we can rightly conclude that his bumping exhibits a pos-tulation for an alley of the old length. If he had wanted to bump, then this very same act of running and bumping would have exhibited a postulation for the new shortened length. To rightly evaluate behavior cognitions, we must, then, at the same time rightly know and evaluate the controlling purposes.[4]

What, now, are the purposes? Fundamentally, as we have already seen, they are persistences to or from. But to or from what? We will answer quite dogmatically, without here attempting to present the argu-ment, that they are persistences to or from, finally and in the last anal-ysis, states of bodily quiescence or of bodily disturbance. External en-vironmental objects are got to or from only as means to or from these bodily states. It goes beyond the task of this paper to argue for a par-ticular enumeration of these final states. Suffice it to say that my pre-dilection is for a relatively short list. Food hunger, sex hunger, shelter demands, excretion demands, fatigue demands, and aesthetic demands complete what I should consider as the final list of ultimate *appetites*, or drives *towards quiescences;* and fear and pugnacity the final list of ultimate *aversions*, or drives *from disturbances*.[5] Others will perhaps not agree with this list. The important point for this discussion, however, is merely the doctrine that all behavior purposes do thus reduce ulti-mately to drives to or from final physiological states, and that all other objects or situations are, in the last analysis, got to or from only as routes or means for getting to or from these bodily states. Appetites and aversions plus external stimuli constitute the final determiners of be-havior. It is the already aroused condition of the appetite or the aver-sion which alone sensitizes the animal to external stimuli and causes him to postulate therefrom the characters of the intervening environ-mental objects which he must traverse or manipulate. Or, putting this pictorially, we may liken the environment to a multidimensional spider's

[4] See also, E. C. Tolman, "Purpose and cognition: The determiners of animal learn-ing," *Psychol. Rev.*, 32 (1925), 285–297. (Reprinted in this volume pp. 38–47.)

[5] See also, E. C. Tolman, "The fundamental drives," *J. Abn. Psychol.*, 20 (1926), 349–358.

web radiating out from the behaving organism in many directions. The far ends of the threads terminate in final to-be-sought-for quiescences, or final to-be-avoided disturbances. Environmental objects and situations are responded to and cognized only in their character of providing bridges or routes along these threads.

Turning, now, to analysis, we shall find that these behavior cognitions subdivide into three types or elements which may be termed respectively: (1) postulations of discrimination features; (2) postulations of manipulation features; and (3) postulations of relative positions and orders among discrimination and manipulation features.

First, *discrimination features*. The release of a behavior act postulates certain stimuli. That is, the going off of that one behavior act rather than of some other constitutes an assertion as to the characters of the stimuli which are present. Consider, for example, the sensory-discrimination experiment as used with the lower animals. The apparatus consists of a rectangular box or choice chamber from which two exits lead. From the standpoint of the animal, say a chicken or a rat, who enters at the end of the box, one exit leads out from the far right-hand corner and the other from the far left-hand corner. A partition projects out from the opposite wall and comes part way toward the animal, separating the ways to the two exits. To choose the right-hand exit, the animal has to pass to the right of this partition; to choose the left-hand one, he has to pass to the left of it. The experimental procedure consists in facing the animal with a pair of cue stimuli, say, two colors, one on the right and the other on the left, but arranging it so that, in any given trial, the one color, perhaps red, will always be on the side of the opened exit, and the other, perhaps yellow, on the side of the closed exit. In other words, if the animal goes toward the red side whether this in the particular trial be right or left, he is allowed to get through and he receives food; but if he goes toward the yellow side, he finds the door shut in his face and may even be punished further by an electric shock. If he is capable of discriminating, he will in time learn always to go toward the red and to avoid the yellow, whichever sides, right or left, these happen to be on in the given trial.

But such behavior illustrates very prettily what I mean by discrimination postulation. For this always-going-toward-the-red rather than toward the yellow must be said to assert, or make a claim as to the specific discrimination difference between these two kinds of stimuli. For a complete definition, however, we need further experiments. We need to try substituting other wavelengths for the given ones to discover which of these others would be accepted as equivalent for discrimination purposes. We should probably find, for example, that quite a large range of long wavelengths could be substituted for the initial red, and another quite large range of shorter ones for the initial yellow. Or in the case of the rat, we might find even that the initial red was really being reacted to as equivalent to no light at all, so that as long as there was some light on one side and none on the other, the animal would continue to react in the same fashion. But, in any case, the first step in our definition would consist in listing all these other color stimuli which could experimentally be substituted for the given ones. But even this would not be enough. For the final definition we should want to know also all about the whole system of interdiscriminabilities for this organism. We should want, in short, to know such a complete system of interrelationships as that which is represented for human beings by the Titchener color pyramid. For the color pyramid, as you will remember, is simply the schematic way of representing the whole system of interdiscriminabilities of visual stimuli for human beings. We need, then, an analogous color pyramid or color polygon for each organism. And not only a color polygon but, of course, also smell, touch, sound polygons. Having such polygons, we should then, finally, define the given postulated discrimination features in any such experiment, first, by listing all the substitutable and all the nonsubstitutable stimuli, and, secondly, by locating these respective substitutable and nonsubstitutable stimuli in their respective places on the given sense polygon.

We must note, however, that what we have thus been saying for these cue stimuli would really apply as well to all the other stimuli involved in such a behavior. Thus, for example, in this same experiment the animal's method of running to the one side or the other expresses not only postulations as to the discrimination characters of the cue stimuli, but also as to those of the visual, tactual, olfactory, and other stimuli coming from floors and walls and doors. The animal only goes the way he does because also of what he postulates as to these other stimuli. But here again experiment would show that certain stimuli could be substituted for these given ones and others could not. So that the final definition of what was postulated would again be in terms of the substitutable stimuli plus their specific positions upon the given sensory polygons for the given animal.

Finally, suppose that instead of a rat or a chick, it was a human being we had been concerned with and that instead of making him run in a discrimination box to the red side or to the yellow, we merely asked him which was red and which was yellow. What more should we have learned? We should have learned that for him a range of wavelengths around the red part of the spectrum can always be discriminated from another range around the yellow part. And we should have located these "reds" and "yellows" upon his color pyramid. But we should have learned nothing else, except, of course, that his color pyramid happened to be like ours and that he had been taught the same names for the "red" and "yellow" bands of the spectrum that you and I have. We should never have learned how these colors felt "inside" his mind, assuming with the mentalists that his mind has an inside. What they may be as private mental "feels," if there are private mental "feels," would not have entered into our account. And, indeed, it never did enter even into the results of the introspectionists, whatever they themselves may have thought to the contrary.[6]

We may turn, now, to the second type of behavior-postulations, that of *manipulation features*. The release of a behavior act postulates in the environment not only certain present and immediately-to-come stimuli, but also what, for want of a better name, I shall call certain specific *supports*. A behavior act postulates, that is, such real physical entities as sizes, shapes, weights, inertias, resistances, to serve as actual supports for itself. In order to stand, to walk, to climb, to run, to swim, to make noises, an organism requires and must have such and such physical supports as a solid surface to walk on, a physical height to climb over, an unobstructed stretch to run in, a liquid to swim in, and a gaseous medium to vocalize with. An organism requires and postulates these supports. That is, to return to the above experiment, the animal's going to either side postulates not only the discrimination characters of the two cue colors and of the visual, tactual, olfactory stimuli from floors and walls, but it postulates also such manipulation support features as the capacity of the floor for holding his weight, and of the geometry of the box for permitting him to turn at such and such points. The organism, in behaving, holds two sorts of intercourse with his environment. He senses it; that is, he postulates stimuli or discrimination features; but he also tries actually to manipulate it; that is, he postulates supports or manipulation features.

To define, now, in any given case these postulated manipulation features, we must discover, first, what other supports besides the given one could and could not be substituted and have the same behavior sustained. Secondly, we must discover also what other responses these given supports could likewise sustain. We must, that is, work out an algebra between physical supports and resultant manipulation features

---

[6] See also, E. C. Tolman, "Concerning the sensation quality: A behavioristic account," *Psychol. Rev.*, 29 (1922), 140–145.

analogous to that algebra which our sense polygons express as between stimuli and resultant discrimination features. We must know that while a thing of the size and shape and weight, etc., of a chair will, for a man, present manipulation features such as to-be-sat-on-ness, to-stand-on-ness, to-jump-over-ness, to-pick-up-ness, and to-use-as-a-weapon-ness; for a rat, it will present quite a different set of manipulation features, those, say, of to-build-a-nest-in-ness or to-hide-behind-ness.

Finally, we may note certain significant and philosophically interesting relationships between manipulation features and discrimination features. Discrimination features function as signs for manipulation features. For instance, I am now leaning (in a somewhat trembling fashion) against this desk. But this particular behavior results first from certain postulated discrimination features which I locate in the desk, those, for example, of its visual size and shape, plus certain of its touch qualities. These act as signs for my further postulation of its manipulability as something capable of being leaned against. The desk, however, has other discrimination features, for example, those of color and temperature, which, however, in this situation do not function as indicating to me anything about its lean-against-ability. Not all discrimination features, then, are in any given situation signs of manipulation features, but certain ones only. But here we strike up against, do we not, the old classical distinction between the "primary" and "secondary" qualities? Visual size and shape, pressure sensations, and the like, are primary qualities. Color and temperature are secondary qualities. The former indicate specific manipulation features; the latter do not. It must be noted, however, that this difference is merely functional and with reference to specific situations. That is, the orthodox list of primary qualities contains those discrimination features whose associations with specific manipulation features are relatively fixed and universal; while the orthodox list of secondary qualities contains those whose associations with specific manipulation features are less consistent and less frequent. Visual and tactual size and shape and number and pressure are pretty uniformly indicative of specific sizes and shapes and weights defined as supports or manipulation possibilities. Colors and temperatures, on the other hand, are not so uniformly indicative. As aforesaid, however, the distinction is only relative. For these so-called secondary qualities do often have definite indicative values, at least for specific situations. Thus, for example, the color may well be the significant cue for the housewife who needs an apple and dives rapidly into box or basket or cooler shelf, half filled, as it usually is, with a medley of oranges, lemons, apples, and tissue-paper wrappings. In such a case it may well be that it is the distinctive *color* of the apple which indicates to her quickly the whereabouts of the latter's specific manipulability features. And there is also the opposite fact. The so-called primary qualities themselves do not always have absolutely fixed and invariable implications,—witness our old friend the bent stick half in water and half out. The difference between primary qualities and secondary qualities is one of degree rather than of kind. It was easier for God (or the devil) to arrange it so that colors and temperatures and tastes can be more easily smeared on and off the surfaces of things than can visual and tactual shapes and sizes and resistances. But that is the only difference. Discrimination features, whether primary or secondary, always remain but discrimination features. Visual and tactual shape and size and resistance, as such, i.e., as pure discrimination possibilities, are no more at one with their indicated manipulation possibilites than are color and smell and taste. Both sets are mere signs for these manipulation possibilities.

We turn, now, to the third type of behavior postulations, that of *positions*, or orders among discrimination and manipulation features. The release of a behavior act postulates not only qualities and meanings, i.e., discrimination and manipulation features, but also orders and sequences or positions among the latter. But first we must note that the discrimination features which serve as signs for manipulation features seem to unite with the latter into what may be called the ultimate units of behavior. These units of behavior, however, can be of very different degrees of generality or extensiveness. For not only "entering an alley," "clawing at a loop," and the like, are to be described as such units of behavior, that is, of discrimination-manipulation wholes, but also such more extended operations as "getting out of the box," "running through the total maze," "buying a house," "going to Europe," or even "embarking upon a career." But in these more extended units it is obvious that the defining discriminations and manipulations must be less specifically detailed than in the cases of "clawing at a loop," and "entering an alley." A wider variety of different particular stimuli and of different particular supports can be substituted in them and have them still preserve their defining characters. All that is necessary is that the general pattern of discriminations and manipulations remain the same. And here, it may be noted, is where the *Gestalt* psychology comes in. For the *Gestalten*, as I see it, are just such discrimination-manipulation units, which, as the *Gestalt* psychologists themselves have emphasized, do retain their specific defining outlines in spite of wide changes and variations among their constituent elements.

Finally, we must note that these discrimination-manipulation units compound together into larger complexes. And such a compound may be formed in either of two ways: (1) two discrimination-manipulation units may come together as two coördinate successive links where the one is merely the necessary forerunner of the other; or (2) they may be combined rather as one superordinate to and inclusive of the other. For example, in the case of the kitten in the puzzle box, the two acts of "getting out of the box" and of "eating che food" are connected in the first fashion, the one merely the coördinate forerunner of the other. The two acts, on the other hand, of "getting out of the box itself" and of "clawing at the loop of string" are instead related in the second fashion, the former as superordinate to and containing the latter. But in both types of case the one act is a means to the other, and, as such, lies in a specific position relation to it. Thus, for example, "getting out of the box" lies primarily in a spatial position with respect to "eating the food," while "clawing at the loop" lies primarily in a mechanical position with respect to "getting out of the box."

Our problem is, then, how and to what extent does the animal postulate these position relations? We require in each case an experimental answer. We might, for example, in the case of our first pair of behavior acts, put the food in other directions outside the box, to discover thus if the directions of the getting out are or are not affected. Does, that is, the animal struggle primarily only against that side of the box which is towards the food, or does he struggle with equal readiness against all four sides? Can his insight into the position of the food "as outside" be defined as recognizing the notion of the box as a four-sided container, or is it limited rather to the notion of it as a mere face-on barrier? For the cat it would probably turn out to be the former. His behavior would probably express an insight into, a postulation of, the four-sidedness of the box. If, in contrast, chickens were put into the same situation, those of us who have kept hens in our youth know full well that they would oscillate back and forth (in the most irritating fashion) on the one side of the box nearest the food. Their position postulations would, in short, be limited to the simpler notion of "face-on barrier."

For the other example, that of pulling the loop of string to get out, we should need to try substituting different actual mechanical connections between string and door; connections which the animal could see and ones which he could not; connections which were simple and direct, or ones which involved higher principles, such as that of the pulley and of the lever; and connections in which the temporal sequence was rapid and ones in which it was slow. But for the cat we should probably find that the loop was merely equivalent to any other part of the cage; that his response expressed no greater mechanical insight into the situation other than, perhaps, that the loop is something relatively loose and shaky. If, in contrast, we were to put a chimpanzee or a child in the same situation, we should no doubt find that the simpler structural connections between string and door would lead to his pulling sooner. The behavior of these animals would, in short, exhibit some mechanical insight. A chimpanzee, as Köhler found, is capable of such manufacturing of tools as the piling of boxes and the fitting of two short bamboo rods together, in order to reach, in roundabout fashion, goals the direct spatial routes to which are blocked. This suggests relatively complex and ramifying systems of spatial and mechanical position postulations in these animals. Discrimination-manipulation objects lie inside one another and beyond one another, spatially, temporally, mechanically. And organisms, in so far as they behave correctly to such complexes and chains of objects, postulate, have insight into, not merely these objects themselves, but also their spatial, temporal and mechanical interrelationships.

We may stop now and sum up the argument to this point. The release of any behavior act expresses, contains immanently within itself, postulations or reachings out. And these are, as we have seen, (1) postulations of specific stimuli or discrimination features; (2) postulations of specific supports or manipulation features; and (3) postulations of specific positions or orders among discrimination and manipulation features. Or, in terms of orthodox tradition, may we not say, postulations of qualities and of meanings and of interrelations among meanings or among qualities. Such are the "in-behavior" ideas. And these ideas are in the most well established habits as well as in the more recent and newly acquired ones. And in defining none of them have we had to rely on introspection or assumed anything as to conscious awareness. The time remaining is short, but we must nevertheless still say a word about this matter of consciousness awareness. What sort of behavior acts would our theory assume as exhibiting not only such postulations, but also what the introspectionists call conscious awarenesses? Our answer is simple. Conscious awareness is for us but a unique type of postulation. It is a postulation which not only postulates but which brings the postulated into the present and makes it one of the determiners of the behavior act itself. And it is achieved whenever an organism is able, instead of actually behaving, to make a mere adjustment for that behavior. Such adjustments bring the postulated results into the present. For consciousness, as Professor Bode would say, is the "bringing of the future into the present."[7] It is a *representation* of results so that the latter can themselves become determiners for or against the act which leads to them. If these represented results are "good," the impulse toward this act can thereby momentarily and suddenly be reënforced; if "bad," it can be weakened. Wherever there is a sudden drop in the learning curve, there there is consciousness. For only by representation of its results (through memory or imagination) could acts hitherto infrequent become thus suddenly and consistently frequent.

By virtue of such representation the organism is able to evaluate the result of his act, and to release it or not to release it, as the case may be. If the result is in harmony with the already released and controlling larger act, then the given act is evaluated as good, if not, it is evaluated as bad, providing the animal has insight into the given position relations. This insight, however, may be of different degrees: (1) the organism may merely "feel" whether these represented results are ones which if actually presented would themselves, given the larger act, lead on to still further behavior. Or (2) if he is of a superior type, he may even represent the results of still further behavior which might lead from these first represented results; and so on through a whole chain of successive representations.

Perhaps this will all be clearer from examples. Imagine again the kitten in the puzzle box or the rat in the maze. Have we anything like objective evidence of consciousness or representation in their cases? The act of clawing at the loop, or of entering a given alley I would assert to be conscious in cases where the animal can be observed to hesitate for a moment between clawing and not clawing or between entering and not entering. I have not myself worked with cats in puzzle boxes, but I have worked with rats in mazes, and I have seen at certain stages in their learning very patent instances of such hesitation at a choice point between two alleys. The rat stops and wiggles his nose from side to side, and then finally chooses. And I have noted further that in such cases he usually chooses the correct one, more often than when he does not hestitate. There are, in short, real little drops in the learning curve at such points. And I assume therefore that there is consciousness. But how much does such representation amount to? My guess is that for these cases of the rat or the cat it amounts to very little. It is probably a representation of only the very immediate consequences of the act, a prevision, perhaps, of the opening door in the case of the cat, or of merely the immediate free space ahead in the case of the rat, of hardly more than is included in the mere perceptual properties of the situation.

---

[7] B. H. Bode, *Creative intelligence*, New York, Holt, 1917, pp. 228–281.

But these represented slightly farther-on-nesses are ones which when actually present have been "good" in the sense of having led successfully on previous occasions to further responses which were consonant with the larger controlling acts. Their representation therefore helps the animal to decide and to release the act leading to them. I doubt, on the other hand, if these animals are capable of anything like long trains of representations based upon these first representations. I doubt if the rat can represent not only the end of the immediate alley, but also the fact that this end opens into such and such another alley, and so on.

Turning, however, to human beings, or to chimpanzees, there are suggestions of just such chains or trains of representations. The chimpanzee was observed struggling to make one longer stick out of two shorter ones, in order to use this latter for reaching the food. Such behavior, when it first occurred in nonroutine, nonautomatic fashion, certainly suggested a representation by the animal of the longer stick and then a further representation of using this longer stick to reach the food. It suggests that he held up the immediate act in the form of a mere adjustment in order to represent its end, and that he then made a still further adjustment to this end in order to represent a still further end, and so on. But if so, then this was in embryo all that we mean by a train of thought or reasoning, as we find the latter in human beings.

But you may ask how, upon such a behavioristic model, can we allow for any but trains of concrete thoughts? How is our behavior model to care for generalized and abstract thinking? How is it to allow for the tedious flights of speculative fancy found in the papers of philosophers or even of psychologists? My answer is that philosophic animals can apparently adjust not merely to absent represented discrimination-manipulation possibilities as well as to present ones, but that they can also adjust to universalized discrimination-manipulation possibilities. For example, they can adjust for and prepare to behave to not merely a given specific pair of pairs, but also to all sets of pairs of pairs. They can declare, in short, that two plus two always equal four. They can abstract in their behavior adjustments from the specialities of a given case and adjust only to its generalities. But, even so, they can not make adjustments to anything other than the behavioristic discrimination-manipulation or interposition properties of objects. The world for philosophers, as for rats, is, in the last analysis, nothing but a maze of discrimination-manipulation possibilities, extended or narrow, complex or simple, universal or particular.

Finally, one last word. I know I can not hope in such a short space to have made this discussion of consciousness and thinking other than hopelessly chaotic and superficial, and particularly I feel certain that the die-hard mentalists among you will feel that I have been illicitly relying on introspection. My answer to this last charge, however, will be that introspection is for a behaviorist also a form of behavior. It is a surprising but none the less purely *behavioristic* fact that human beings can not only discriminate and manipulate in gross manner but they can also perform the very refined behaviors of using gestures, verbal or otherwise, to influence and to manipulate their fellows. They can say: "See this desk I am leaning against," or "Hear this noise I am making," or "Note this all-gone feeling I now have in the pit of my stomach," or "Let me tell you what I represent to myself if I try to describe all human activities on the analogy of a rat in a maze."

Human beings can do all these things, but they can not convey *per se* private mental contents to their fellows. If their fellows do not understand what they are talking about, then all they can do is to point and grossly to behave. Or, better yet, they can take their fellows over to a really good laboratory and show them a really good rat in a really good maze, and say, "See, this is what I mean, this is the sort of thing that is going on in my mind." I may have private mental contents, but if I have, only God and myself will know them. All you can ever know is what postulations and representations are waiting to get themselves expressed in my behavior, as those of the rat there are getting themselves expressed in his.

7

A BEHAVIORIST'S DEFINITION OF CONSCIOUSNESS

[*Psychological Review*, NOVEMBER, 1927]

THIS PAPER[1] should have been called "The frantic attempt of a behaviorist to define consciousness." In fact, the doctrine I shall present seems even to me quite unprovable and to you it will no doubt seem something far worse. And yet so great is my faith that behaviorism must ultimately triumph that I should rather present even the following quite doubtful hypothesis than hold my mouth and say nothing. If we behaviorists can not present good theories, we can at least present as many bad ones as possible in order that by their successive refutation we may be forced finally either into discovering the correct theory, or, if there be none, into abandoning our behavioristic adventure altogether.

Before, however, attempting my definition of consciousness, let me first briefly outline the nature of behavior as I see it. Every behavior act, in so far as its continued going off is contingent upon there proving to be such and such specific features in the environment, must be said in so far to postulate or cognize those features. For example, when a rat, after learning, is ready to enter only the white alley of a discrimination box, and not the black alley, the continuance of this "white-entering" behavior must be said to express a cognitive postulation as to the difference between white and black. Further, the fact that the continuance of this tendency to enter the white and not the black is also contingent upon the further circumstance that there prove to be a difference between food and nonfood on the two sides of the box must be said to express also a cognitive differentiation between food and

---

[1] Read before the Western Psychological Association, Los Angeles, June 17, 1927.

nonfood. And, thirdly the continuance of this entering of the white rather than the black must be said to express in addition a cognitive differentiation as to the relative sign relationships of white and black— the one as indicative of the food and the other as indicative of the non-food. For, if any one of these three sets of environmental facts should suddenly change, this behavior act would break down. Thus if there ceased to be a difference between the white and the black, or between the food and the nonfood, or between the respective sign relations of the white and the black with regard to food and nonfood, the consistent entering of the white and avoidance of the black would no longer continue. In short, the continued going off of this white-entering behavior act assumes, postulates, these three specific sets of environmental facts and relations.

But this which we have thus proved for the discrimination box behavior holds, it would seem, in a similar manner for all behaviors. Every behavior act, in going off and being what it is, expresses, implies, certain specific characters in the environment. And this is so because the continuance of its going off can be shown to be contingent upon there actually proving to be such characters in the environment. If these expected characters are not found, the act sooner or later ceases or modifies itself. Behavior is driven by organic needs, and in going off it postulates that the environmental characters and relations are such that it will prove an appropriate behavior for satisfying those needs. The going off of a particular act postulates a particular complementary character in the environment. And this is to be assumed as true for all behavior acts whether new and just learned or old and well-established by custom. The only condition is that these acts show themselves ready for alteration, if things go wrong.

In spite, however, of this conclusion that practically all behaviors are thus cognitive or postulative, we must note the further fact that many of these cognizing and postulating behaviors are none the less quite obviously automatic and unconscious. For a behavior to be postulative and cognitive, it is not necessary that it also be conscious. A well-established and quite automatically functioning habit act cognizes and postulates the environment, in our sense that its continuance is contingent upon the environment proving actually to be so and so. But such a habit act may none the less be quite unconscious.

What, then, we must now ask, is the further occasion and cause of consciousness? Our answer will be that *wherever an organism at a given moment of stimulation shifts then and there from being ready to respond in some relatively less differentiated way to being ready to respond in some relatively more differentiated way, there is consciousness.* For example, let us assume that our rat has up to some given occasion been responding in undifferentiated fashion to the white and black alleys. He may, perhaps, have been treating them both as distinct from some third chromatically colored alley, but as between these two, the white and black themselves, his behavior has not distinguished. On this particular occasion, however, we assume that something internal happens, such that he then and there switches from not being ready to respond to them as undifferentiated to being ready to respond to them as differentiated. The moment of this switch is the moment of consciousness. The organism then and there becomes conscious of the difference between black and white. On all the previous occasions his behavior treated the black and white as alike. On the occasion when the switch occurs his behavior first starts to treat them as different. It is this change to the new differentiation which we define as consciousness. The behavior after such a switch may in time become just as automatic as the behavior before it. Acts which imply more cognitive differentiation may be just as automatic as ones which imply less cognitive differentiation. It is only the switch-over when it occurs in a given moment of stimulation that defines consciousness.

What, now, is the mechanism of such switch-overs? In order to answer, we shall have to consider a new principle. This new principle is that organisms, at least the higher ones, are to be assumed capable not only of actual behaviors but also of what may be called mere behavior adjustments. The nature of these behavior adjustments is to be assumed such that they in some manner bring the animal into contact with the same stimulus results with which he would be brought in contact, if he should actually behave. The results of any proposed act may thus by means of a mere feint or adjustment to that act be brought into the present and became a conditioner for or against the act. To make an adjustment to an act is to achieve a *representation* (based, of course, upon what has happened upon previous occasions when this act or similar ones have actually been performed) of the probable stimulus results to be expected from the act.

This doctrine of an ability by virtue of mere behavior adjustments to represent the probable results of acts may well strike you as a pretty mystical affair. It may sound to you unworthy of consideration by any hard-headed scientist, let alone a behaviorist. And yet, I would ask you, what is Watson's own doctrine of implicit or subvocal speech, in so far as it has any cogency, other than a specific account of just such behavior adjustments? Watson, of course, does not call them behavior adjustments, but his gestures and subvocal contractions seem to have been devised by him to serve the very function which we are ascribing to the behavior adjustment. His doctrine has cogency only in so far as he implies that gestures and subvocal speech serve to bring (i.e., represent) to an acting or listening organism the type of stimulus results to be expected from an actual overt behavior, if it were carried out. The baby, when ruminating on what it wants, says subvocally among other things the word "doll." But this saying of "doll" serves to represent the type of stimuli to be expected if the baby were actually to go and get the doll. If these represented doll stimuli are satisfactory, the child performs the actual act of going and getting. If not satisfactory he rehearses, subvocally perhaps, the names of other toys.

The above is, of course, not quite the way Watson's own argument reads. It is, however, I believe, the way it should read, and it is only because of such an implied reading that his argument has such cogency as it seems to have. I present this account to you here, however, not to ask you to accept the doctrine of subvocal speech and subgesture as such, but rather to woo your minds gently to my own more general notion of the behavior adjustment. The behavior adjustment, whatever its neurological or physiological character, is to be conceived functionally as a surrogate for actual behavior—and a surrogate which somehow serves to bring into the present, that is to make then and there active upon the organism, the stimulus results to be expected from the corresponding actual behavior.

Assuming for the purposes of argument that you accept this doctrine, the next step will be to declare that it is these behavior adjustments which produce or *are* consciousness. When a rat on some given occasion switches over from a condition of nonreadiness to discriminate white and black to one of readiness to discriminate them, and, as we have said, thereby becomes conscious of the difference between them, this switch-over and this consciousness are mediated, we shall now declare, by a behavior adjustment. In this case we shall assume it is a behavior adjustment to the act of running and looking rapidly from the one color to the other. The stimulus results which would come from such an actual running or looking would presumably be a complex pattern containing both the run-from color and the run-to color. The rapid passage from the one to the other would, that is, presumably result in a sort of Gestalt (?) containing both the colors set off in juxtaposition one against the other. And the adjustment to such a running would be to bring this resultant Gestalt into the moment before actual behavior. Thus, it would be possible for the animal, when faced with either color alone, to respond nevertheless discriminatively to the difference between them. Another point, however, must now be noted, namely, that after this new differentiating behavior has once become established, consciousness and the behavior adjustment can apparently drop out and yet the new discrimination behavior continue.

We must assume that the complex stimulus pattern of white in juxtaposition to black, or vice versa, is still needed for the continuation of the discriminating behavior. But we shall assume that eventually this complex pattern results automatically by pure associative extension from the white stimulus alone or the black stimulus alone. Simple redintegrative bonds must become established whereby the stimulus results from running back and forth are now automatically fused into either the white or the black stimuli alone.

So much for the consciousness of white versus black. We saw, however, at the beginning of this paper, that the total behavior of choosing one alley rather than the other involves not only this differentiation of white from black, but also a differentiation of food from nonfood. And it involves likewise a differentiation of the specific sign connection of white from that of black. We now assert that the initial appearance of these other two differentiations also involves consciousness. And they also are to be explained by the functioning of behavior adjustments.

The switch-over at some single moment of stimulation from not being ready to differentiate between food and nonfood to being ready to differentiate between them would be mediated by a behavior adjustment for running rapidly from the one goal to the other. Such a behavior adjustment would present the complex Gestalt result of the two types of goal compared one against the other. And the mediating presence of such a Gestalt would constitute a then and there consciousness of the food or the nonfood character of the particular goal presented or represented.

Finally, the switch-over (on any given occasion) from not being ready to treat the sign relationship of the black and the white as different to being ready to treat them as different would also be due to the mediating function of behavior adjustments. In this case the behavior adjustments would be those for actually going down the presented alley and reaching the to-be-expected food or nonfood result. Thereby a fused Gestalt would be produced in which the presented stimulus, white or black, not only would be set over against its comparison color but also would be enlarged by its to-be-expected food or nonfood result. Only on the basis of this total Gestalt would the behavior of entering or not entering ensue.

To recapitulate, we would suppose the rat's total process of learning to be something as follows: First, the animal, after a greater or smaller number of trials, would come, when faced with the white or the black, to make an adjustment for running back and forth. And he would thereby become conscious of the whiteness or blackness. Similarly, when faced with the food or the nonfood, he would make an adjustment for running back and forth and thus become conscious of the foodness or nonfoodness. Finally, when faced with the white or the black, he would also make an adjustment to entering that one or the other and thereby become conscious of the to-be-expected food or nonfood result. On the basis of all three such adjustments, resulting, let us say, in one grand total Gestalt, he would respond. This total Gestalt would contain the differentiation of white from black, of food from nonfood, and of the sign relationship of white as leading to food from that of black as leading to nonfood. And on the occasions of its first appearances there would be consciousness. On later occasions this grand total Gestalt would eventually occur by mere associative extension, without the intervention of behavior adjustments, i.e., without consciousness.

One last word. You will perhaps be doubtful that the lowly rat is capable of all this. So, I think, am I. The important point is merely that if a rat learns consciously, the above gives a perfectly objective definition of how he might do it. It may be that he learns unconsciously.[2] If he learns unconsciously, then we should have to assume that the changes from the readiness for undifferentiated behavior (i.e., behavior mediated by very simply "Gestalted" stimuli) to the readiness for differentiated behavior (i.e., behavior mediated by more complexly "Gestalted" stimuli) occurs somehow automatically between trials. We would then assume no mediating adjustments to introduce these changes. We should be forced to suppose rather that the initial stimuli somehow grow large and properly "Gestalted" by mere mechanical accretion.

---

[2] Though the recently reported results of McDougall and his son (*J. Comp. Psychol.,* 7 (1927), 145–176) tend to minimize the probability of such unconscious learning.

8

SIGN-GESTALT OR CONDITIONED REFLEX?

[Psychological Review, MAY, 1933]

THE GENERAL FACT that specific acts tend to be learned or not learned according to the "goodness" or "badness" of their consequences is an empirical generalization with which, I suppose, we would now all agree. Our disputes will arise not with respect to this empirical fact but rather with regard to the hypotheses we would adopt for its underlying explanation. The "trial and error" psychologists would explain this influence of consequences upon the learning by their laws of "effect." They would say that those stimulus-response connections which are followed by "good" effects, whether these latter be conceived as pleasure, increased sensory consequences, or what not, will be strengthened, whereas those which are followed by "bad" effects will be weakened. And they will hint at various neurological concepts to explain this back-action of effects upon learning. But it is not this trial and error doctrine, in any of its forms, in which I am interested in this paper.[1] Rather I wish now to draw your attention to a conditioned response doctrine of consequences.

At first blush it might seem that the conditioned response psychologists could have no doctrine of consequences. For in their original and pristine statement they seem to assert that a response gets learned (i.e., attached to a new stimulus) in so far as that new stimulus has been presented enough times preceding or just simultaneously with an original stimulus. Good or bad consequences do not come into the picture. It is the mere concatenation of the two stimuli which does the work.

---

[1] Read before the American Psychological Association, Ithaca, New York, September 8, 1932.

And yet the conditioned response psychologists, at least those in this country, do have a doctrine of consequences. And one can but admit that they, in achieving it, have been both "as wise as serpents and as harmless as doves." For they have invented a way of allowing for the different effects of good and bad consequences and yet at the same time of apparently still adhering to their original *bona fide* conditioning principles. Let me illustrate in terms of a concrete experiment.

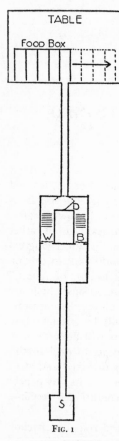

FIG. 1

Figure 1 shows the ground plan of a discrimination box similar to one which I have been recently using. B and W are black and white curtains hanging just behind the two exits from the choice box. They are interchangeable. The task is always to choose the white curtain. D is a door which in each trial is so placed that, if the animal chooses the white curtain he gets to the food, whereas, if he chooses the black he runs into a blind alley and also he can be given an electric shock in this blind alley. How do our conditioned response friends explain such a discrimination learning?

They argue somewhat as follows: Learning consists in conditioning a positive response to the white curtain and a negative response to the black curtain. The rat learns to enter the door which, in the given trial, has the white curtain behind it because this white-curtained door, as stimulus, is followed by a free open path and by food. And to such free open path and food the positive responses of approach and of eating are already attached. That is, the unconditioned positive responses which the animal makes to the food or to the free open path get conditioned back to the stimulus, white-curtained door, which always precedes them. Similarly the rat learns *not* to enter the black-curtained door because this latter, as stimulus, is always followed by the further stimuli of blind end and electric grill to which latter negative responses are already attached. And these negative responses get conditioned back to the black curtain which just precedes them.

It appears that what our conditioned response friends really do is to divide all responses into two sorts—positive and negative. And they argue that in a trial and error situation the acts which get learned are those which result in bringing the animal into the presence of further stimuli to which positive responses are already attached. And the acts which do not get learned are those which result in bringing the animal into the presence of further stimuli to which negative responses are already attached. These resultant positive and negative responses get conditioned back to the cue stimuli. It must be noted, however, that the positive and negative responses which thus get conditioned back may in concrete terms be as different from the original responses from which they are supposed to be derived as entering is from eating or as not-entering is from jumping back and squealing. But this last is a little point which is not stressed by the theory. Our conditioned response friends are truly both serpentish and dovelike.

But let us not be too captious. For it must be admitted that this conditioned response formula, even though it be thus a bit—shall we say—jesuitical, is really surprisingly workable. It can be applied usefully to most discrimination box and maze problems² and, as such, it seems to provide a helpful schema for holding together past results and for predicting future ones. Nevertheless my purpose here must be to show that there are (or at any rate there ought to be) types of maze or discrimination box finding for which this all-useful though emasculated conditioned response formula will not hold.

By way of a first example, let me return to an experiment of my own which used a discrimination box like that just shown. After having, as part of another problem, overtrained rats in this discrimination box, I tried putting them directly into the food compartments and shocking them then and there. Then I carried them immediately around to S and started a run in the usual fashion. My assumption was that as a result of all their preceding training, in which they had been running through the box as the way to get to food, the rats would have built up what in my barbarous terminology I have called sign-gestalt expectations.³ These sign-gestalt expectations I assumed would be to the effect that the earlier parts of the discrimination apparatus would have become a sign or a set of signs to the rats that the encountering of the

---

² This elaboration of the conditioned reflex formula is probably to be credited in the first instance to Smith and Guthrie [14], to Wilson [18] and to Frank [2]. See also Guthrie [4]. Recently it has been further elaborated in a series of striking articles by Hull [7, 8, 9, 10, 11]. Finally, for a criticism of it see Williams [17].

³ For a further elaboration of this concept of the sign-gestalt-expectation, see Tolman [15], chapters ix, x, xi and xxi.

food compartments was to be achieved by running through this discrimination apparatus. And, if the rats had built up such sign-gestalt expectations, I assumed further that a single experience of the changed character of the food compartments (or, as I should put it, this changed character of the significates of the sign-gestalts) should have been enough so that upon being reintroduced to the signs (that is, to the first parts of the discrimination box) the rats would at once have inferred or remembered this new changed character in the goal compartments. And hence they should have refused to run.

But alas, no such thing. Each rat (I must confess that I tried it with only four), after having been shocked in the food compartment and then carried to the starting point, immediately dashed off gaily and just as usual through the whole discrimination apparatus and bang whack into the very food compartment in which he had just been shocked. If the rats had sign-gestalt expectations, then sign-gestalt expectations are not as intelligent as I have supposed them to be.

Furthermore, after some more days of the original training I tried a second procedure. I ran the rats through the discrimination box first and gave them their shocks only then when they had reached the food compartments at the termination of such a run. I then ran them a second trial. And on this second trial they all balked before finally getting to the food. In this second procedure the rats first ran the discrimination box and received the shocks immediately after such runs. And this procedure worked. They all made the connection and refused to run on an immediately subsequent trial. In the former procedure, on the other hand, the rats were put into the food box and shocked there first without any just-preceding run; and it failed. They did not make the connection. (I may remark parenthetically that I tried both procedures several times with plenty of additional straight training in between and that I am convinced of the general validity of the results, at least for the special conditions of my experiment.)

But what is the significance of this difference in outcome? Obviously our conditioned response friends will immediately say: "Of course, in the case when the rats had just been run through the box before being shocked in the food compartment the negative response to the shock had a chance, by virtue of the just preceding run, to get conditioned back to the various stimuli of the discrimination box. But in the other procedure in which the discrimination box was not run through just prior to experiencing the shock in the food compartment there was no such chance for the negative response to the shock thus to become conditioned back. Hence the difference in the two outcomes."

Discretion is, no doubt, the better part of valor. So I suppose I must admit that it does look as though the conditioned response people were here going to be justified. And yet I am not quite ready to be completely and finally downed. Thus, first of all as a very general alibi, I would point out that even though further work does continue to verify the above findings—even though it be indicated consistently and repeatedly that a change in goal character can be carried back to the apparatus leading to that goal only if the stimuli of the apparatus have just preceded those of the new goal,—still this very fact is one which it took a sign-gestalt psychologist to discover. In other words, I would venture to assert that a dyed-in-the-wool, or I should say a drunk-from-saliva, conditioned responser would never have thought of even trying such an experiment. The sign-gestalt hypothesis has to that extent justified itself. It has initiated an interesting and illuminating experiment which was necessary to prove its own downfall.

But anyway I still have in addition a couple of more specific alibis. The foremost of these would be to assert that the negativity of my results (that is, their negativity from my own sign-gestalt point of view) may possibly have been due to one particular feature of my special set-up. For it must be noted that I tried this experiment only after my rats had had a very great deal of overtraining. And this may have meant that they had become what Gilhousen would call "fixated"[4] before the experiment began. That is, if the change in the character of the goal had been made earlier, the rats might still have been able to respond to it in true sign-gestalt fashion. And the fact that under the conditions of the experiment, as I carried it out, they did not make this sign-gestalt adjustment may mean merely that at the time of the experiment they had sunk to the level of something much more automatic and "fixated"— something, if you will, like a true conditioned response. And we would then conclude that whereas under such overtrained conditions learning would follow conditioned response principles, at earlier stages in the learning curve it would follow sign-gestalt principles.

Finally, my last alibi lies in the results of another somewhat different set of experiments already on record. These are the experiments of Hsiao [12] and of Honzik and myself [16] with what we called the "insight" maze. We found that under certain conditions a rat will avoid a given alley entrance not only when he has experienced that this alley

---

[4] For the original discussion of this concept of "fixation" see Gilhousen [3] and for a subsequent further experimental investigation of it see Krechevsky and Honzik [13]. Finally, for still other investigations of what seems to be essentially the same phenomena but which has been called by them "Behavior Constancy" see Hamilton and Ellis [1, 5, 6].

entrance itself is followed by a negative-evoking stimulus (in this case
a block) but also when he has experienced this negative stimulus (block)
merely as the result of another alley entrance which debouches into the
former one.

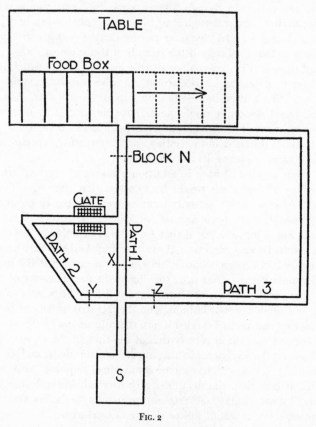

FIG. 2

Figure 2 shows the ground plan of the elevated maze which was used
by Honzik and myself. It will be observed that path 2 debouches into
path 1 and that block N makes path 2, as well as path 1, useless. In the
preliminary training the rats were forced down all three paths in an
irregular order by putting blocks near the entrances of any two of the
three paths at such points as x, y, and z and they soon learned, as the
result of this preliminary training, first to try path 1 and then, if this
was blocked at x, to try path 2 and only then, if this also was blocked at

y, to try path 3. But, finally, in the test trial (and it is only this test trial which will interest us here) the block was inserted at N which, as has been noted, is in the common segment of paths 1 and 2. In this test trial the rats as before entered path 1 first but they found themselves blocked at N and hence retraced. Then, however, instead of next trying path 2, as they had practically always done before, they now immediately chose path 3. In other words, it appears that the negative-evoking character of N was carried back not only to the stimuli at the entrance to path 1, which stimuli had actually just preceded it, but also to the stimuli at the entrance to path 2, which stimuli had never thus preceded N.

Here, evidently, the conditioned response formula will not and does not suffice. To explain *these* results some other formula must be found. And I suggest something like my sign-gestalt formula as the proper substitute. The rat because of all his preliminary training is ready after he has found the block at N to cognize that he will in all probability meet this same block N if he now enters path 2. For he has built up sign-gestalt expectations in the sense that the entrance to path 1 has become for him a sign for the coming of the common segment and that the entrance to path 2 has also become a sign for the coming of this same common segment. So, now, when he discovers the negative character, N, in this segment as a result of entering it from path 1, he necessarily infers this same negative character to be met as a result of entering it from path 2.

So much by way of alibis. Let me sum up.

1. A change from positive to negative goal character if met by the rat just after an actual run affects his behavior on the next trial. This finding can be explained by the conditioned response formula, or at any rate by that jesuitical form of it which passes current among psychologists in this country.

2. A change in goal character (or rather in this case in the character of a part of the maze just proximate to the goal) which a rat meets at the end of one path will carry back to a second path which the rat has already learned as debouching into the first. This finding cannot however be explained by the conditioned response formula. It suggests something more like the sign-gestalt formula.

3. Finally, a change from positive to negative goal character which the rat experiences quite *de novo*, without, that is, having just run over the path which leads to the goal (although he has previously frequently been over this path as the way to get to the goal) does not affect his behavior on the next trial. At least it did not under the special conditions of the experiment as I carried it out. This negative finding forces

us to conclude either that the conditioned response doctrinaires are to some extent correct after all, or else that my animals, because of over-training, were unduly "fixated." If this latter were the case, we might conclude that the sign-gestalt formula is appropriate only for the earlier stages of learning, and not for the later ones.

But obviously many more experiments are needed. Some of these I hope to carry out myself in the near future.

REFERENCES

1. Ellis, W. D. and J. A. Hamilton, "Behavior constancy," *J. Gen. Psychol.* (in press).
2. Frank, L. K., "Suggestions for a theory of learning," *Psychol. Rev.,* 30 (1923), 145–148.
3. Gilhousen, H. C., "An investigation of insight in rats," *Science,* 73 (1931), 711–712.
4. Guthrie, E. R., "Conditioning as a principle of learning," *Psychol. Rev.,* 37 (1930), 412–428.
5. Hamilton, J. A. and W. D. Ellis, "Behavior constancy in rats," *J. Genet. Psychol.,* 42 (1933), 120–139.
6. ———, "Persistence and behavior constancy," *J. Genet. Psychol.,* 42 (1933), 140–153.
7. Hull, C. L., "A functional interpretation of the conditioned reflex," *Psychol. Rev.,* 36 (1929), 498–511.
8. ———, "Simple trial-and-error learning; a study in psychological theory," *Psychol. Rev.,* 37 (1930), 241–256.
9. ———, "Knowledge and purpose as habit mechanisms," *Psychol. Rev.,* 37 (1930), 511–525.
10. ———, "Goal attraction and directing ideas conceived as habit phenomena," *Psychol. Rev.,* 38 (1931), 487–506.
11. ———, "The goal-gradient hypothesis and maze learning," *Psychol. Rev.,* 39 (1932), 25–43.
12. Hsiao, H. H., *An experimental study of the rat's "insight" within a spatial complex,* Univ. Calif. Publ. Psychol., 4 (1929), 57–70.
13. Krechevsky, I. and C. H. Honzik, *Fixation in the rat,* Univ. Calif. Publ. Psychol., 6 (1929), 13–26.
14. Smith, S. and E. R. Guthrie, *General psychology in terms of behavior,* New York: Appleton, 1921, pp. 119–130.
15. Tolman, E. C., *Purposive behavior in animals and men,* New York: Century, 1932.
16. ——— and C. H. Honzik, *"Insight" in rats,* Univ. Calif. Publ. Psychol., 4 (1930), 215–232.
17. Williams, K. A., "The conditioned reflex and the sign function in learning," *Psychol. Rev.,* 36 (1929), 481–497.
18. Wilson, W. R., "Principles of selection in trial-and-error learning," *Psychol. Rev.,* 31 (1924), 150–160. (An amplification and statement of the Smith & Guthrie theory.)

9

GESTALT AND SIGN-GESTALT

[*Psychological Review,* SEPTEMBER, 1933]

IN THE PRESENT article I wish to point out some of the similarities and differences between sign-gestalts and true Gestalten. For sign-gestalts, as I have conceived them,[1] are, it would seem, only in some measure of the nature of the true Gestalten of Gestalt psychology proper.

Sensationalism, perceptualism, propositionalism.—Perhaps the most significant way in which sign-gestalts can be set off, for purposes of contrast, from true Gestalten is to point out that sign-gestalts constitute the third term in a progression beginning with the sensations of Structuralism as the first term and passing through the Gestalten of Gestalt psychology as the second term. Or, to put it still another way: whereas Structuralism is a "sensationalism" and Gestalt psychology a "perceptualism," Sign-Gestalt psychology is, I would assert, a "propositionalism." That is, whereas according to Structuralism an organism responds to a complex of stimuli by a congeries of pointlike "sensations" and "images" and according to Gestalt psychology by a configurated "percept," according to Sign-Gestalt psychology it responds rather by some total "proposition" or "propositions" (i.e., by a sign-gestalt or sign-gestalts).

The "percepts" of Gestalt psychology cannot we are told be analyzed into mere algebraic sums of sensations and images. For according to Gestalt psychology the organism always responds with an indissoluble "group" or "figure on ground" or "step up phenomenon" or "phi movement" or whatever. Such a total percept includes, to be sure, those

---

[1] For a first statement concerning sign-gestalts see Tolman [10], especially chapter ix and following.

aspects of quality, intensity, extensity, duration, which the sensationalistic Structuralist abstracts out and makes all important. But these
latter according to Gestalt psychology no longer stand alone, each separate in its own right. The organism never just senses—always it "perceives." But, turning now to Sign-Gestalt psychology, it will be asserted
that an organism does not even just perceive, rather it always goes still
further and "propositionalizes." And this proposition even though it
contains the "figure on grounds"—the percepts—of Gestalt psychology

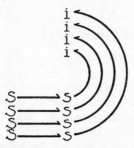

Structuralism. Sensations (s) and images (i) combined in association by "and"
relations only.

Gestalt psychology. The total circle
represents sensory qualities together
with "shape," "movement," "figureness
and groundness," "Sachlichkeit," etc., all
indissolubly bound up together into one
configurational whole.

is never completely and without remainder analyzable into the latter.
The "figure on grounds," etc., of Gestalt psychology are always caught
up into some larger whole (i.e., *sign-gestalts*),—containing signs, significates and means-end relations.

   Before going ahead to expand this comparison, I must hasten however to point out that from a purely historical point of view it is not
of course altogether fair. For just as there were undoubtedly features
of the Gestalt psychology doctrine of "perceptualism" already inherent
in historical Structuralism, so there are undoubtedly, and perhaps to
an even greater extent, features of a sign-gestalt doctrine, or "propositionalism," inherent in present-day, i.e., historical, Gestalt psychology.
My purpose in stating and enhancing the sequence is therefore not that
of assigning or withholding credit, historically speaking, to or from
actual schools but rather that of emphasizing and bringing to the fore
a purely logical relation. Historically it may well be that there have
never actually been any pure sensationalistic Structuralists nor any
pure Gestaltists as I am respectively defining these two. There were fore-

runners of Gestaltism in historical Structuralism and there are very considerable forerunners of what I am calling Sign-Gestaltism in historical Gestalt psychology. It seems permissible, however, for purposes of logical clarity to imagine a pure sensationalistic Structuralism and a pure perceptualistic Gestaltism over against which to set a pure propositionalistic Sign-Gestaltism.[2]

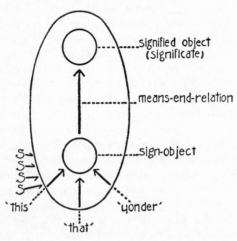

Sign-Gestalt-Expectation

Sign-Gestaltism. A sign object located by some sort of a "this" or a "that" leading by a means-end relation to a signified object.

Granting then that it is but such logically idealized schemes which I am presenting, let me offer the following three diagrams to indicate this interrelation between Structuralism, Gestaltism, and Sign-Gestaltism.

Let me illustrate by a concrete example. Consider yonder chair. According to the Simon-pure Structuralist (as we are conceiving such a hypothetical gentleman) the visual stimuli coming from such a chair will be thought to evoke in a human observer merely visual sensations plus some kinesthetic sensations from the eyes plus some tactual and kinesthetic images corresponding to the sensations which he would get from hand and arms and legs if he were actually to touch the chair.

---

[2] This need for distinguishing between the contents of a doctrine as a mere "geographical-historical" accident and the contents of a doctrine as a specific logical entity has been neatly pointed out by Lewin [2], p. 390. Unnecessary argumentation and confusion are sure to arise if such distinctions are not kept in mind.

According to a Simon-pure Gestaltist (again as we are conceiving such a one) these visual, kinesthetic and tactual stimuli will evoke a unique visual, tactual and kinesthetic configuration which will contain visual and tactual and kinesthetic qualities but will in addition present such properties as "figure-on-groundness," "form," "solidity," "stationariness," "such and such internal accents," etc. Finally, according to the Simon-pure Sign-Gestaltist (as we conceive the latter and naturally I am surest of him) these same visual stimuli will be thought to evoke not just this configuration as a mere "perceived" given, but rather some specific larger whole in which this merely pictured (i.e., perceived)[3] configuration will itself be embedded as one term in a larger means-end "proposition" such, as that: "this chair, if sat on, will lead to rest (or its reverse)"; or "that chair, if placed against the wall, can be stood upon like a stepladder to reach this picture"; or "yonder chair, if placed near a table and sat upon, will make writing possible"; or "that chair over there, if placed near such and such other furniture, will form an aesthetically pleasing whole"; or "this chair, if kicked out of the way, will conduce to the catching of yonder escaped white rat"; and the like.

Discriminanda, manipulanda, means-end relations.—But in order to indicate more clearly and in more detail just what this progressive order between Structuralism, Gestalt psychology and Sign-Gestaltism really means it will be helpful to introduce some still further terms. And to this end I wish to use three new pairs, viz., "discriminanda" and "discriminanda expectations," "manipulanda" and "manipulanda expectations," "means-end relations" and "means-end expectations."[4]

Discriminanda and discriminanda expectations.—Discriminanda is my name for those properties of objects wherein, in purely sensory fashion, such objects differ one from another. This term is, in short, a substitute for the Sensationalist's term "sense qualities" (when those latter are conceived as actual existents in the objects). Discriminanda are investigated by arrays of sensory-discrimination experiments. By such experiments it is determined what the given environmental situ-

---

[3] It is obvious that throughout the discussion I am restricting the terms "perceive," "percept," "perception," etc., to only one of their several manners of being used. I am using them, that is, to cover only that which is given merely as a presented entity—a something with, to be sure, shape, form, etc., but quite divorced from any necessary further and "practical" implications. Actually, of course, the textbooks tend to play fast and loose with the term perception. They usually begin by defining it in this restricted way but are apt, then, in subsequent use, to stretch it to cover what I am here calling practical (i.e., means-end) meanings as well. But it is for these practical "means-end" meanings that I am suggesting the further term "propositions."

[4] For a previous discussion of discriminanda and manipulanda see Tolman [10] chapter v, and for a previous discussion of means-end relations and means-end expectations see Tolman [10], chapter xi and following.

ation offers to the given organism in the way of *possible* sensory discriminations. Discriminanda are thus the *actual* discrimination possibilities
of the given environment which result from the nature of the environmental object and from the sense-organ make-up of the species of individual animal in question. Discriminanda are the actual sense-quality
differentiations which, given the make-up of the environment and the
sensory capacities of the organism, are actually there to be *enjoyed* in
the given situation; if the organism will but do so.

Discriminanda expectations, on the other hand, are the cognitive
sets or determinants aroused in the individual organism on the given
occasion. Such sets prepare the animal for there being such and such
actual sense qualities (discriminanda) then and there present (actually
to be "enjoyed"). But such expectation sets may or may not be confirmed and supported by the actual facts of the environmental situation.
They are not, for example, confirmed and supported in cases of illusion
or hallucination. Discriminanda expectations are, in short, my substitute for the Sensationalist's concept of "sensations," as mere subjectively
aroused effects in the organism. (Just as discriminanda were my substitute for his concept of the sense qualities actually present in the environment.)

It is to be noted further that the reasons why I prefer these terms
(and concepts) discriminanda and discriminanda expectations to the
older ones of sense qualities and resultant sensations are two. In the
first place the concepts of sense qualities and sensations appear to me
undesirably and unnecessarily mentalistic and subjective. By discrimination and other experiments I can learn all there is to know both
about the discriminanda which a given situation can present to a rat
and also all about the momentary discriminanda expectations which
such discriminanda do actually arouse in him at the given moment
but I can hardly be said to learn much of anything about the possible
sense qualities or his actual sensations (not, that is, if these terms are
understood in their usual mentalistic way). And so also for a fellow
human being,—I can learn all there is to know about another man's
discriminanda and discriminanda expectations by gross discrimination
and other experiments (very often similar to those I would use with the
rat but often differing, in that instead of involving gross behavior they
involve merely verbal reports) and yet as a result of neither such method
do I really learn anything about this other man's private mental "feels."[5]

---

[5] For an expansion of this argument concerning discriminanda vs. sensations see
also Tolman [10], chapters xvi and xxv. Also for what is essentially the same argument
see C. I. Lewis [6] and [7], p. 76 f. and Rynin [9].

In a word, discriminanda and discriminanda expectations are my names for and understanding of, sense qualities and sensations *when these are defined objectively and in the same ways for both men and the lower animals.*

Secondly, I prefer the concept of discriminanda expectations to that of sensations also because the former includes openly and avowedly the implication of "objective reference"—an implication explicitly denied to "sensations." Sensations were conceived as nought but dead givens. They were not conceived as properly speaking in any way pointing outside themselves to the real sense qualities. For me, on the other hand, the discriminanda expectations have as part of their very warp and woof this pointing-outwardsness. When a rat or a human being has the discriminanda expectation of "dark" he then and there "expects" that this expectation is going to continue to be confirmed and supported by an actually present environmental situation—that, to wit, he can continue to "enjoy" and have commerce with such a darkness. Such a darkness is not reacted to by him as to a mere fantasy of his own creation. It is responded to as to a in-some-way-objectively-caused darkness (even though when sophisticated he may realize that on occasion this objective cause is one residing wholly in his own physiology) which he can continue to "enjoy."

Turn now to our next pair of concepts.

Manipulanda and manipulanda expectations.—Under these two terms I would introduce two more—in this case almost completely new— notions. By manipulanda I would understand those properties of objects which actually support (i.e., make possible) *motor manipulations.* And it is to be noted that, since the types of possible motor manipulation will vary with the structure of the species, one and the same objective environment often must offer quite different manipulanda to different species of organisms. Or, to put it another way, manipulanda bear the same relation to the motor-organ developments of species that discriminanda do to sense-organ developments. For just as its sense organs will determine what discriminanda a species is capable of, the motor organs of a species will determine what manipulanda it will be capable of. One and the same environmental object will afford quite different manipulanda to an animal which possesses hands from what it can and will to an animal which possesses only a mouth, or only a bill, or only claws. Grasp-ableness, pick-up-ableness, throw-ableness, heaviness (i.e., "heave-ableness") and the like—these are manipulanda. And it is obvious that they will be present in different measure and in different fashion for species which possess different equipments in the way of prehensile and locomotor organs. The environment will offer quite different actual ranges and orders of grasp-ableness, heaviness, and the like, to an animal with only a bill from what it will to one possessing hands. And it will present quite different manipulanda in the way of spatial directions and distances to an organism like a rat with a body length of only six inches but with four feet to what it will to a human biped with two legs, but with each of these some three feet long. Or, again, the same environment will present quite different ranges and orders of solidity,—i.e., stand-on-ableness, rest-in-ableness, and the like—to a species with the muscles and the general form of a gorilla from what it will to puny man or to a mere finned fish.

Again, just as one can distinguish between discriminanda as the sensory qualities (defined in terms of the sense-organ capacities of the given organism) actually offered by a given environmental set-up and the momentary discriminanda expectations aroused in the organism (which latter discriminanda expectations may or may not correspond to such actually present discriminanda); so one must distinguish between the manipulation possibilities, i.e., the manipulanda, actually presented by such an environmental set-up and the momentary manipulanda expectations (which may be more or less veridical) arising in the organism as a result of that set-up. Manipulanda expectations, like discriminanda expectations, are sets or preparations aroused in the organism, which may or may not be confirmed and supported by the actual entities truly present then and there in the environment.

Manipulanda expectations and Gestalt.—Another point may now be made. It must be pointed out, namely, that manipulanda expectations as just defined seem to be closely allied to the very features which Gestalt psychology has especially brought to our attention, i.e., to "figure and ground," "form," "solidity," "movingness" (or its reverse), "size," and the like. Or, in other words, whereas our concept of discriminanda expectations seems to coincide rather neatly with the orthodox concept of sensation qualities such as color, temperature, odor, pitch, visual size, visual form, etc., our manipulanda expectations seem to correspond more closely to those special new sorts of characters of *total* configurations which it has been the virtue of Gestalt psychology to indicate and bring to the fore. In short, what I am here asserting is that "figure-on-groundness" and "shape," "size," *Sachlichkeit* (i.e., solidity, etc.), are really in the last analysis manipulatable properties. I am asserting that "figureness" is probably in the last analysis nothing but pick-up-ableness; that "groundness" is similarly perhaps nothing but walk-about-on-ableness or reach-about-on-ableness; that "size" and "shape" are nothing but further specifications of pick-up-ableness; tha "solidity" is probably rest-on-ableness or obstructingness or heave ableness (heaviness); that "movements" are undoubtedly nothing bu such and such types of run-after-ableness; and so on.[6]

Manipulanda (i.e., configurating properties) and "primary quali ties."—Another point concerning manipulanda must now also be noted

[6] Experimental evidence to support such a contention is, of course, wanting. believe, however, that such evidence could be collected. What one would have to d would be, by experimentally controlling the larger means-end relations (see below' experimentally to induce in the given subjects a determined upon manipulatory prc pensity. Then one would present these subjects with an ambiguous stimulus situatio to see if, as we are assuming, this induced manipulatory propensity would enter in an

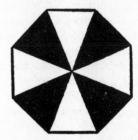

tip the scale so that the ambiguous stimulus situation would now take on for the give subject the configurational property corresponding to this induced propensity. Lc me illustrate by an example.

"Figure" and "ground" as manipulanda expectations are, I have just suggestec "pick-up-ableness" and "reach-about-on-ableness" respectively. To prove this exper mentally I would attempt something as follows. First I would select an ambiguou figure and ground drawing such, for example, as the Rubin cross, and choose two colo (perhaps black and white) such that in a large unselected mass of people there woul be found an equal propensity when naïve and untrained to see either the one or th other color as "figure." I would then select two large groups of observers and subje one of these groups to a preliminary training in which for a long succession of white an black stimulus dots, presented tachistoscopically, they made for the white stimulu dots picking up movements with respect to little objects presented in a container; whil for the black stimulus dots they made merely pushing away movements with respe to these same little objects. And the other group I would subject to just the revers training. That is, I would have these latter pick up for the black stimuli and push away for the white. I would then expose the Rubin cross for a brief instant tachisto scopically to both groups. And, if my experiment were successful, I should expect tha the group trained to pick up for the white stimulus dots would see a white cross a figure on a black background and that the other group, exposed to the reverse trainin, would see a black cross as figure on a white background.

So much for a mere suggestion. Similar experiments could, I believe, be worke out for other types of configurational property—i.e., for "grouping," "shape," "size, "solidity," "movingness," etc., which would show that these also, as expectations in th organism, are nothing but manipulanda expectations,—i.e., expectations, or sets, i the organism whereby he is prepared to grasp, to heave, to chase, to push against, an the like in such and such ways.

Manipulanda, or as we have just further identified them the configurating properties of Gestalt psychology, are also, I believe, closely related to the "primary qualities" of English empiricism. Thus, for example, Locke's list of the "primary qualities" comprised, it will be remembered: solidity, extension, figure, motion, number, and situation (i.e., spatial position?) [8]. But are not these, I would ask, almost identical with the grasp-ableness, the heave-ableness, the run-after-ableness, the sit-on-ableness, etc., which have just been defined as manipulanda (or configurating properties)?

The so-called primary qualities and the so-called secondary qualities are of course, in the first instance, both mere discriminanda—i.e., mere stimulus qualities to be differentiated so and so. They are nevertheless different from one another in that the primary qualities do, I believe, tend to exhibit a more consistent and persistent set of correlations with manipulanda than do the secondary qualities. The primary qualities (e.g., the visual and tactual and kinesthetic discriminanda of size and shape and resistance) do, that is, seem to have much more consistent and persistent correlations with such manipulanda as specific pick-up-ableness, sit-on-ableness, stand-on-ableness, heave-ableness, and the like, than do secondary qualities such as color or odor or temperature.

These differences are, however, ones of degree only. For sometimes a color or an odor or a temperature may be quite as persistently and consistently correlated with a given set of manipulanda as is a size or shape. Trees, as a given relatively definitive group of manipulanda, are, that is, almost always "green." And they are about as consistently green as they are consistently of any persistent *visual* and *kinesthetic* and *tactual* size or shape or resistance. The difference between the primary and the secondary qualities is thus, in the last analysis, due merely to the fact that it was easier for God, or the devil, to smear on and off colors, odors, tastes, temperatures without upsetting the underlying manipulanda than it was to smear on and off different visual and tactual and kinesthetic shapes and sizes and resistances. [10, p. 89 f.][7] But this is the only difference. And it is, as we have seen, one of degree only.

Means-end relations and means-end expectations.—With these two terms I would now introduce still another pair of concepts. By means-

---

[7] Some slight confusion must perhaps be guarded against in the reading of the argument here because the words, "shape" and "size" and "resistance" seem to be used under ordinary circumstances to apply indiscriminately to what I am here specifically keeping separate, viz: to "size" and "shape" and "resistance" as true manipulanda, i.e., as defined in the last analysis in terms of "stand-on-ablenesses," "heave-ablenesses," and the like; and to size and shape and resistance as but the mere *visual* and *tactual* and *kinesthetic* discriminanda correlates of such manipulanda.

end relations I wish to designate those interrelational properties between environmental objects,[8] whereby the "enjoyment of" (i.e., the
"commerce with") the discriminanda and manipulanda constitutive of
one such object will (or will not) actually lead on to an immediate possibility of "enjoyment of" (commerce with) the discriminanda and manipulanda of such and such other environmental objects.

An organism immersed in his environment comes into contact at a
given moment with a certain group of stimuli. As a result of these
stimuli he "expects" to be able to enjoy (to be able to have intercourse
with) such and such a set of immediate discriminanda and manipulanda—or, as I have called it, such and such a "sign object." But it is to
be noted that in addition to, or rather simultaneously and circumam-
biently with, this expectation of a more or less immediately present
sign object, the organism has aroused in him a *further expectation* that
this sign object, if thus actually had intercourse with (i.e., if actually
enjoyed), will, or will not, lead on so and so to the presence of such and
such further objects (sets of discriminanda and manipulanda)—or, as I
have called these latter, such and such "signified objects," or "significates." Such *expectations* of leading-on-ness (or not-leading-on-ness)
are what I would define as means-end expectations.

To sum up, it appears that it is the actual leadings-on or not-leadings-
on,—including such subvarieties of this function as "obstructing,"
"being an alternate to," "being a shorter way than," or "a longer way
than," or "farther off than," and the like,—which constitute the means-
end relations; and it is the aroused preparatory sets in the organism for
such possible leadings-on, or not-leadings-on, and their various subvarieties which constitute what I would call the means-end expectations.

The environment as so envisaged is thus naught but a very field or
tissue of means-end relations. It is a *means-end field* in which the various
component objects and situations appear ineluctably in their roles of
possible, or impossible, good, or bad, better or worse, *means* to, or from,
such and such other objects or situations.[9] Objects (and situations) provide easy or difficult routes (or perhaps, contrariwise, barriers) to or
from other objects. And the defining "easynesses" and "difficulties" of

---

[8] I throughout use the term "object" not only to apply to the relatively sharply
outlined environmental entities for which the word is usually reserved but also to apply
to those more amorphous, less distinct, environmental entities for which the term
"situation" is more ordinarily adopted.

[9] This concept of the environment as a means-end field follows closely upon Lewin's
concept [3, 4] of it as a "psychobiological field." And it is here in this conception of
Lewin's that Gestalt psychology has probably most clearly and obviously already fore-
stalled my sign-gestalt "propositionalism."

these routes are of course dependent in the last analysis upon the given organism's make-up. They rest finally upon the functioning of some internal physiological principle of "least effort." Objects which present "short" (i.e., easy) routes do so because the given organism's physiological internal constitution so makes them. And objects which present "long" (i.e., difficult) routes do so because that is the way again that this same internal physiological mechanism of least effort affects them. The means-end field and its constituent facts of distance and direction are superimposed upon some more fundamental underlying logic,— some logic of physiological "least effort";[10] though as to the details of this latter we are, it must be admitted, now almost completely ignorant. Finally, however, it must be emphasized that even though this underlying mechanism determinative of means-end characters be thus as yet unknown to us we are nonetheless at present able to go on discovering and asserting various facts and principles at the psychological or means-end level itself.

Means relations and means expectations versus position relations and position expectations.—It must be noted next that in the further analysis of this concept of the means-end field it will be helpful to make a subdistinction. We will, that is, find it helpful to distinguish two subvarieties of means-end relations. The one set will be called simply "means relations" and the other "position relations." This distinction is a purely functional one. It arises out of the fact that, in so far as there is a means-end field, in responding to any sign object or signified object in that field not only must the organism be sensitive to the character, or relations, of that object as providing a short or long (direct or indirect) "means" to or from such and such other objects; but also he must be sensitive to the complementary "position" of that object as a something which in its turn is to be got to or from. Any environmental object provides not only routes to or from other objects but also presents concomitantly a complementary character of having its own "position," i.e., the character of an object which in its turn may be easily, or difficultly, or so and so got to or from. Objects have "means relations" by virtue of the manner in which they afford routes to or from other objects, and they have "position relations" by virtue of the manner in which such and such other objects would provide routes to or from them.

Or, putting it another way, any object in a means-end field is to be depicted as presenting to the organism both a set of "means" lines radiating *from* it and a set of "position" lines radiating *towards* it. A

---

[10] For bringing to the fore the need of this concept of physiological least effort we must thank both Gengerelli [1] and Wheeler [11].

given object will be selected and responded to by the organism partly because this object appears to present short "means" lines to some further more ultimately desired object and partly because it appears also to have short "position" lines leading to the immediate presence of it itself. Such a distinction between the two kinds of lines is obviously, however, purely functional. It depends upon the side from which the given object is considered. As an object to be got to means-end relations are called "position relations"; as an object to be used to get to some other more distant object, means-end relations are called "means relations." This, however, is in the last analysis solely a functional difference.

In so far as the organism is responding to relations of how to get to an object, the organism may be said to be experiencing "position expectations" relative to that object. In so far, on the other hand, as the organism is responding to the relations involved in using the given object in order to get to or from further objects the organism may be said to be experiencing "means expectations" relative to the former object.

The spatiomechanical conception of the means-end field.—There is one other point which must be stressed. This concept of the means-end field as I have thus suggested it, is obviously built up very largely upon spatiomechanical lines. I have been assuming, that is, that the means-end interrelations of objects to one another and to the organism may be translated for purposes of the present psychological discussion primarily into simple spatial and mechanical symbols.[11]

And assuming such a spatial mechanical symbolization I would now suggest some six subvarieties of component variables. These I would name as: "direction," "distance," "direct open pathness," "obstructingness," or, as I shall hereafter call it, "barred pathness," "round-about pathness," and "tool pathness." One object lies in means-end terms relative to another first of all and most generally in such and such a "direction" and at such and such a "distance." But such directions and distances will, it appears, always be more specifically qualifiable as "direct" or "barred" or "round-about" or of the nature of a "tool." The means relations and the position relations are in the first instance directions and distances but secondly such directions and distances will further specify themselves in terms of their "directness" and "openness" or their "barredness" or their "round-about-ness" or their "tool characters."

---

[11] It is to be pointed out that again it was Lewin [See 3 and 4 as well as 5] who first pointed the way to such a spatiomechanical envisagement.

Direction will, in general, be that property inherent in a means-end field whereby a certain set of means objects arrange themselves into some natural order or sequence relative to their "goodnesses" or "badnesses" as presenting routes to or from specified further objects. Those means objects which afford the better, i.e., the shorter, routes will be said to point in the more "direct" directions; whereas those which afford the poorer, i.e., the longer, routes will be said to point the less direct directions.

And *distance* will thus be a correlative concept to that of direction. In any type of means-end set-up, distances will be the property which is expressed by the relative *preferabilities* of the various alternative directions. The more preferable directions will present the shorter distances; the less preferable, the longer distances.

A *direct open path* in any means-end set-up will be defined as one without obstacles—i.e., as one in which the type of activity necessary to reach the further object is direct and constant in kind (i.e., constant in direction).

A *barred path* in contrast will be defined as one in which some change in "direction," i.e., in the type of "activity," is necessary to get on. A barred path will be one which requires a "round-about path" to circumvent it.

A *tool path* will be defined as one in which intercourse with one object brings with it willy-nilly intercourse with some other object so that this latter intercourse brings the organism into the presence of the desired further object (just as intercourse with the one end of a lever causes the other end to achieve such and such another desired intercourse).

Examples of means-end relations represented in spatiomechanical terms.—In order to make both the possibility and the desirability of such a spatiomechanical symbolization of many various types of means-end relations clearer, it will be helpful to give some concrete illustrations.

The first and most obvious type of case will be that in which the actual set-up is in truth spatial and mechanical. In such an instance the various objects in the given means-end environment will be removed from the organism and from one another in actual spatial and mechanical ways. But it is to be emphasized that even in such a case it will probably turn out that the means-end distances and directions do not actually or exactly correspond with the underlying spatial distances and directions. For example, it has been found that rats when well motivated by hunger will prefer (i.e., choose) the shorter of two paths to food and in the same degree apparently to which actually they

can differentiate between those two paths in terms of the spatial manipulanda which they experience in running over them. Under such conditions they exhibit Weber's Law.[12] That is, they will differentiate and
prefer any path if it be approximately one-tenth shorter than the other
alternative path. In such a case means-end distances and spatial manipulanda distances probably correspond. Suppose, however, to assume a
purely hypothetical case, never yet as far as I know actually tried out,
that the rats be run with considerably less hunger, in such a distance
discrimination set-up. I would now bet that under such conditions their
choices of the shorter path will not be so refined and will not correspond
to their previously discovered discriminanda and manipulanda capacities. I am betting that now they will accept as equivalent (i.e., *as far as
their means-end purposes go*) paths which are not identical for them
in spatial discriminanda or manipulanda—i.e., which differ from one
another in actual spatial lengths by considerably more than one-tenth.
Assuming such an outcome, then we should have to say that, whereas
as far as the rats spatial discriminanda or manipulanda go an increase
in spatial distance of one-tenth would continue to constitute a true
change in spatial discriminanda and manipulanda, that under conditions of less motivation, such a spatial change need not involve a corresponding means-end change. Under less hunger a path which as a set
of spatial discriminanda and manipulanda can be differentiated as
somewhat shorter or longer from another path may, from a *means-end*
point of view, be accepted as exactly equal in length to that other path.

Or, consider a hypothetical case with a human being. Suppose the
matter be one of selecting one among a number of almost equally good
means-objects—say pencils. And suppose that half of these pencils be
at actual spatial distances anywhere from three feet to three yards from
the individual whereas the other half of them are at spatial distances
of one hundred yards or more. In such an instance it seems to me pretty
certain that, as far as means-end distances would be concerned, the
individual would exhibit no distinction between the three-foot-distant
pencils and the three-yard-distant pencils. All the pencils within these
two extremes would probably for most means-end purposes be grouped
together as "near" as contrasted with the group of one-hundred-yard-
distant pencils which would be classed as "distant." And yet as far as
actual spatial discriminanda and manipulanda were concerned this
individual would of course still be able to distinguish between the three-
foot-distant and the three-yard-distant.

[12] See Yoshioka's experiment [12] for an extremely careful and elaborate investigation
of this point.

So much for examples to suggest that even when the actual discriminanda and manipulanda stuffs of the given set-up are primarily spatial what we are calling the means-end distances need not be the same as these discriminanda and manipulanda distances.

Consider now, however, a type of instance in which the actual stuff of the situation is not really spatial at all. Social situations are particularly good examples. Lewin has presented many illustrations of such social situations with young children and he has shown that these situations also can be fruitfully translated into spatio-mechanical diagrams.[13] For example, he draws the following picture to represent the case of a child who is offered a reward by an adult for the performance of an unpleasant task— together, at the same time, with a threat of punishment if he does not perform the task. R is the reward; T, the undesired task; C, the child; and P, the threatened punishment. Lewin thus conceives the situation as one in which the child is placed in a "field" in which the task and the threatened punishment are in opposite "directions." To "go towards" the task is to "go away from" the punishment and vice versa. Again, the reward is drawn as "lying beyond" the task as it can be reached only by "going through" the task. The heavy lines bounding the whole rectangle are "barriers" which "enclose" the situation, in the sense that, due to the power of the adult, the child can't "escape out of" doing either the one or the other. Finally the degree of freedom "open" to the child before it makes up its mind to do either the one or the other is represented by the "size" of the middle "area" in which the child is thus represented as "confined." If this area is drawn as small, it means that the choice is very imminent and the child can have little free play before making up its mind, that is, before going over into the "area" of either the task, T, or the punishment, P. Whereas if this middle area is drawn larger, it means that the child will have a much "bigger" opportunity to play "about" before doing either the task or receiving the punishment.

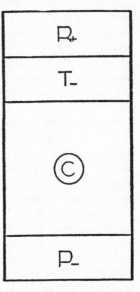

In such an illustration it is quite obvious that the true discriminanda

[13] Adapted from Lewin [4], p. 54.

and manipulanda stuffs of the situation are not by any means primarily spatial, and yet it is equally obvious that such nonspatial, but social, materials can be quite readily translated into the simple spatial and mechanical concepts of areas and barriers, etc., placed so and so relative to one another.[14]

Finally, however, even though in the end it should turn out that these spatiomechanical diagrams and concepts are not adequate for certain and all types of means-end feature, and even though some other more comprehensive type of representation must finally be found, nonetheless it still seems desirable for us now to go on pushing these spatio-mechanical concepts as far as we can. For whatever we succeed in stating in these terms now will undoubtedly be more readily translatable in the future into whatever other terms may then have to be substituted for them.

Recapitulation: discriminanda, manipulanda, means-end relations.—To sum up, according to Sign-Gestalt psychology, environmental objects offer not only discriminanda and manipulanda but also means-end relations. And these means-end relations may for convenience be subdivided further into "position relations" radiating towards a given object and "means relations" radiating from that object.

The stimuli from such environmental objects therefore tend to evoke in the organism not only discriminanda expectations but also manipulanda expectations and means-end expectations (this last subdivided as we have seen into position expectations and means expectations). Not only does the organism "sense" such and such objects as presenting such and such discrimination possibilities, but further he also "perceives" in these objects concurrently such and such correlated manipulation possibilities. And, thirdly, he also concomitantly "propositionalizes" in them such and such associated means-end possibilities,—i.e., that they present such and such "positions" as entities to be got to or from and likewise that they present such and such "means" as paths for the getting to such and such other entities.

Finally, as a last word.—It is to be emphasized that all three kinds of expectation are interactive, conjoint and mutually interaffecting. That means-end expectations determine manipulanda expectations and

---

[14] An examination of the figurative building up of language suggests that such a spatial transformation or analogy has always played an instinctive part throughout the history of thought. Thus, for example, in the paragraph above it was only by putting in quotation marks that I felt I could bring it sufficiently home to the reader that I was here using the words in question in their explicitly *spatial* sense because one and all of these words are so commonly used in means-end discussions without stopping to realize their actual spatial significance.

that the latter determine discriminanda expectations is often almost as true as the reverse. Indeed it has been the function and thesis of Gestalt psychology to indicate the second step—i.e., the partial dependence of the component discriminanda expectations upon the characters of the including and circumambient manipulanda expectations. So it shall now in analogous fashion be the function and thesis of Sign-Gestalt psychology to emphasize the former step—viz., the, at least partial, dependence of the manipulanda expectations in their turn upon the including and circumambient means-end expectations. That sign-gestalts determine Gestalten is just as true and important as that the latter determine "sensations."

REFERENCES

1. Gengerelli, J. A., "Preliminary experiments on the causal factors in animal learning," *J. Comp. Psychol.*, 8 (1928), 455–458; 377–384.
2. Lewin, K., "Gesetz und Experiment in der Psychologie," *Symposion Phil. Zsch. f. Forsch. u. Aussprache*, 5 (1927), 375–421.
3. Lewin, K., *Die psychologische Situation bei Lohn und Strafe*, Leipzig, S. Hirzel, 1931, p. 67.
4. Lewin, K., "Environmental forces in child behavior and development." Chapter 4 in *Handbook of Child Psychology*, ed. by C. Murchison, Worcester, Mass., Clark University Press, 1932, pp. 94–127.
5. Lewin, K., "Untersuchungen zur Handlungs- und Affect-psychologie." I through XI, *Psychol. Forsch.*, 7–16 (1926–1932).
6. Lewis, C. I., *The pragmatic element in knowledge*, Univ. Calif. Publ. Philos., 6 (1926), 205–227.
7. Lewis, C. I., *Mind and the world order*, New York, Charles Scribner's Sons, 1929.
8. Locke, J., *Essay concerning human understanding*, Book II, chapter 8.
9. Rynin, D., "The nature of communication," *J. Philos.*, 29 (1932), 505–515.
10. Tolman, E. C., *Purposive behavior in animals and men*, New York, Century, 1932.
11. Wheeler, R. H., *The science of psychology*, New York, Crowell, 1929.
12. Yoshioka, J. G., *Weber's law in the discrimination of maze distance by the white rat*, Univ. Calif. Publ. Psychol., 4 (1929), 155–184.

10

PSYCHOLOGY VERSUS IMMEDIATE EXPERIENCE

[*Philosophy of Science,* JULY, 1935]

IN THIS PAPER[1] I am going to try to indicate my notion concerning the nature and subject-matter of psychology.[2] I am a behaviorist. I hold that psychology does not seek descriptions and intercommunications concerning immediate experience[3] *per se.* Such descriptions and attempts at direct intercommunications may be left to the arts and to metaphysics. Psychology seeks, rather, the objectively stable laws and processes governing behavior. Organisms, human and subhuman, come up against environmental stimulus situations and to these stimulus situations they, after longer or shorter intervals of time, behave. The laws and processes determining this their behavior are stable in objective terms. Even in the cases where the organism is oneself, these determining causal factors can and must—for the purposes of psychology—be stated objectively. It is true that in these latter instances, in which the animal in question is oneself, one may in one's role, not of a psychologist, but of an artist or a metaphysician, attempt to describe and convey to another man one's own facts of immediate experience. But such a description and report of immediate experiences, except in so far as this report

---

[1] Presented before the Kosmos Club of the University of California, February, 1935.

[2] For a previous but less completely thought through statement of the position to be presented here see E. C. Tolman, *Purposive behavior in animals and men,* New York, Century, 1932, especially chapters xxiv and xxv.

[3] I shall throughout use the phrase "immediate experience" to designate the immediately given preanalytical complex (To borrow Professor Loewenberg's term. Cf. J. Loewenberg, "Pre-analytical and post-analytical data," *J. Philos.*, 24 (1927), 5–14.) as this appears to the naïve man and before the subtleties of philosophical and scientific analysis have been applied to it.

is itself a form of behavior and therefore like all other behaviors the basis for an investigation of the objective laws and processes underlying it, will not, for the purposes of the psychologist, add anything essentially new to the picture. Experience *qua* experience, while of concern and interest to the man in the street, the philosopher and the poet, does not enter as such into the laws and equations of psychology,—in so far, at any rate, as psychology is to be considered as a science.

In order, however, to lend such a doctrine cogency I need to begin at the beginning. I must attempt to review, at least briefly, the situation relative to the problem of knowledge as this problem has in the past appeared to the philosopher and to the psychologist, and as it now appears to me.

Ever since the time of Descartes the so-called relativity of sense perception has been of prime concern to the philosopher. It is because of the facts of sense relativity that there arose most of the technical issues of modern philosophy. And it is largely in terms of those facts that the traditional, prebehavioristic, notion of the subject matter of psychology arose.

By way of recalling to you what is meant by this matter of sense relativity let me quote some passages from Bertrand Russell.

"To make our difficulties plain," he says, "let us concentrate attention on the table. To the eye it is oblong, brown and shiny, to the touch it is smooth and cool and hard; when I tap it, it gives out a wooden sound. Any one else who sees and feels and hears the table will agree with this description, so that it might seem as if no difficulty would arise; but as soon as we try to be more precise our troubles begin. Although I believe that the table is 'really' of the same color all over, the parts that reflect the light look much brighter than the other parts, and some parts look white because of reflected light. I know that, if I move, the parts that reflect light will be different, so that the apparent distribution of colours on the table will change. . . . It is evident . . . [therefore] that there is no colour which preeminently appears to be the *the* colour of the table, or even of any one particular part of the table . . . it appears to be of different colours from different points of view, and there is no reason for regarding some of these as more really its colour than others. Thus colour is not something which is inherent in the table, but something depending upon the table and the spectator and the way the light falls on the table."[4]

He then goes on to indicate that the situation is similar for all the

---

[4] Bertrand Russell, *The problems of philosophy,* Home university library of modern knowledge, no. 35, New York, Holt, n.d., p. 11 f.

other properties of the table. Not only its color but its texture, its shape, its size depend upon, are relative to, the position and character of the percipient. And, if we include also the facts of illusions, dreams, false memories and hallucinations with these of sense perception we are easily led to the dogma of Bishop Berkeley that there is no "real" table but only "ideas" of a table. Or, if one will not go as far as that, then one may be led at least to the position of the dualists, who, since there do seem to be some quite independent features of order and character in our sense perceptions, hold that the world is to be dichotomized into two sets of entities. On the one hand, there are the immediate sense data—the immediate colors, feels, shapes, images, etc., in and of themselves. No misconceptions, errors or illusions about these sense data are possible. They are what they are. They are immediately given. But, on the other hand, there are also according to this doctrine independent material objects behind and causing such sense data. These independent material objects are known mediately. They are known indirectly through the sense data.

It was the assumption of this sort of a dualism which became the starting point for modern physics and modern prebehavioristic psychology. And it must be granted that the sort of a picture therein presented still dominates much of our thinking. We still often tend to conceive of the mental as an array of immediately given sense data and to think of different sets of these arrays as private to each one of us. The physical, on the other hand, we tend to conceive as an independent and for the most part only mediately known set of entities behind these our several private sensory arrays. The fact that such a view persists means, of course, that it is, in some degree and in some manner, pragmatically workable. I shall, nevertheless, in the rest of this paper attempt to get you to adopt a somewhat different view. I shall abandon this conception of two sets of metaphysical stuffs—a physical world really "out there" to be studied by physics and a series of private mental worlds each in our own respective heads or minds to be studied by psychology. Such a conception does not seem to be as successful for a philosophy of science as does the more modern view for which I am now going to argue.

I shall hold that immediate experience just as it appears, contains quite as much objectivity as it does subjectivity. Immediate experience, as initially given, is not my private world or your private world. It is not something to be studied primarily by psychology. It is, rather, an initial, common matrix out of which both physics and psychology are evolved. It is the only tangible real that we have. Physics does not present another real behind that of immediate experience. Nor does psychology, as such, study this real of immediate experience in a more firsthand way than does physics. Physics is a set of logical constructs—a set of rules and equations whereby we are aided in finding our way about from one moment of immediate experience to another. Further, and this purports to be the only new and specific contribution of this paper, psychology is, I shall argue, but another such set of logical constructs, another such set of rules and equations, which, when added to those of physics, will give us still further aid in finding our way about from one moment of experience to the next.

There is, if you will, still left in my universe a dichotomy, but it is a dichotomy not between physical entities, and mental entities, but between both of these as mere logical constructs, on the one hand, and immediate experience as the actually given, rich, qualitied, diffuse, matrix from which both sciences are evolved, on the other. The purpose of science, of psychology as well as of physics, is not to describe and relive experience but merely to explain it,—to help in predicting and controlling it,—or to use Professor Pepper's term, to give map accounts of it.[5] My dichotomy will be between reality and its maps and not between two types of reality.

By way, now, of introducing this point of view more specifically let me return to the facts of sense perception. And let me present them again in the light of some of the more recent work in this field.[6] In particular, I have in mind the experiments and theoretical analyses of Brunswik.[7] Brunswik's doctrine is that in any perception the organism "intends" certain objective environmental characters. The absolutely correct values of these characters can be determined only by measurement—that is, by the sorts of procedure introduced and exploited by physics. But immediate perception makes a stab at arriving at these characters or, to use Brunswik's phrase, perception "intends" or "expects" these characters. Further, these perceptual intentions and expectations succeed in "attaining" or "achieving" the real values of the characters sometimes with more and sometimes with less success. Again, these environmental characters which Brunswik finds to be "intended" in perception can, for the purposes of the present argument be divided

[5] S. C. Pepper, *Categories: Studies in the problem of relations*, Univ. Calif. Publ. Philos., 13 (1930), 73–98.

[6] That is, such work as that of Brunswik, Katz, Hering, Bühler, Gelb, Koffka, Kardos, Thouless, E. R. Jaensch, on the so-called problem of "Dingkonstanz." For references, see L. Kardos, "Ding und Schatten: Eine experimentelle Untersuchung über die Grundlagen des Farbensehens," *I. Abst. Zeitschr. f. Psychologie*, Ergänzungsband 23 (1934), and E. Brunswik *vide infra*.

[7] Egon Brunswik, *Wahrnehmung und Gegenstandswelt—Grunglegung einer Psychologie vom Gegenstand her*, Leipzig und Wien, Deuticke, 1934.

into two sub-classes: (a) characters which are relatively independent and which may be said to inhere in the things or bodies themselves; and (b) characters which are dependent and determined not only by the character of the thing in question but also by the special relations of this thing to be percipient. The first I shall label "independent properties or qualities" or simply "independents" and the second, "perspective properties or qualities" or simply "perspectives." It also appears that in the usual case the individual is much more likely in perception to "intend" an "independent" than he is to "intend" a "perspective." Furthermore, it appears that he is likewise more nearly successful in perceptually "attaining" or "achieving" independents than he is in perceptually attaining or achieving "perspectives." His perceptual expectations are usually more nearly verified by the corresponding measurements when he has intended the independent object than when he has intended the perspective of that independent object.

Let us take a concrete example. Suppose you now actually look, at two tables or two men—one, say, twenty feet away and one, say, ten feet away. Both, I feel sure, will now look to you as about the same size. In other words, the chances are great that, at this moment without any special preparation, you will perceptually "intend" and approximately "attain," not the perspective sizes, but the independent sizes of these two tables or men. These independent sizes are the same irrespective of their relative distances from you. If, on the other hand, you now set yourselves to perceive the "perspective" or "projective" sizes you can probably, to some extent, do so, but your degree of attainment will, I am sure, be far less than when you perceived the independent sizes. That is, I defy any one of you, unless you have had special training, now to "see" the twenty-foot-away table or man as twice as small as the ten-foot-away table or man. Only if you have had considerable special training as an artist or if you abandon perception per se and resort to a measuring technique such as holding up a pencil and marking off the projections of the two tables upon it, will you succeed in somewhere near approximating these their relative perspective sizes.

And the situation, which thus holds for perception of sizes, also holds in analogous fashion for the perception of all other qualities, such for example as color. When one perceives the color of yonder table one may intend either the true independent color or the immediate perspective brown or white or yellow which is due to one's specific position and to the special lighting of the moment. But the surprising thing is that also in this case of color what one more often intends and approximately attains in his seeing is the true independent object-color and not the momentary perspective color. Russell was, in short, factually wrong when he implied that for all of us and ordinarily "the parts that reflect the light 'look' much brighter than the other parts, and that some parts look white because of reflected light." Actually, it is usually only in our moments as would-be artists or as would-be introspective psychologists that we can intend and come near attaining these immediate perspective values. For most of us, most of the time, the table looks the same brown all over.

Or consider the case of shape. One of Brunswik's students did an experiment in which the subjects had to compare the shape of one ellipse rotated out of the face-on plane with the shapes of a series of ellipses of different proportions lying squarely face on. And it was found that the rotated ellipse tended, unless special instructions were given, to be identified with a face-on ellipse having approximately its, the rotated ellipse's, true shape and not with one having the rotated ellipse's foreshortened shape. Again, the independent quality, in this case, shape, was perceptually intended and approximately attained and not the immediate perspective quality.

In a word, it appears that in all the different modes of sense perception the subject may perceptually intend and more or less successfully achieve or attain either an independent or a perspective. But he more frequently intends the independents than he does the perspectives. And his degree of perceptual achievement or attainment also is usually greater when he intends the former.[8]

If we return, now, to our initial discussion, it appears that what we there called sense data we are now calling perspectives and that what we there called the reality behind such sense data we are now calling the independents. But such a distinction no longer seems fundamental. The really important distinction now seems to lie rather between both perspectives and independents as perceptually intended, expected and more or less successfully attained environmental object characters, on the one hand, and the to-be-discovered laws and equations which determine the nature and functioning of such "intentions," "expectations," and degrees of "attainment," on the other.

[8] It is, of course, to be noted that in the case in which he perceptually "intends" an independent, the special circumstances of the latter, such as its distance, its special lighting, its plane of rotation and the like also affect the individual's sense organs and must so to speak be taken into account by the perceptual apparatus, if the approximately true values of the independent is to be attained. But this the perceptual apparatus inevitably does, and the final product in no way presents psychologically a more "derived" character to the percipient than in the case where he is perceptually intending not the independent but the perspective.

Immediate experience is a matrix which contains *both* perspectives *and* independents perceptually (and also, as we shall see, memorially and hypothetically) intended. It also contains the rudiments of measurements, that is, it contains the moments in which these perceived, remembered, or hypothesized qualities are checked by measurement and found to have been more or less successfully attained. Immediate experience as thus composed is rich, qualitied, but perhaps in large part ineffable, that is, logically incommunicable from one sentient being to another. It is, however, real—the most real reality that we can have or desire. Its lack is that it does not provide in itself, or only in minor degree, its own rationale. It does not contain written on its face the rules whereby the particular perceptual, memorial, or hypothetical intentions occur nor whereby these prove to have been more or less successful in their attainment. It is such rules which physics and psychology taken together seek to supply.

As to the difference between physics and psychology my further thesis will now be that whereas physics is the system—the rationale—which attempts to explain all the possible "independents" and "perspectives" any organism could conceivably intend and attain in given environmental set-ups, psychology is the system—the rationale—which attempts to explain what perspectives and independents the particular organism or type of organism, on the given occasion, will actually (perceptually, memorially, and hypothetically) intend; and why these intentions will have the specific degrees of success or failure of attainment that they do. In the rest of this paper I shall attempt to elaborate this thesis for psychology. The "logical positivists," that is such men as Wittgenstein,[9] Schlick,[10] Carnap[11] in Europe and Bridgman,[12] C. I. Lewis,[13] Feigl and Blumberg[14] in this country, have already done the task for physics. But no one as yet, so it seems to me, has satisfactorily done it for psychology.[15]

But first let me point out that, since according to this doctrine psychology will be concerned only with developing a system of *rules or*

---

[9] L. Wittgenstein, *Tractatus Logico—Philosophicus,* Kegan Paul, 1927.

[10] M. Schlick, "Positivismus und Realismus," *Erkenntnis,* 3 (1932), 1.

[11] R. Carnap, *Der Logische Aufbau der Welt,* Weltkreis-Verlag, 1928.

[12] P. W. Bridgman, *The logic of modern physics,* Macmillan, 1927.

[13] C. I. Lewis, *Mind and the world order,* Scribner's, 1929.

[14] H. Feigl and A. Blumberg, "Logical positivism," *J. Philos.,* 28 (1931), 281.

[15] Carnap and Feigl have, to be sure, prepared the way, but they have done it only for "molecular behaviorism" and not for "molar behaviorism." R. Carnap, "Psychologie in Physikalischer Sprache," *Erkenntnis,* 3 (1932), 107–142. H. Feigl, "Logical analysis of the psychophysical problem: a contribution to the new positivism." *Philosophy of Science,* 1 (1934), 420–445. A point of view similar to that presented here but not worked out in detail for psychology seems to be that of the zoölogist, Russell. Cf. E. O. Russell. "The study of behaviour," *Nature,* 134 (1934), 835–839.

equations, this absolves it from any attempt at trying to depict what is going on in the other man's mind. As psychologists we do not seek to relive and describe the other man's immediate experiences. Such a reliving must be left, as we have said, to metaphysics, or to poetry, or to common sense—that is, to whatever disciplines as may concern themselves with immediate experience, *per se.* Psychology, as such, is concerned only with such objectively definable variables as the intentions, expectations, attainments, immanent in the behavior of organisms. Psychology as such is objective and behavioristic.

But behaviorism, as we shall now see, may take either of two courses. On the one hand, it may seek to develop a set of what may be called molecular or microscopic concepts. These are essentially physiological. This form of behaviorism attempts a complete neural, glandular and visceral picture. And a large part of what today is known as behaviorism is of this form. But there is also, I would contend, a second type of behaviorism which seeks rather to develop a set of molar or macroscopic concepts concerning what I shall designate as "behavior readinesses." This second form of behaviorism seeks to describe and explain behavior in terms of such "readiness variables." And these latter it fashions directly from the more surface facts of behavior itself. This molar form of behaviorism does not deny the possibility and need of neural and glandular concepts but it prefers to leave the latter to the adequately trained physiologist.

Both varieties of behaviorism start with the same initial facts: (*a*) the fact that organisms, human and sub-human, come up against environmental stimulus situations and suffer from internal physiological disequilibriums; (*b*) the fact that as a result of such stimulus situations and such internal upsets these organisms behave; and (*c*) the fact that the nature of this their resulting behavior is determined by a set of intervening variables to be conceived as lying in the organism. But, whereas the molecular behaviorist—that is, the behaviorist with physiological bent—seeks to state the nature of these intervening variables in terms of such concepts as chemical or other physical action in the sense organs, innate and acquired neural pathways, sympathetic system reverberations, and the like, the molar behaviorist seeks to state the intervening variables as specific types of behavior readiness or, in more common sense terms, as objectively definable "demands," "intentions," "expectations" and "attainments." The physiological behaviorist states the laws of visual perception in terms of photochemical actions on the retina, convergence of the two eyes, biretinal disparity, lens accommodation, and neurological processes in optic thalami and cortex. The molar behaviorist states the laws of perception in terms of objectively defined behavioral conditions of "intention" and "expectation" as these have been discovered by Brunswik and his students, and as they may also be discovered by animal psychologists. There will, of course, be no conflict between the two behaviorisms. Each will play into the hands of the other. The molecular physiological variables will, of course, underly and may, if you will, be said to explain the molar variables of "demand," "intention," "expectation." But these latter still have to be discovered and schematized at their own level. In other words, the psychologist in the guise of the molar behaviorist, still has, I would assert, his own job to do and can still properly demand his own place in the sun.

But let me be more specific. Both types of behaviorism begin by listing four independent or causal variables, as follows: (1) the environmental stimulus set-up, this may be symbolized by S; (2) the specific heredity of the given organism, this may be symbolized by H; (3) the specific past training of the organism, to be symbolized by T; and (4) a releasing internal condition of physiological appetite or aversion, to be symbolized by P. The independent variables S, H, T and P are the initial causes for the final resulting behavior. And, if we symbolize the latter by B, then a total equation of the form

$$B = f_1 (S, H, T, P)$$

can be written.

The determination of the actual form of this function f_1 will constitute the final goals of both molecular and molar behaviorisms. But, further, as has already been implied, both these disciplines are forced to take one more step in common. That is, they both find that in order to proceed, they now have to subdivide this one final equation into two sets of subordinate equations, of the forms:

$$B = f_2 (I_a, I_b, \ldots I_n)$$

and

$$I_a = f_3^a (S, H, T, P)$$

$$I_b = f_3^b (S, H, T, P)$$

$$I_c = f_3^c (S, H, T, P)$$

etc.

In these equations, $I_a, I_b, \ldots I_n$ represent what I have called "intervening variables." And it is obvious that once these have been properly chosen and the functions f_2 and f_3 been determined then it will be possible to solve for the final total equation $B = f_1 (S, H, T, P)$. But at present both molecular and molar behaviorisms are far from this final step. Both are still trying to work out their respective intervening I's. And only very tentatively and inadequately are they as yet making suggestions concerning f_2 and the f_3's.

But now, finally, let me turn to the task of stating my own particular conceptions concerning the I's and their connecting functions. I define the I's as behavior readinesses. And I would divide them into two main groups which I shall designate, respectively as *demands* and *cognitions*. In attempting to illustrate for you the nature of these latter I shall for the most part present the case for rats. For these are the organisms that I know most about. I will, however, as a sop to you as my readers throw out a few suggestions now and then relative to human beings. Turn, first, to the demands. These are to be further differentiated into (1) *ultimate demands* and (2) *subordinate demands*.

1. By the *ultimate demands* I would conceive behavior readinesses which appear in, and are defined by, three sets of facts: (*a*) the going off of positive and negative consummatory responses; (*b*) the propensity to persist through trial and error to and from locales where the goal objects appropriate to such positive or negative consummatory responses have been found on previous occasions; and (*c*) the tendency which appears for an animal in successive trials to select shorter routes to and from such locales. These three behavioral facts I take as indicative of, or as the logical positivists might say, as the pointer readings for, three types of ultimate demand which I shall designate as: (*i*) the demand *for* a positive goal object; (*ii*) the demand *against* a negative goal object; and (*iii*) the demand *for* "short" distances to a positive or from a negative goal.

i. Under the heading *demands for positive goal objects* I conceive a set of variables (i.e., behavior readinesses) such that when any one of them is operative it will act to produce a specific positive consummatory response, if the appropriate goal object be present. It will also operate, if this goal object be absent, to produce a persistent exploratory activity until an instance of this appropriate type of goal object has been found. The list of such positive demands would, in the case of rats, be comprised, I believe, by (*a*) the demand for food; (*b*) the demand for sex objects; (*c*) the demand for explorable alleys; (*d*) the demand for dark places in which to hide; and (*e*) the demand for warm soft places in which to go to sleep.

Turning to human beings, I suspect that the list of the ultimate positive demands would be much the same. It also is probably largely, if not wholly, comprised by the demands for food, for sex objects, for explorable alleys, for dark places in which to hide, and for warm soft places in which to go to sleep. It may, however, turn out that in addition there must also be included in the list for men an ultimate demand for harmonious sense impressions, an ultimate demand for the company of one's fellows and perhaps an ultimate demand for the social approval of one's fellows.

ii. Demands against negative goal objects. Under this head of negative demands I would conceive a set of variables which would be respectively operative in producing (in the case of rats) negative consummatory responses (a) in the presence of electric grills, (b) in the presence of surrounding and hampering barriers (including the ends of blind alleys), (c) in the presence of open exposed fields, and (d) in the presence of powerful noxious stimuli. Each such negative demand would also operate to produce a persistence through trial and error to get away from a locale where an instance of the given type of negative goal object has already been found.

For men also I suspect the list of ultimate negative demands would be much the same. For them also it would, I believe, include and probably be wholly comprised by: demands against electric grills (or other pain-inducing devices), against surrounding and hampering barriers, against open exposed fields, and against powerful noxious stimuli.

iii. By *demands for "short" routes* I conceive still another set of intervening variables. That is, "demands for short routes" would be my name for the tendencies which appear in behavior to select, after learning, short paths rather than long ones to positive goal locales and from negative goal locales. Furthermore these tendencies to learn to take the short routes include not only the tendency for spatially short routes but also that for temporally short ones and finally that, also, for what, for want of a better name, we may call force-resisting short routes. For it appears that, if there be two alleys to the same positive goal or from the same negative goal which differ in spatial lengths, rats will learn (within the limits of their ability to discriminate) to take the spatially shorter.[16] Similarly, if there be two paths of equal spatial lengths but of which one involves a longer temporal distance than the other—due to the insertion of a longer delay chamber—rats will also learn (again within the limits of their abilities to discriminate) to select the temporally shorter.[17] And, finally, if there be two strings, with food cans

[16] Cf. J. G. Yoshioka, *Weber's law in the discrimination of maze distance by the white rat*, Univ. Calif. Publ. Psychol., 4 (1929), 155–184.

[17] Cf. E. G. Tolman and C. F. Sams, "Time discrimination in white rats," *J. Comp. Psychol.*, 5 (1925), 255–263.

attached, which are of equal lengths and which take approximately equal times to pull in but of which one has a lighter weight attached to it than the other, again rats will learn to pull in first (within the limits of their abilities to discriminate) that with the lesser force re- sistance—that is, that with the lighter weight attached.[18]

And for human beings, also, I suspect that this same list of demands or tendencies for short routes likewise holds. For men likewise, seem wherever they can, to take the spatially short, the temporally short, and that which in terms of the force to be overcome is "short."

2. But let us turn now to my second main group of demands—the *subordinate demands*. Under this heading I shall lump (*a*) demands for specific types and instances of goal objects and (*b*) demands for specific means objects. In the case of rats there is some slight evidence for the *a*-type in that it appears that these animals perform less well, when a new food is substituted at the end of the maze in the middle of learning for one used up until that time. This evidence, however, is not very overpowering.[19] And for the *b*-type of case—that in which a characteristic and specific type of means object sets up in its own right— there is in rats still less evidence. In other words, these animals have not as yet been shown to become permanently attached to, say, pink alleys rather than to white or, if you will, to California redwood mazes, rather than to the white pine mazes imported from New England.

For men, on the other hand, both the above kinds of subordinate demand seem to make up the very breath and substance of life. In short, the whole body of both what the anthropologists find in the way of specific culture patterns and what psychologists find in the way of indi- vidual idiosyncrasies seem to consist for the most part, psychologically speaking, in acquired specifications of ultimate goals or in acquired adherences to specific types of means objects, which latter then often set up in their own right. And such specifications and settings-up, once established, acquire a strangle hold. If a man grows up in a social group in which one type of food, sex object, explorable alley, dark place in which to hide, or warm soft place in which to sleep, is current, and then is transported into another social group in which other types of food, sex object, dark place, and feather bolsters instead of blankets are provided, he will most certainly languish and he may even die. And a man does die, or almost so, for Camels rather than Lucky Strikes, for

---

[18] T. L. McCullough, "Performance preferentials of the white rat in force-resisting and spatial dimensions," *J. Comp. Psychol.*, 18 (1934), 85–112.

[19] M. H. Elliott, *The effect of change of reward on the maze performance of rats*, Univ. Calif. Publ. Psychol., 4 (1928), 19–30.

Bull Dog Drummond rather than Prince Albert, for food at the Men's Faculty Club rather than the very same food—only better—at the Women's Faculty Club. And we professors would come to love our money, if we had it, not only for what it would buy, but for its own sake. And, as it is, we have some of us become misers as to our books and even some few of us as to our pocket matches.

The above is a very sketchy account. But it indicates the general nature of my doctrine that ultimate and subordinate demands are one type of intervening variable—one type of "behavior readiness" or "I"— between stimuli, physiological conditions, heredity and training, on the one hand, and final behavior, on the other. We have, however, not only the task of discovering these I's, but also that of discovering the forms of the functions f_3 which attach them to the initiating S's, H's, T's and P's as well as the form of the function f_2 which connects them, along with the cognitions, to the final resulting behavior, B. But these are questions all still for the future. One can, perhaps, already guess that it is probably a very simple function which attaches the ultimate demands to the physiological conditions, the appetites and the aversions of the given species—(i.e., to P and to H). But the further complications which arise in the cases of subordinate demands are still very far beyond us.

Let us turn now to the cognition variables. They also I shall divide into two subtypes which I shall call (1) *differentiations (i.e., intentions, expectations, and attainments as to qualities)* and (2) *hypotheses (i.e., intentions, expectations, and attainments as to relations)*.

1. It is under the *differentiations* of quality that the perceptual intentions and attainments investigated by Brunswik and his students would be classed. And it is pertinent to our present argument now to emphasize that the procedures and resulting definitions of these workers were perfectly objective. A subject was required, say, to pick out of a series of cubes of varying sizes one, which at a distance of 6 meters appeared equal in size to a standard 6 cm. cube at a distance of 1 meter. If under such conditions he picked out, on the average, a cube about 7 cm. on a side, it could be concluded that he was intending the independent size of the 6 cm. standard cube and missing it by about 1 cm. If, on the other hand, he picked out a cube at 6 meters about 15 cm. on a side, then it could be concluded that he was intending the perspective size of the standard 6 cm. cube. But in this latter case his attainment was proportionally far less. He should have picked out not a 15 cm. cube but a 36 cm. cube at 6 meters to equal the 6 cm. cube at 1 meter.

The experiments were, in essence, purely behavioristic. They were

the kind of experiment we can and do do with animals. The only difference is that with animals we usually require them not to equate but
to discriminate between a given pair of entities. We teach an animal to
go to the larger of two doors or, in the case of a chimpanzee, to pull in
with a stick the larger of two boxes. We teach him this first when both
doors or both boxes are at an equal distance from him. But then we
place the actually larger box or the actually larger door at a greater
distance, so that it now subtends a smaller visual angle—presents a
smaller perspective size.[20] And we discover perhaps to our amazement
that even under these latter conditions he will still choose this same
objectively larger box or door, in spite of the fact that it now "looks"
smaller. That is, we discover that the animal, as well as the man under
ordinary conditions, perceptually "sees," that is, intends and approximately attains, the independent sizes of objects and not their momentary perspective sizes.

Turn, now, to memorial differentiations of qualities. These likewise
are to be discovered and defined quite objectively. Consider, for example, the so-called "delayed reaction" experiment as used with the
lower animals. The animal in question is taught first that of two doors,
the one which in any given trial is lighted, always leads to food, whereas
the other always leads to punishment or to lack of food. He is then
introduced into the choice chamber while the light is still on, but the
latter is turned off for a longer or shorter time before he is allowed to
make his choice. If after this delay-interval he can still choose correctly,
we are able to say, quite objectively, that there was operative in him
at the moment of choice an intervening variable to be called the memorial differentiation of the previously lighted character of the given
door. A certain past but now absent environmental quality is determining his present behavior.

And when one examines the so-called memories not of the lower
animals but of one's fellow men one's procedure is really the same. One
discovers from their words, if not from their gross behaviors, what the
past environmental properties are to which they are now reacting. And
one can check up on those past environmental properties so as to measure the degree of attainment in these their present memorial assertions.

---

[20] W. Köhler, "Optischen Untersuchungen am Schimpanzen und am Haushuhn,"
Abh. d. Kgl. Preuss. Akad. d. Wiss.: Phys-math. Kl. Nr. 3 (1915), p. 29.
———, "Ueber eine neue Methode zur psychologische Untersuchung von Menschenaffen," *Psychol. Forsch.*, 1 (1922), 390–397.
For similar experiments indicating that hens respond to independent colors and not
perspective colors see D. Katz und G. Révész, "Experimentelle Studien zur vergleich-
enden Psychologie," *Zt. f. Angew. Psychol.*, 18 (1921), 307–320.

Their words will not provide any essentially different type of information from that which one obtains from the nonverbal behavior of a rat or of a chimpanzee. With all three species one presents certain objective stimulus situations and observes certain resulting successes or failures in a later behavior. And to explain such successes in all three cases one is forced "logically to construct" a type of intervening variable to be called the memorial differentiation of a past environmental quality or property.

It is, nonetheless, interesting and seemingly significant that in the case of men we do thus have, in addition to gross behavior with its successes or failures, verbal reports. And it will be of course part of our final task as psychologists to decide upon the further nature and meaning of such verbal reports. At the moment, however, I shall make but one suggestion with regard to them. I shall suggest that an essential feature of a certain type of verbal report or introspection is that, in it, the individual "intends" his perspectives as well as some independent. A perspective is, as we have seen, perfectly objective. The size of the projected image resulting from a given cube, placed at a given distance, is just as objective as is the independent size of that cube. But I believe that it will be found that it is only in introspection that an organism can actually intend and behave relative to such projected images. In fact, no experiment so far as I know has as yet ever appeared in which even a chimpanzee, to say nothing of a rat, could be shown to be responding, not to the independent size or shape or color of an environmental object, but merely to its momentary perspective size or shape or color. This is not to say that the values of the perspective sizes, shapes and colors do not affect and indeed often distort an animal's response to the corresponding independents. It is, however, to say that an animal's behavior always seems to "intend" the independent qualities and never the perspective ones.

And so it is also for memory. Rats or chimpanzees can never seem to intend merely the present perspective effects of a past light. We men, on the other hand, when in introspecting about our memories we report visual images, internal speech and the like, are, it would seem, reporting just such present perspectives. That is, we are reporting that in addition to what we take to be the actual independent qualities of the given past object there are also before us, here and now, at the moment of recall, such and such immediate perspective effects. These immediate perspective effects—these visual, auditory, kinesthetic images, or this internal speech—are objectively definable entities which in introspection we intend and sometimes with more and sometimes with less success attain.

The degree of our attainment is, however it must be noted, much more difficult to measure than it is in the case of the perceptual intention of perspectives. For images and internal speech, as objective properties, seem to be located inside our nervous systems somewhere. And that makes it difficult for their true values to be independently determined by the experimenter. Hence it is now, given our present techniques, almost impossible for an experimenter to conclude exactly in how far the given introspecting individual is successfully reporting—successfully "attaining"—his actual images and his actual internal speech. But this is not a fundamental difficulty. The account of memorial perspectives, i.e., of visual and other images and of internal speech which now gets into our psychology, while certainly far less reliable and less valid than our accounts of perceptual perspectives, is nonetheless, I would declare, quite as objective.

2. But let us turn, now, to brief consideration of the second main subtype of cognitive behavior readiness, what I called *hypotheses;* or intentions, expectations and attainments as to relations. Suppose a rat be run in a successive discrimination box. Such a box is an apparatus in which the animal has to choose one of two doors at each of four successive choice points. One of the two doors at each such point is lighted and one is dark. The lighted door may be either the one on the left or the one on the right in chance order. Thus at each such point the animal has the possibility of responding either on the basis of light-darkness or on that of right-leftness. Suppose, now further, that it be arranged by the experimenter that the correct choices shall in a day's series of 10 trials, or 40 choices in all, fall an equal number of times to the left and an equal number of times to the right, and suppose it also be arranged that the correct door be an equal number of times a dark door and an equal number of times a lighted door. Under these conditions it was found by Krechevsky,[21] whose experiments it is I am reporting, that the rat will pick up one systematic way of behaving after another. In the first two or three days he may pick up, say, the propensity of choosing always the right-hand doors. But then he will shift sooner or later to some new propensity, to that say, of choosing only the left-hand doors; and then still later to that of choosing alternate right and left doors; or he may shift to choosing all the lighted doors, irrespective of side, or all the dark doors, or to choosing alternately light and dark;

---

[21] I. Krechevsky, *"Hypotheses" versus "Chance" in the pre-solution period in sensory discrimination-learning,* Univ. Calif. Publ. Psychol., 6 (1932), 27–44; "The docile nature of 'hypotheses,'" *J. Comp. Psychol.,* 15 (1933), 429–433; *The genesis of "hypotheses" in rats,* Univ. Calif Publ. Psychol., 6 (1932), 45–64.

and so on. Each such systematic propensity will be adopted for a time and then dropped in favor of some other. And, following Krechevsky, we may now define each such intervening condition (or "I") in the organism, behind any one such systematic way of behaving, as a hypothesis.

A hypothesis, behavioristically, in other words, is to be defined as nothing more nor less than a condition in the organism which, while it lasts, produces just such a systematic selectivity in behavior. Further, it appears that such a hypothesis or selectivity is equivalent to an intention or assertion of a specific relation as obtaining in the environment. In the above case these assertions are to the effect that it is such and such types of door which lead on and such and such other types which are closed. The rats assert—hypothesize—that it is the right-hand doors, or the left-hand doors, or alternate right and left doors or dark doors, or whatever, which, as such, lead on. And when any one such assertion proves incorrect, an animal sooner or later drops it for a new one.

In the experiment as thus far described, the problem given to the animals was actually insoluble. The correct doors were, that is, determined by chance. And no hypotheses—none of the systematic selectivities in the behaviors of the animals—could prove successful. This meant that during the entire duration of the experiment the rats kept shifting from one hypothesis to another. In other experiments, however, the situation was different. Thus in one case it was arranged that after a rat had once adopted some hypothesis with a given degree of consistency the experimenter then made that hypothesis correct. Under these conditions the animals persisted in their now correct hypothesis throughout the entire remainder of the investigation. Or, again in still another set-up, a certain hypothesis was made correct from the very beginning. In such a case the rats might begin with various wrong hypotheses. But they always ended sooner or later with the single correct one. So much for rats, let us turn now to human beings.

In men, also, a hypothesis is fundamentally, I believe, no more than a similar behavior readiness. It is a condition or set which produces consistent selectivity of behavior relative to some type of environmental relation. But in men there are, to be sure, complications and refinements. Men can introspect. And when they introspect they tell us that it is not essential to their hypotheses that these issue into actual behavior. Hypotheses, they say, can be purely "mental." Furthermore, as thus mental, they can be "mentally" tested out to see if they are going to work before they go over into actual behavior. And, if they won't seem to work, they can be rejected. Now these introspections concerning hypotheses cannot be completely ruled out of court. They have to be considered further. But, first, it may be well to note that to be thus conscious and intropectable is not always inevitable even for human hypotheses.

Thus, for example, in certain multiple choice experiments with human subjects—a type of experiment very similar to Krechevsky's discrimination-box experiment just described with rats—Warner Brown and Miss Whittell[22] found cases in which the human subject arrived at the correct solution without, however, himself being able consciously to formulate the nature of his hypothesis. The individual chose the correct door every time (in this case not a door but a counter representing a door) without, however, being able to say what it was that defined his choice. He was not conscious of his hypothesis and yet this hypothesis successfully governed his behavior. We must conclude, therefore, that to be conscious—to be introspectively formulable—is not essential to even human hypotheses. The fundamental essence of any hypothesis is not, it would seem, whether it be conscious or not but the fact that it is a condition in the organism which sets the latter, whether human or subhuman, for a certain systematic selectivity of behavior. In the case of a man this condition may not get over into actual behavior but its significance and meaning is that, if it did get over into behavior, it is such and such behavior which it would determine. A hypothesis is defined by the fact that it would determine the choosing of left-hand doors rather than right-hand doors, or that it would determine the "apple polishing" of some instructors and the avoiding of all others.

Consider now, however, the further problem that a human hypothesis *can* be conscious and also that when conscious it can be held up and tested out before going over into gross behavior. What further points do these facts involve? It seems to me that perhaps there are two such points. The first is similar to that already made for the case of perceptual and memorial differentiations, it is the fact namely that in introspection a man can apparently intend the momentary perspective properties as well as the independent property. And so now in the case of hypotheses, here also a man can apparently in introspection "intend" not the independent relation but rather the momentary perspectives corresponding to that independent. He can intend, that is, the momentary immediate effects in himself—the immediate visual, auditory-kinesthetic, organic images, or whatever they may be which result from the external independent relation. And a large part of what we are wont to demand in

---

[22] W. Brown and F. Whittell, "Yerkes' multiple choice method with human adults," *. Comp. Psychol.*, 3 (1923), 305–326.

the laboratory in the way of introspection is just such a reporting of these immediate perspectives.

But there is a second more important feature involved in hypotheses as conscious,—the fact, already noted, that they can be mentally tested out. We must conceive, that is, that in human beings and perhaps also in some of the lower animals—certainly in the monkeys and the great apes—consciousness allows for a playing off of one intention, one behavior readiness, against another. It is thus that the possibility of arriving at modified and improved sets of these intentions or behavior readinesses is achieved. The conscious organism checks his hypothesis against his memories or against his perceptions. And, if necessary, he changes his hypothesis accordingly. He hypothetically expects all dark doors to be open. And then he memorially intends the openness or closedness character of the last dark door. And he remembers, say, that it was not open but closed. The two intentions—the two sets of behavior readiness—are thus at variance. He therefore corrects the former in the light of the latter. This sort of procedure, which seems to be limited to us men and to perhaps some of the higher animals, is certainly most remarkable. And it needs a lot more in the way of a successful analysis and study than any psychologist has yet succeeded in giving it. I see no reason, however, to suppose that it involves anything of a fundamentally different order from the sort of facts that we have already considered. It is another feature about the nature and functioning of the intervening variables—the intervening behavior readinesses. But, as such, it can likewise be taken care of, I would declare, in purely constructuralistic logical terms. For the purposes of psychology this capacity of the higher organisms to check up their intentions one against another can not require us to introduce into our account new variables of a nonobjective or experiential order. Science is, and must remain, a map and not turn into a reliving even when it has to concern itself with consciousness.

So much for a brief and inadequate consideration of the cognition variables—the differentiations of qualities and the hypotheses as to relations. There is one final set of problems still left over which we cannot attempt to treat now and our answers to which would still leave much to be desired. These are questions concerning the nature of the functions f_3 which connect the cognition variables to the independent variables and of the function f_2 which connects the cognition variables along with the demand variables to the final behavior B. As regards the functions in the class f_3 we already know some of the answers. They are the laws of sensory capacity, memory, learning and reasoning, which we to some extent now have. But even as regards them there is obviously still much more to be done. And as to the function f_2 we are as yet almost completely in the dark. There is at present one psychologist, Lewin,[23] who, I think, is doing something very important in this direction. But the whole affair is still too complicated for me to attempt to indicate it here.

This completes my argument. It has been long and, I fear, obscure. Therefore in conclusion I would like briefly to enumerate what seem to me to have been the most important points:

1. Modern psychology and modern physics starting from early noted facts concerning the relativity of sense perception were led to make a distinction between sense data, as immediately given and to be studied by psychology, and real material objects behind such sense data, to be studied by physics.

2. The more recent work on perception such as that of Brunswik and his students leads us now, however, not to the distinction between sense data and hypothetical reals behind such sense data, but rather to one between the perceptual intention of perspectives and the perceptual intention of independents. And both these types of intention are objectively discoverable and definable logical constructs.

3. The true dichotomy is not, therefore, between sense data and physical reals but between the logical constructs of both physics and psychology, on the one hand, and the matrix of immediate experience, on the other.

4. In the case of psychology the logical constructs to be evolved are necessarily those of a behaviorism.

5. A behaviorism seeks to write the form of the function f_1 which connects the dependent variable—the behavior, B—to the independent variables—stimulus, heredity, training, and physiological disequilibriums, S, H, T, and P.

6. The determination of this final function is, however, at present too difficult and behaviorism breaks its task down into two steps by the insertion of intervening variables $I_a, I_b, I_c, \ldots I_n$.

7. It appears further, however, that there can be two different types of behaviorism and that the nature of these intervening I's will be conceived differently by each of these types.

8. The one type, which I have called "molecular behaviorism," and which, as I see it, is more nearly the task of the physiologist than of the psychologist, tries to work out these I's in detailed neurological and

[23] Cf. K. Lewin, "Environmental forces," in *Handbook of child psychology*, ed. by C. Murchison, 2d rev. ed. Worcester, Mass., Clark University Press, 1933.

glandular terms. The other type, which I have called "molar behaviorism," and which as I see it is the task of the psychologist proper, tries to work out these I's at a more macroscopic level in the guise of "behavior readinesses." These behavior readinesses are to be conceived as correlated with the underlying molecular I's but as having their own level of description.

9. These molar I's or behavior readinesses would, according to my doctrine, be divided further into "demands" and "cognitions." The demands would then further subdivide into ultimate and subordinate demands and the cognitions into "differentiations" (or intentions as to qualities) and "hypotheses" (or intentions as to relations).

10. These demands, differentiations and hypotheses are all demonstrated and defined by objective experiments—the sorts of experiments that we can perform with animals as readily as with men. They are, in short but logical constructs. They are not relivings of immediate experience. Psychology like physics deserts immediate experience and leaves it for the philosopher, the poet, or the proponent of common sense.

11

OPERATIONAL BEHAVIORISM AND CURRENT TRENDS IN PSYCHOLOGY

[Proceedings of the Twenty-fifth Anniversary Celebration of the Inauguration of Graduate Studies at the University of Southern California, 1936]

I AM GOING to present a brief statement of my own brand of psychology. I shall here call it Operational Behaviorism. And I shall try to show that the principles of such an operational behaviorism will help to illuminate the interrelationships between the types of psychological experiment now actually current.

Before proceeding with the detailed presentation of my system, let me note in an aside that the term "operational" has been chosen with two different meanings in mind. In the first place, I have chosen it to indicate a certain general positivistic attitude now being taken by many modern physicists and philosophers and for which Professor Bridgman [1] [2] has selected this word "operational." In this sense, an operational psychology will be one which seeks to define its concepts in such a manner that they can be stated and tested in terms of concrete repeatable operations by independent observers. In this sense, to quote from S. S. Stevens, "a term or proposition has meaning (denotes something) if, and only if, the criteria of its applicability or truth consists of concrete operations which can be performed." [12, p. 517 f. See also 11.] The behaviorism which I am going to present seeks, then, to use only concepts which are capable of such concrete operational verification.

But, in the second place, I have also chosen this designation, "operational," because of what seems to me a second connotation which in connection with the word "behavior" it tends to have. For behavior as the thing observed also turns out to be essentially an activity whereby the organism in question "operates." In behaving, an organism, as Brunswik [3] puts it, "intends" and more or less successfully "conquers" its environment. It operates on its environment by such intendings and conquerings.[1]

To sum up, then, I will call mine an operational behaviorism because (a) my type of psychology would self-consciously seek to discover the concrete operations which an experimenter, or any observer, has to carry out to test the applicability or nonapplicability in any given instance of a specific psychological concept or proposition; and because (b) the observed behavior itself turns out to be a set of operations performed by the observed organism relative to its own environment. In a word, the activities of both of us, the observing and conceptualizing organisms, and of them, the observed and behaving organisms, are all ultimately to be characterized as operations of organisms upon environments.

To return, now, to the specific presentation of my system. The final dependent variable in which, as a psychologist, I am interested is behavior. It is the behavior of organisms, human and subhuman, which I wish to predict and control. As a psychologist I shall not attempt to describe immediate experience. The problem of immediate experience— the problem, that is, of some ultimate statement concerning that initial, as Professor Loewenberg [10] calls it, "preanalytical" matrix out of which both physics and psychology have developed—is either a problem for the philosophers or it is no problem at all. But, in any case, immediate experience can no longer, I would assert, be conceived as the special province of psychology any more than it is to be conceived as the special province of physics. For psychology, like physics, must now take immediate experience for granted and then proceed to develop maps, rules, and equations for finding one's way about. Physics develops one type of such a map and psychology another, and the two maps are ultimately to be fitted together so as to make complete prediction—complete finding of our way about—possible.

The particular map, the particular subset of predictions, in which psychology is interested concerns the to-be-expected behavior of organisms—the behavior to be expected from other organisms, and the behavior to be expected from ourselves. And in these predictions, mental processes, whether they be those of another or of ourselves, will figure only in the guise of objectively definable intervening variables. Or (to borrow a phrase from William James) the sole "cash-value" of mental

---

[1] See also my own previous analyses of behavior [13] and [14].

processes lies, I shall assert, in this their character as a set of intermediating functional processes which interconnect between the initiating causes of behavior, on the one hand, and the final resulting behavior itself, on the other.

Organisms of given heredities, given kinds and amounts of previous training, and given maturities are immersed in environments and are driven by conditions of physiological disequilibrium. And because of these environments and these disequilibria, they behave. Mental processes are but intervening variables between the five independent variables of (1) environmental stimuli, (2) physiological drive, (3) heredity, (4) previous training, and (5) maturity, on the one hand, and the final dependent variable, behavior, on the other.

Let me indicate this situation symbolically. Let S stand for environmental stimulus condition, P for the conditions external and internal whereby physiological drives are defined, H for heredity, T for previous training, and A for age or maturity. We may then write the general equation:

$$B = f_1 (S, P, H, T, A)$$

B is some function f_1 of S, P, H, T, and A. Given this equation, mental processes are concepts which arise when we attempt further to elaborate the nature of this f_1 function. For it is a very complicated function—at least for all cases save those, perhaps, of such very simple behavior as reflexes and tropisms. It is in fact so complicated that we at present seem unable to state it in any single simple statement. We find, rather, that we have to handle it by conceiving it as broken down into successive sets of component functions. These component functions connect the independent variables to logically constructed "intervening variables," and then connect these intervening variables in their turn to one another and to the final dependent behavior. We may symbolize such intervening variables as I_a, I_b, I_c, ... I_n. And, if we do so, we may then write in place of the original single function, $B = f_1 (S, P, H, T, A)$, various sets of component functions of such forms as:

$$I_a = f_2^a (S, P, H, T, A)$$

$$I_b = f_2^b (S, P, H, T, A)$$

$$I_c = f_2^c (S, P, H, T, A)$$

or:

$$I_g = f_2^g (I_a, I_c ... S, P, H, T, A)$$

or finally:

$$B = f_2^x (I_a, I_b, I_c, I_f ... H, T, A)$$

It is such intervening I's, whether simply or complicatedly related to the independent variables and to one another, which are all that my operational behaviorism finds in the way of mental processes. These I's are "demands," "discriminanda," "manipulanda," "means-end fields," "traits," and "capacities," and the like. They are objective entities defined in terms of the f_2 functions which connect them to the S's, P's, H's, T's, and A's, on the one hand, and to the final B, on the other.

It is to be pointed out, however, that there is also a second way of trying to conceive and define a set of intervening I's—the physiological way. But when this physiological way is taken, the result is to be called a physiological rather than a psychological operational behaviorism. In such a physiological operationalism the interconnecting I's would be conceived and defined as such and such specific central and peripheral disturbances in the nervous system, as conditioned reflex connections, as anticipatory goal reactions, as cerebral potential gradients, as glandular secretions, and the like. Science demands, of course, in the end, the final development of both sorts of behaviorism. And the facts and laws of physiological behaviorism, when obtained, will presumably provide the explanation for the facts and laws of psychological behaviorism. But the psychological facts and laws are also to be gathered and established in their own right. A psychology cannot be explained by a physiology until one has a psychology to explain. Further, it appears to me that it is primarily the job of us psychologists, or at any rate of the "purer" among us, to gather the psychological facts and laws and to leave it to our less pure, physiologically minded brethren to gather the neurological, glandular, and biochemical data which underlie such psychological facts and laws.

Confining myself, then, from here on to psychological operational behaviorism, let me attempt to sketch in the general outlines of the latter. For, as I see it, such a psychological operationalism does no more than give a list of, and attempt to indicate the true functional interrelationship between, the actual types of experiment being done today in psychology.

Psychological operationalism presents three main theses:

1. It asserts a list of intervening I's.

2. It asserts certain laws or functions whereby these I's result from the S's, P's, H's, T's, and A's, and from each other.

3. It asserts certain further laws or functions whereby the final behavior B results from combinations of these I's, as well as from S's, P's, H's, T's, and A's.

The schema on page 120 indicates my formulation of these three assertions. This schema is, of course, tentative. It will surely need re-vision before it can be adopted wholeheartedly. I present it, neverthe-less, because I believe it to be correct in essence. I believe that even now it is a pretty fair summary of what psychology today is actually, opera-tionally, doing.

The causal sequences run from left to right and are indicated by arrows. The final dependent variable—behavior—is at the extreme right. The initial and independent variables, the S's, P's, H's, T's, and A's, are at the extreme left.

The final dependent behavior has three component aspects. Some-times it is one and sometimes it is another of these aspects which the given experiment is interested in. No one of these aspects can, of course, be missing, but a given experiment can vary one of them somewhat independently of the other two. They are (a) direction, (b) quantity or persistence, and (c) efficiency or skill. That is, concretely speaking, a behavior is (a) a doing of one thing, a taking of one direction rather than another: it is speaking certain words rather than other words, sitting in a chair rather than walking about, going into one maze alley rather than another maze alley, or the like. And it is (b) a taking of this direction with a certain degree of intensity or persistence as measured concretely in terms of percentage of animals in the given situation who do it, or by the amount of distraction that has to be introduced before it is interrupted, or by some other quantifying technique. And it is (c) the exhibition of a certain degree of efficiency or skill as measured by time, waste motion, or some similar measure. Thus, for example, in a given discrimination problem, using Lashley's technique, the rats (a) jump to one door rather than the other; (b) they do this a certain percentage of times; and (c) they exhibit a certain degree of skill in their actual jumping technique. In different experiments it might be different ones of these three subvariables the causal antecedents of which one is particularly interested in determining.

The initial independent variables, indicated at the left, subdivide into two groups: S's and P's, on the one hand, and H's, T's, and A's, on the other. The former may be characterized as releasing variables. It is these S's and P's which set behavior going. The H's, T's, and A's, on the other hand, are to be designated as the governing or guiding vari-ables. Heredity, previous training, and given maturities do not, as such, initiate behavior. But they do govern or guide in a very fundamental way the final character of the behavior which is initiated by given S's and P's. These governing or guiding H's, T's, and A's have been in-dicated as working together in subgroups.

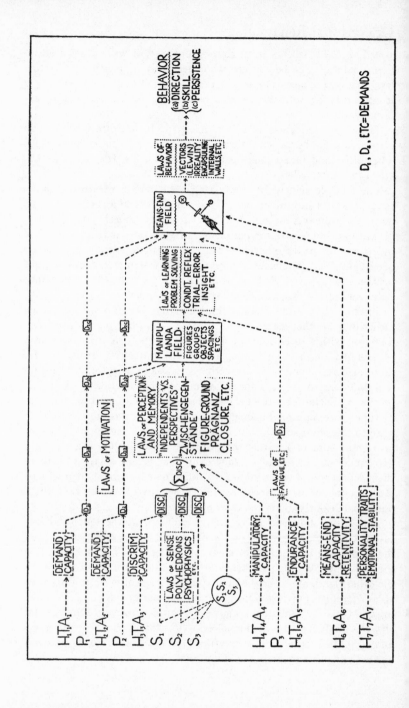

Operational Behaviorism

There are also two types of intervening variable. These have been indicated as surrounded by solid lines and by dash lines, respectively. Those surrounded by solid lines are to be characterized as mental events whereas those surrounded by dash lines may be characterized as mental traits or capacities. The traits and capacities are the relatively direct products of the H's, T's and A's. The events are the products of the S's and P's combined with the traits and capacities.

The functional causal relations are indicated by the arrows with the legends enclosed in dotted lines.

Now, I would insist that the different chapters in modern experimental psychology, as we know them today, are located by such a diagram. That is, each chapter, it seems to me, chooses as its topic some one minor group of the intervening variables, or else the final behavior itself, and then discusses the immediate functional dependencies or laws—the arrows—whereby these variables depend upon various of the preceding variables in the schema.

Thus, for example, the chapter on Motivation is concerned, obviously, with the demands, designated as D_1, D_2, D_3, et cetera, and the laws or functions whereby these latter depend upon the P's and upon the motivation capacities deriving from H_1, T_1, A_1; H_2, T_2, A_2; and H_5, T_5, A_5.

The chapter on Sensory psychology concerns the discriminanda, $Disc_1$, $Disc_2$, $Disc_3$, et cetera (my name for sensations and images), and the way in which these depend upon the S's and upon sensory capacities.

The chapter on Gestalt psychology—the Gestalt psychology, that is, of perception and immediate memory—concerns what I have labeled the "manipulanda field" and the laws of Pragnanz, Closure, Good Gestalt, Zwischengegenstände (Brunswik), etc., whereby this manipulanda field depends upon the discriminanda, upon the pattern relations among the stimuli (indicated on the diagram by $S_1 S_2 S_3$) and upon capacities.

The chapter on Problem Solving, Learning, and Reasoning concerns the means-end field and the laws of conditioned reflex, trial and error, and insight, whereby this means-end field results from the manipulanda field, from demands, and from the intellectual and motor capacities deriving from H_6, T_6, A_6.

Further, a chapter which I would call that of Behavior Dynamics concerns the final dependent behavior and the latter's immediate dependence upon the means-end field and upon capacity factors and upon traits, such as emotional stability, deriving from H_7, T_7, A_7. It is the laws of this latter chapter which, as I see it, Professor Lewin [9] has been pioneering with regard to.

Finally, there would be a chapter, or rather many chapters, on Individual Differences. These chapters would concern themselves with the nature of the trait and capacity factors and with the laws of their dependence upon the H's, and T's, and A's. And the question which gives rise to the most disputes would be that as to whether these capacity and trait factors and the H's, T's, and A's which underlie them are relatively many (and specific) or relatively few (and general).

But, by this time, I am sure that the critic must be up in arms. How, he will ask, are the intervening variables ever arrived at? All that one has overtly in any experimental setup are, by hypothesis, the left-hand independent variables, on the one hand, and the right-hand dependent behavior, on the other. All that one has actually to operate with are physiological drives (defined in terms of time since last feeding, since last copulation, or the like), environmental stimuli (defined in physical or common-sense terms), heredity (defined by breeding charts and the traits of ancestors), and age (defined by number of days and hours since birth, or, if one is being more precise, since insemination), on the one hand, and the finally observed behavior, with its special characteristics of direction, persistence and skill, on the other. Whence, then, come our notions and definitions concerning the intervening variables?

My answer is as follows: In certain carefully chosen, controlled and "standard" experimental setups, one tries to hold all but one, or one small group, of the independent variables constant and studies the functional connection between the variations in this one independent variable, or this one limited group of independent variables, on the one hand, and the correlated variations in some quantitatable feature of the final behavior on the other. For example, one holds all the independent variables but, say P_1 (time since last feeding) constant. And in doing this, one chooses certain "standard" values for all the other independent variables such as P_2, S_1, S_2, et cetera. And then, under these conditions, one observes the correlations between the variations in P_1, on the one hand, and the resulting variations in some aspect of the behavior B, on the other.

For example, let us suppose it to be a case of rats, and let us suppose that the feature of the behavior which is in question is the percentage of entrances into the correct alley for groups of rats that have already thoroughly learned the maze. Under such conditions, as we vary P_1 (time since last feeding), we shall obtain some curve such as the following (page 123) between this B (percentage of entrances into the correct alleys) and P_1.

This curve holds, of course, in the first instance only for one given value of H_1, T_1, A_1. We shall assume, however, that the same general form of curve will be obtained whatever the values of H_1, T_1, and A_1 (i.e., of heredity, previous training, and maturity). The effects of these different values of H_1, T_1, and A_1 will, we shall suppose, be simply to give new values to the constants or parameters which determine the height and curvatures of this curve.

We must now, however, make one further assumption. We must suppose that we have chosen the constant "standard" values, which we have

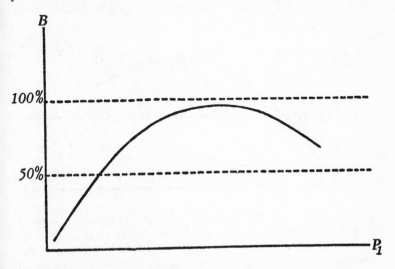

given to all the other independent variables, P_2, P_3, S_1, S_2, et cetera, in such a fashion that this general curve between B and P_1 which we have thus obtained really mirrors directly the functional relation between P_1 and *an intervening variable* D_1 (the demand for the given type of food.) In other words, we must assume that we have chosen a setup such that the variations in the selected aspect of the behavior mirror directly those of the desired intervening variable and that we can therefore rescore and relabel our curve as shown on page 124.

Of course, the obtained behavior does actually depend upon a whole welter of other variables—general stimulus setup, number of previous presentations, other physiological drives, and the specific heredity factors, training factors, and maturity factors, as well as upon P_1. So that we are assuming that the "standard" values which we chose in this experiment for these other variables were such that they did not distort the picture. That is, we are assuming that we have obtained this functional relationship between P_1 and D_1 under standard conditions so that this same relationship will also hold between P_1 and D_1 under all conditions, even though under many of these other conditions it will no longer appear simply and directly in some single aspect of the behavior.

Or, consider the findings of Warden [15] and his co-workers as to the functional relation between P_1 (time since last feeding) and B (number of crossings of the electric grill). Now it is obvious that the interest of such an experiment also depends upon assumptions similar to the

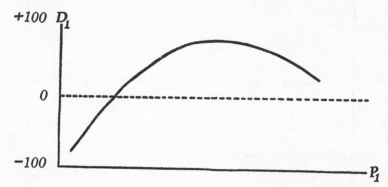

above. The first of these assumptions is that the details of the Warden experimental setup (that is, the values given by the experiment to all the other variables: type of obstruction box chosen; location of the reward object; length of time allowed for crossings; et cetera) have all been chosen so that the obtained behavior (number of crossings in twenty minutes) mirrors directly the intervening variable D_1 (demand for the given food). And the second implicit assumption is that the relationship which is thus found between D_1 and P_1 is a characteristic and true relationship—one not limited for its validity to this one type of obstruction apparatus or to the other specific conditions. It is assumed, in short, that the same true relationship, the curve for which we have just drawn hypothetically as the result of the supposed maze experiment, will be found. It is assumed, that the Warden obstruction technique is a "standard" experimental setup which uncovers a true, relatively universal relationship between P_1 (hunger) and D_1 (demand for the given food)—a relationship which will also hold for other situations—for other mazes, discrimination boxes, and the like—even though it may not appear simply and directly in any of these other situations. Indeed, it even seems to be assumed by Warden and his co-workers that this relationship thus found between P_1 and D_1, using the obstruction-box technique on rats, is the one which also holds for human beings in general life situations. It is assumed, in short, that this relationship holds not only for different values of the S with the given H_1's, T_1's, and A_1's, (rats) but also for quite different values of such H_1's, T_1's, and A_1's, (i.e., those of men).

But all such assumptions are ticklish and of very uncertain justification. And yet, however dangerous and open to pitfalls they may be, such types of assumption are, I am convinced, the sort which in psychology we actually do employ today. We do assume intervening variables, and we do try to work forward to them from the independent variables and backward to them from the resulting behavior. We do suppose (in spite of all the complexities) that we can determine in carefully chosen "standard" experimental setups certain relatively unique true functions connecting these intervening variables to specific groups of independent variables. That is, we do assume that, when we carefully select our experimental setups, these intervening variables will be betrayed directly in the selected quantified feature of the resulting behavior. And we do suppose that the relationships thus obtained are true and persistent ones which will also obtain in other conditions where the given intervening variables are no longer directly mirrored by any single simple aspect of the behavior.

Turn now, to another example, the typical discrimination experiment. It is obvious that in this type of experiment we seek to hold all the P's and all the H's, T's, and A's, and all the other S's (than the one type of S that we are specifically investigating) constant. And then we seek to establish a general and universally true relation between the variation in this one type of S and the given resulting type of discriminanda (i.e., sense qualities). And we assume that this obtained relation between the values of this type of S and the values of the resulting discriminanda betrays itself in its true form under these standard conditions of such a discrimination experiment. So that we suppose that we thereafter know this relation between this type of S and this type of Disc (between, for example, S_1 and $Disc_1$), even when under other conditions than such a discrimination experiment this relation no longer, as such, appears directly in the final behavior.

So much for suggestions as to what we may call, perhaps, the "first-line" intervening variables—the D's and the Disc's. But it appears, looking at the diagram, that there are also "second-line" and "third-line" and perhaps still further removed intervening variables. Examples of such second- and third-line variables are the manipulanda field and the means-end field. How do we ever arrive at notions and definitions of these? My answer is that we first assume that we already know the functions which connect the preceding intervening variables to the independent variables. And then we use these preceding intervening variables as independents.

For example, in the study of the manipulanda field we assume that we already know what discriminanda will, under the ideal conditions of a Titchenerian, or a psychophysical, experiment, result from the given sense stimuli. We also assume that we have average standard individuals with standard capacities. And then we proceed to investigate the laws or the function by which given S's plus their temporal and spatial patterns plus the manipulanda traits and capacities of the given species produce the manipulanda field. And we assume that this manipulanda field, under these conditions is betrayed directly by some chosen aspect of the resulting behavior. That is, we devise experiments whereby certain obtained variations in B can be assumed to be direct expressions of "figure ground," "grouping," or other "gestalt formations," and of whether it is the "projected" or the "independent" size that is intended [14] and the like. In short, we do experiments using sizes, weights, groupings, movements, et cetera, similar to those of Klüver [6] with monkeys or of Hertz [4], [5] with blue jays or of Wertheimer [16], Köhler [7], Koffka [8], and Brunswik [3] and their co-workers, with human adults.

Again, having thus assumed that we know all the functions which produce the demands, the manipulanda field and the various capacities so that, given the values of the independent variables, we can read off by means of these functions the correlated values of these demands and manipulanda fields, we then proceed to study the laws of learning, conditioned reflex, trial and error, and insight, whereby the manipulanda field plus the demands produce such and such a final means-end field.

And, finally, assuming that we now know the means-end field—assuming, that is, that we know the organism to be responding relative to such and such goals, so and so far off, with such and such obstructions between him and these goals—then we proceed to study the final function connecting the characters of this means-end field with the final behavior. And we discover such laws as those which Lewin [9] has brought to our attention and which he has characterized by such phrases as "resolution of vectors," "going out of the field," "encapsuling oneself," "flight into an irreality plane," "relief of internal tensions," and the like. These are the final types of function which connect behavior to the preceding means-end field and to the personality factors resulting from H_7, T_7, A_7.

Operational Behaviorism

In order to make the schema still more real, let me point out, further, just where some of the other chapters of modern psychology would fall.

The chapter on Psychoanalysis would concern itself with P_2 whether this type of P is one or many, and with the question of the heredity and training variables, H_2 and T_2, whereby hierarchies and interactions of the subordinate demands, D_2a, D_2b, et cetera, are established. It would also concern itself with the building up of special social features in the means-end field and with facts concerning introspectability and nonintrospectability arising out of such social features.

The chapter on Motor Skills would concern the manipulation capacities and the laws of their dependence upon heredity differences H_5, on training differences T_5, and upon mere maturation differences A_5.

The chapter on Learning, Reasoning, and all the higher thought processes would be concerned with the development of the means-end field and its dependence upon H_6, T_6, A_6, and upon the manipulanda field.

The chapter on Feeling and Emotion would, I believe, fall in three places. In part it would be a discussion of a peculiar type of discriminandum, resulting from interoceptive stimuli. In part it would be a discussion of the laws of motivation whereby the D's derive from the P's. And in part it would be a discussion of certain features of the final behavior dynamics as these are affected by emotional stability and the other personality traits deriving from H_7, T_7, A_7.

And, to repeat once again, the chapter or chapters on Individual Differences would concern itself with the question of in how far H_1, and H_2, and H_3, et cetera, up to H_7 are mutually independent of one another. And it would also raise the question as to whether each one of these itself may not really represent a bunch of several or perhaps many independent subvariables.

So much for my attempt to indicate the general operational meaning of the schema. You may, if you will, cavil at its details. But I doubt if you can get away from the general proposition which the schema embodies; namely, that we do in psychology assume intervening variables more or less like the ones I have suggested, and that we do attempt to define these intervening variables by going at them experimentally, i.e., *operationally*, from the two ends.

If you will have none of such a schema, then there are but two alternatives left to you. Either you must return to good old-fashioned introspectionism or you must wait for the appearance of a more refined neurology and physiology. Either you must assume that you know the intervening variables in some immediate direct fashion—not only your own but also of the other fellow and those of the rats who can't tell you about them—or else you must wait until physiology and neurology can give you all the actual neural and physiological disequilibria, and genes, on the one hand, and final resulting behavior, on the other. But, if you adopt either of these two alternatives, it seems to me that you may as well confess that for the present you must give up psychology altogether.

One last word. Some one is sure to ask: But what about introspection? Is not introspection after all, at least in the case of men, a significant method by which one can get at and define these intervening variables in a direct and really reliable fashion? I doubt it. I believe that introspection is a form of social response—a type of final behavior which would appear at the right on our diagram like any other behavior but one which has very complicated conditions. And I do not believe that this introspection behavior in a standard experimental setup is of a sort to mirror most types of intervening variables any more successfully and truly than do more gross, less social forms of behavior. In fact, it seems to me obvious and already well demonstrated that in most cases introspective behavior is far less successful in such a direct mirroring than are more gross forms of behavior; for these latter are not, as is introspection, subject to distortion by being directed toward an audience. The very essence of introspection lies in the fact that it is a response to audiences—external and internal. And, such being the case, it seems less likely to mirror most types of intervening variable so directly and correctly as do more gross nonsocial forms of behavior.

The above does not, of course, however, preclude the proposition that, where the intervening variable in question is, as in psychoanalysis and in many personality studies, itself some complicated resultant of the social situation, that then such an intervening variable can, and perhaps must, be mirrored by introspection. For example, one of the most significant findings of psychoanalysis is that introspection is impossible or violently distorts in some situations but is valid and adequate in others.

To sum up, then, the validity of introspection is, as I see it, restricted to one special type of investigation—the type of investigation where what we are primarily concerned with are those intervening variables (whatever they may be) which underlie the ability or nonability of being able "to talk about it." But in the other, far greater majority of psychological investigations, this ability or nonability "to talk about" is not important or determinative. And, indeed, when it is called into play, it is apt to lead to decided errors relative to the other types of intervening variable with which, in such cases, we are concerned.

Let me recapitulate:

1. I have tried to present and defend an "operational behaviorism."

2. Such an operational behaviorism comprises two main principles: (a) It asserts that the ultimate interest of psychology is solely the prediction and control of behavior. (b) It asserts that psychological concepts, i.e., the mental capacities and mental events—may be conceived as objectively defined intervening variables. And it asserts that these intervening variables are to be defined wholly operationally—that is, in terms of the actual experimental operations whereby their presences or absences and their relations to the controlling independent variables and to the final dependent behavior are determined.

3. I have presented a tentative schema for such intervening variables.

4. I have asserted that the different chapters of modern psychology find their natural locations on this schema.

5. I have denied that introspective behavior provides any *sui generis* type of information concerning the intervening variables. Introspection is just one more behavior which will in some cases (but in other cases most certainly will not) provide a good, standard experimental setup for discovering and studying specific types of intervening variable.

REFERENCES

1. Bridgman, P. W., *The logic of modern physics*. New York: Macmillan, 1928.
2. Bridgman, P. W., "A physicist's second reaction to mengenlehre," *Scripta Mathematica*, 2 (1934), 101–117.
3. Brunswik, E., *Wahrnehmung und Gegenstandswelt: Grundlegung einer Psychologie vom Gegenstand her*. Wien: Deuticke, 1934.
4. Herts, M., "Beobachtungen an gefangenen Rabenvögeln," *Psychol. Forsch.*, 8 (1926), 336–97.
5. Hertz, M., "Weitere Versuche an der Rabenkrähe," *Psychol. Forsch.*, 10 (1928), 111–41.
6. Klüver, H., *Behavior mechanisms in monkeys*. Chicago: University of Chicago Press, 1933.
7. Köhler, W., *Psychologische Probleme*. Berlin: Springer, 1933.
8. Koffka, K., *Principles of Gestalt psychology*. New York: Harcourt, Brace, 1935.
9. Lewin, K., *A dynamic theory of personality*. New York: McGraw-Hill, 1935.
10. Loewenberg, J., "Pre-analytical and post-analytical data," *J. Philos.*, 24 (1927), 5–14.
11. Stevens, S. S., "The operational basis of psychology," *Amer. J. Psychol.*, 47 (1935), 323–30.
12. Stevens, S. S., "The operational definition of psychological concepts," *Psychol. Rev.*, 42 (1935), 517–27.
13. Tolman, E. C., *Purposive behavior in animals and men*. New York: Century, 1932.
14. Tolman, E. C., "Psychology vs. immediate experience," *Philos. Science*, 2 (1935), 356–380.
15. Warden, C. J., *Animal motivation: Experimental studies on the albino rat*. New York: Columbia University Press, 1931.
16. Wertheimer, M., *Die Abhandlungen zur Gestalttheorie*. Erlangen: Verlag der Philosophischen Akadamie, 1925.

12

THE ACQUISITION OF STRING PULLING BY RATS—CONDITIONED RESPONSE OR SIGN-GESTALT?

[Psychological Review, MAY, 1937]

IT HAS BEEN demonstrated by McDougall and McDougall [9], Adams [1], and McCulloch [11] that rats, and not merely monkeys and apes [see Köhler, 8, and Klüver, 7] can be taught to pull in food by means of attached strings. The initial training-in of such a string-pulling habit in rats requires, however, a special sort of procedure. From some recent experimentation with this procedure and from analysing it while in progress, I feel that it offers a nice problem for theories of learning.

I propose, therefore, to present here a somewhat detailed description of this initial training-in of string pulling and then on the basis of this description to seek to indicate why the sign-gestalt theory[1] seems to fit the account better than a conditioned reflex theory.

DESCRIPTIVE ANALYSIS OF THE ACQUISITION OF STRING PULLING

McCulloch describes the technique which he used in inducing string pulling, as follows:

On the first day each animal was placed in a discrimination box and allowed to nibble from the food pan at the front of the box [i.e., the pan was already drawn in as far as it would come under the wire at the front of the box] about one gram of the standard food reward. He was then removed. This procedure was twice repeated. No additional food was given. On the second day the same procedure was followed. On the third day the rat was placed in the box

---

[1] See Tolman [14], [15], [16], [18], [20], [21].

and allowed to nibble from the pan. While he was eating, the tray was slowly drawn away from him. (At this time the tray weighed 50 grams.) He would clutch at the pan and draw it back again to a position in which food could be obtained. This procedure was repeated. The tray was drawn under the lower wire until it was barely within the rat's reach, and he was allowed to draw in the tray for food.

The tray was then drawn through the animal's paws until it was quite beyond reach. At this time a string extended from the food pan and passed under the lower horizontal wire to the rear of the discrimination box. In a very short time the rat would draw in the tray by means of the string. Sometimes he would secure the food by striking the string in his scrabblings for the food pan, sometimes he would clutch the string and draw it in, and infrequently he would seize the string with his teeth. After he had drawn the string a short distance for a few times, the tray was removed farther on successive trials. The first day's training ceased when an individual had drawn the string a distance of 50 cm. [11, p. 91 f.].

From having now, myself, carried out and watched this procedure on numerous occasions, I believe that this description can be expanded and separated into relatively specific steps. These different steps can be epitomized as shown in table 1.

Let me point out certain features of this table. Columns 1, 2, and 3 represent successive moments in time. Column 3 presents the consummatory situation of eating from the pan. This terminates the behavior in each step of learning. In step *a* this consummatory situation is all that there is. I have indicated this fact by placing "rat eats" in all three columns. In steps *b, c,* and *d,* this consummatory situation is presented first but then it is interrupted and the animal returns to its only after the proper new response of pulling in (perhaps as yet in only a relatively embryonic form) has appeared. Finally, in steps *e* and *f* the consummatory situation is not present before the response proper. The new stimulus is alone there and only if the animal makes the proper response to the latter does he arrive at the consummatory situation.

Finally, note the methods of hastening and reviving the response. Of these, *x, y,* and *y′* all appear to be means of enhancing the new stimulus—the string—whereas method *z* consists in bringing back one or more of the earlier steps (with their responses and the final consummatory situation resulting from such responses).

With, now, such a concrete and analysed picture before us, let us see how far each formula—the conditioned response formula or the sign-gestalt one—may be made to fit this picture. I begin with the former.

TABLE 1

	Column 1		Column 2		Column 3	
	Stimulus	Response	Stimulus	Response	Stimulus	Response
			I. PRELIMINARY TO LEARNING			
(a)	Pan in	Rat eats	Pan in	Rat eats	Pan in	Rat eats
			II. BEGINNING TO INDUCE LEARNING			
(b)	Pan in	Rat eats	Pan pulled away gently when rat's foot is on edge	Rat pulls pan nearer again	Pan in	Rat eats
(c)	Pan in	Rat eats	Pan pulled almost out of reach	Rat scrabbles and catches hold of pan with mouth or paws and pulls in	Pan in	Rat eats
(d)	Pan in	Rat eats	Pan pulled away just out of reach but still very visible; string	Rat scrabbles and catches string with mouth or paws and pulls in	Pan in	Rat eats
			III. APPEARANCE AND DEVELOPMENT OF RESPONSE PROPER			
(e)			Pan apparently present in visual or olfactory terms but out of reach; string	Rat seizes string with mouth or paws and pulls in	Pan in	Rat eats
(f)			String	Rat seizes string and keeps on pulling for quite a time	Pan in	Rat eats
			IV. METHODS OF HASTENING AND REVIVING RESPONSE			
(x)			Pan or string pulled from rat with some force	Rat exhibits opposing and contesting tug and then continues to pull string	Pan in	Rat eats
(y)			String with food smeared on it	Rat picks up string to eat food and after eating starts to pull string	Pan in	Rat eats
(y')			String jiggled	Rat seizes string and pulls	Pan in	Rat eats
(z)	Return to earlier stages a, b, c, and d.					

The Conditioned Response Formula Applied to the Acquisition of String Pulling

The conditioned response theory, as I understand it, finds but four essential factors in any case of learning:

I. An initial *unconditioned stimulus.*

II. An *unconditioned response* originally evoked by this unconditioned stimulus.

III. A new *to-be-substituted stimulus,* which in the typical experimental procedure is made to appear in temporal contiguity just before and then for a short time simultaneously with the unconditioned stimulus.

IV. The new finally *conditioned response.* This conditioned response is either the original unconditioned response itself, or something closely related to it (i.e., some fractional component of it or an anticipatory form of it) which comes to be made to the new to-be-substituted stimulus alone, even when the unconditioned stimulus no longer follows.[2]

Let us look, now, for these four types of factor in the account given above. I think a conditioned response theorist would be led to identify these four factors as follows:

I. The *unconditioned stimulus* he would identify as the food in the pan (i.e., the stimulus which appears in column 3 at all stages of learning).

II. The *unconditioned response* he would identify as the eating of this food from the pan (i.e., the response which appears in 3 at all stages of learning).

III. The *to-be-substituted stimulus* he would identify as the string itself. (This appears in column 2 in steps *d, e,* and *f.*)

IV. The *conditioned response* he would identify as the seizing and pulling of the string (i.e., the response which appears in column 2 in steps *d, e,* and *f*).

What, now, is to be said about such a conditioned response interpretation? Personally, I tend to find three difficulties with it.

First, the learned (i.e., the supposedly conditioned) response of pulling the string is not, as it seems to me it should be according to a strict conditioned response interpretation, either the original unconditioned response of eating or a response "closely" related to the latter. It is neither eating itself, a fractional component of eating, nor an antici-

[2] I have here assumed that those holding to a conditioning theory of learning adopt essentially the "substitute stimulus" notion of conditioning. For an extraordinarily clear and cogent analysis of both the facts and the theories of "conditioning" see Hilgard [3], [4].

patory form of eating. If this pulling of the string is nonetheless to be conceived as the conditioned response, then the conditioned response formula must be elaborated in some way so as to include, among the conditioned responses, responses such as this one of string pulling, which are defined merely by the fact that they *lead to* the presence of the unconditioned stimulus.

Skinner [13] alone among the conditioned response theorists seems to have been aware of this need for an elaboration of the formula and to have sought to take care of it by proposing a second paradigm for conditioned responses. In this second variety of conditioned response the *to-be-learned* response is not the original unconditioned response but a new quite different response which precedes the appearance of the unconditioned stimulus. That is to say, whereas the paradigm for the classical type of conditioned response is

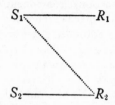

that for this new type proposed by Skinner is

$$S_1 \text{————————} R_1 \text{————————} S_2 \text{————————} R_2$$

In this latter the unconditioned response is $S_2 \text{————————} R_2$ and the conditioned response is $S_1 \text{————————} R_1$. Obviously this second paradigm fits the present case in the form:

$$\begin{array}{cccc} S_1 & R_1 & S_2 & R_2 \\ \text{String————} & \text{Pulling————} & \text{Food————} & \text{Eating} \end{array}$$

The difficulty, however, with this analysis of Skinner's is, as I see it, that the pulling is not, on its first appearance, a response to the given string alone but a response rather to a whole complex relational situation. (See third objection below.) I would assert, in short, that the fact and nature of such a relational complex constitutes an important feature of the causal set-up—a feature which even Skinner's improved analysis fails to care for.

Second, the conditioned response formula seems to me inadequate in that the two stimuli and the two responses which are picked out in the above example by the conditioned response formula are not, it must be observed, stimuli and responses in any strict physiological sense.

They are not physiologically, but environmentally defined affairs. Thus food and string, as visual, olfactory and tactual stimuli patterns, may be quite different from occasion to occasion. They retain their respective identities from time to time only by virtue of their environmental "meanings." And eating and string pulling, as responses, do not correspond to specific and invariant sets of muscle contractions, but are only identifiable through successive times in terms of environmentally nameable "manipulations." If the conditioned response formula is to be retained, then it must also be elaborated and "loosened" in some such meaningful manner. That is to say, it must be loosened so as to allow both "stimuli" and "responses" to be identifiable in terms of relatively gross and meaningful characters and not in terms of any precise or necessarily constant sense-organ and muscle processes.[3]

Third, even supposing that the above two difficulties can be obviated, there still remains another fundamental difficulty with the conditioned response formula as applied here. This lies, as I see it, in the fact that such a conditioned response account allows no place for certain very important features of the actual causal situation. The only causal condition out of which learning arises, is, according to the theory, the mere temporal contiguity of the to-be-substituted and the conditioned stimuli. But in the present case the mere presence of the string and the subsequent presence of the food pan is never enough as such, to cause the rat to learn to pull the string. The tendency to pull the string has to be induced by pulling the pan just out of reach and thereby releasing a general scrabbling (*vide* table 1, steps *c* and *d*). The string pulling appears at first, in short, merely as a component within the more general response of scrabbling. And to release the latter a complex situational whole has to be presented. Further, the string pulling, as such, only gradually becomes independent and specifically released by the string itself. And it appears that in this gradual development it has to be helped further by such devices as: "jiggling the string" (y'); "smearing food on the string" (y); or "pulling the string away and evoking a contesting tug" (x); and "then continually returning to and reviving the original situation of food can just being pulled away" (z). The value of these devices likewise would be accorded no place in the pure

---

[3] Skinner [12] and Guthrie [2] among the conditioned response psychologists have overtly taken cognizance of this situation. But I do not feel that they have been altogether successful in their attempts. For there is a big difference between admitting that stimuli or responses probably vary from time to time and being able to give any account of (in truly stimulus response terms) why they can, nonetheless be called identical with their former selves. It is this latter requirement which I think both Guthrie and Skinner have failed to satisfy.

conditioned response account.[4] Or to sum it up, the conditioned response formula seems to me to leave out of its causal account: (1) the
fact of the causal significance of the initial complex relational whole:
"food can presented and then pulled just out of reach"; (2) the fact
that this situational whole releases initially merely the general response
of scrabbling towards the food can; (3) the fact that string clutching
and pulling thus appear in the first place only as components within
this more general scrabbling; and (4) such facts as that pulling the
string away from the rat; jiggling the string, and returning again to
the original total situational whole of food-can-present-then-pulled-
away are causally important not only in originating but also in reviving
the final perfected string-pulling response.

So much for my criticisms of the conditioned response account. Let
me present now my suggested substitute for the latter—a sign-gestalt
account. In the next two sections I shall present, first, a general outline
of the sign-gestalt theory, and then, second, a specific application of it
to this present case of string pulling.

The Sign-Gestalt Formula

The essence of the sign-gestalt account of learning is that learning
consists in the formation of new sign-gestalt expectations—hypotheses
[20, 21]—with respect to the more distant stimulus objects to be reached
as a result of behaving (or not behaving) to certain more immediately
present stimulus objects. Or, expanding this statement further, the
doctrine may be summarized as follows:

1. Learning, when it occurs, arises as a result of some specific sequen-
tial pattern (spatial and temporal) of environmental stimulus objects
presented to the animal on one or more successive occasions.

2. The consequently evoked state or process—"intervening variable"
[17]—in the animal resulting from this presentation of the given environmental sequence is called a sign-gestalt expectation or group of
expectations or "hypotheses." Learning may be defined as the formation
of such expectations—hypotheses.

3. What is meant by any such expectation or hypothesis is merely
some "set" or process in the organism which is "adjusted" to the fact
that a given spatially and temporally immediate stimulus object is
going to lead, as the result of a particular type of behavior (or lack of

---

[4] I am not denying that a complicated form of the conditioned response doctrine
such as that which Hull has been brilliantly elaborating [see, for example, 6] may
eventually succeed in getting such factors in. But I, personally (I admit that I am
prejudiced), always have a feeling that Hull's assumptions are too *ex post facto* to be
altogether helpful.

behavior) on the part of the animal, to such and such a spatially and temporally more distant stimulus object.

4. The outward expression of such an acquired set is that the animal (given the proper conditions of motivation) tends to behave to the more immediate stimulus object in either the way to get to or the way to avoid such more distant stimulus objects.

5. If the environment changes so that the one stimulus object plus the given behavior no longer leads to the other stimulus object, then this set with its consequent behavior will under normal conditions sooner or later tend to disappear (i.e., to be unlearned again).

6. The laws and principles of learning are simply statements of those types of environmental sequence and the conditions of their presentation which favor the establishment of such corresponding sets—sign-gestalt expectations.

7. Finally, I would find it convenient to distinguish some seven different kinds of learning corresponding to some seven distinguishable classes of such environmental sequence. For the laws of any one of these seven different types of set-up may well prove to be somewhat different from those for each of the others.

Let us briefly review each of these seven classes. They may be named as: (1) *substitute-stimulus learning* (i.e., conditioned reflex learning proper); (2) *signal learning;* (3) *trial-and-error learning;* (4) *trial and error plus signal learning;* (5) *delayed-reaction learning;* (6) *inferential learning;* and (7) *inventive learning.*[5]

1. *Substitute stimulus.*—In substitute-stimulus learning (or conditioned reflex learning proper) the environmental conditions out of which the new sign-gestalt expectation is formed consist simply in the presentation on successive occasions of two stimulus objects in immediate temporal succession. In the formation of the conditioned response the second stimulus object is made by the experimenter simply to follow the first without any activity or intervention on the part of the experimental individual. As a result, the latter develops an "expectation" that the second stimulus object is going to follow the first. This expectation

---

[5] In a recent previous presentation [18] of my doctrine of learning I distinguished but four classes of learning, viz: conditioned reflex learning; sign learning: trial and error learning; and higher forms of learning.

The present seven classes have been obtained from the above four as follows. What I there called conditioned reflex learning I am now calling substitute-stimulus learning. What I there called sign learning I am now calling signal learning. What I there lumped into the one class of higher forms of learning I am here subdividing into delayed-reaction learning, inferential learning, and inventive learning. And, finally, I am here adding one wholly new class which I designate as trial and error plus signal learning.

betrays itself in the going off, at about the appropriate time interval after the first stimulus object, of the behavior appropriate to the second stimulus object.

2. *Signal learning.*—The environmental conditions for signal learning are very similar to those for substitute-stimulus learning. Again the new expectation is simply that such and such a first stimulus object is going to be followed by such and such a second stimulus object. But, whereas in the conditioned response proper the fact which testifies to and measures the strength of this expectation is the fact that the animal comes to release, as a result of the first stimulus object, the behavior appropriate to the second, in signal learning the behavior which testifies to the new expectation is, rather, a behavior of "getting ready for" the coming of the second stimulus object. A typical example of what I am thus designating as signal learning would be the behavior of my dog who, when she hears the sound of my approaching car (first stimulus) has come to make the preparatory response of coming forward and being ready for the appearance of the car itself with me in it (second stimulus). Or, another example would be that of Wever's cat [23] which upon the hearing of the tone came to hold its breath ("flutter" response) in preparation for the coming of the electric shock. Similar behavior was also obtained by Upton [22] and Horton [5] with guinea pigs.

3. *Trial and error learning.*—In trial and error learning the animal acquires an expectation to the effect that such and such an immediate stimulus object will, *if behaved to in such and such a way,* lead to such and such a further stimulus object. And it is the readiness-to-go-off (or in some cases *not* to go off—i.e., when such further stimulus objects are bad) of this mediating behavior which testifies to and defines trial and error learning. The classical examples are, of course, puzzle-box and maze learning.

4. *Trial and error plus signal learning.*—The environmental conditions here are a combination of those for trial and error learning and those for signal learning. As in trial and error learning the animal acquires an expectation to the effect that, *if he behaves* in such and such a way to such and such an immediate stimulus object, such and such a further stimulus object (i.e., food or punishment) will result. But this is complicated by the further expectation that this result will come only if the first stimulus object is also accompanied by a certain type of signal. The classical example is discrimination-box learning.

5. *Delayed-reaction learning.*—The environmental conditions for this are similar to those for the just preceding type save that in delayed-reaction learning the signal is made to disappear before the mediating

behavior is allowed. The expectation must carry over from the time the signal was present to the time in which the response is permitted.

6. *Inferential learning.*—I have coined this term to apply to those cases of learning in which the expectation that an immediate stimulus object is going to lead to another stimulus object arises not out of having gone from this first stimulus object to the second but rather from the presentation to the animal of the second stimulus object, *per se,* as so and so located within a larger total field which has also been presented. Typical examples of what I mean are the Tolman-Honzik "insight" maze [19] and the Maier "reasoning" experiments [10]. After having learned the general path sequences, the animal is given a reward or barrier or punishment directly at some specific locus at a point distant from the entrance and is then carried back, or allowed to go back, to the entrance and is required "inferentially" to expect this distant reward or punishment so that he thereupon takes (or avoids) the appropriate new path for getting to such more distant point.

7. *Inventive learning.*—The environmental conditions for inventive learning are ones in which a required more distant stimulus object can be reached only by a *new* type of behavior. The animal has to respond in a new way to a first stimulus object which before learning he has ignored. The present case of string pulling is an example. Also as examples under this head will come all the cases of learning to use tools such as are reported for example by Köhler [8].

Let us turn then in the next section to further analysis of such inventive learning as applied to the present case of string pulling.

THE SIGN-GESTALT FORMULA FOR INVENTIVE LEARNING AND THE ACQUISITION OF STRING PULLING

As we have just seen the sign-gestalt formula reserves the rubric "inventive learning" for those cases, such as the present, in which the new sign-gestalt expectation—the new set—which the animal achieves involves a new behavior, i.e., a type of behavior not exhibited in the given situation previous to learning.

Rats have probably some innate propensity to pull strings [9]. But in the environmental set-up of the present example they do not exhibit this propensity until after learning has been achieved.

I conceive the situation as follows. Before learning the stimulus object "pan pulled in with food in it" releases the sign-gestalt expectation which may be epitomized by the experimenter by the words "going to pan equals going to food." Also before learning there is in addition the further sign-gestalt expectation to be epitomized as "scrabbling towards pan just out of reach will bring pan and food within reach."[6] But learning consists in the establishment of the new expectation "pulling string will bring pan and food within reach." The way in which this new expectation is brought about seems to be by a clever manipulation by the experimenter so that the expectations present before learning lead "by chance" (i.e., so far as the animal itself is concerned) to the new response. And sooner or later the animal then "gets" the required new expectation in the sense that he now does the new response of "pulling the string"—not accidentally as a mere part of "scrabbling" or of "eating food off the string" or of "responding to an opposing tug" but de novo. He responds in this new way directly because he has acquired the new sign-gestalt expectation (the new set).

The laws for such a case of inventive learning thus become a series of statements as to those types of condition which favor this going off of the string pulling de novo and not just as a component within "scrabbling" or "eating food off the string" or whatever it may be. These laws are undoubtedly first of all those of frequency and recency. The more frequently and recently string pulling has been made to occur as a part of "scrabbling" or as an associated element in "eating food off the string," the more likely it would seem that the animal will, on a subsequent occasion, proceed to pull the string directly.

There must, however, be other laws besides these of frequency and recency. Learning to pull the string does not occur, or at least so I am assuming, merely as the result of a simple associationistic attachment of the pulling response to the string stimulus. Mere frequency of string pulling as a component within "scrabbling" or within "eating food off the string," etc., does not simply, as such, attach this string pulling to the stimulus of "string leading into box." But rather, according to my belief, it is the repetition of such occasions of induced string pulling together with the resulting further stimulus situation of "pan drawn in and food within reach" which causes a new sign-gestalt expectation to develop. That is to say, if the induced string pulling did not result in the subsequent stimulus situation of "pan within reach," any amount

---

[6] I cannot emphasize too strongly that when we thus express the content of sign-gestalt expectations in words we do not mean to imply that such expectations also exist in this verbal form in the rat or indeed that they constitute any sort of conscious process in the rat. A sign-gestalt expectation is simply a set in the animal defined by the fact that it leads to a certain type of behavior in the given situation and that it only continues to lead to this behavior so long as a certain arrangement of objects in the environment does actually obtain. The "set" and the resulting behavior are appropriate to this environmental arrangement and prove to be contingent for their continued occurrence on successive presentations of this arrangement. This is all there is (in a good operationalism) to such sign-gestalt expectations.

of chance string pulling would not cause this string pulling as such to be stamped in.[7] It is not the mere frequency with which string pulling occurs in the presence of the string but also the frequency with which this response leads to the resultant further stimulus situation of "pan and food within reach" which determines learning.

But there are still other conditions for such learning. Such learning as we are conceiving it, is the growth of a new sign-gestalt expectation. And the occurrence of the learned response is in itself merely an external evidence (given such and such demand conditions) of this new expectation. Hence among the conditioners of this new expectation should be ways of presentation of the whole set-up which will tend to be more favorable to the development of the new set than will others. Learning in the present case is the growth of the expectation "pan to be pulled in by string" out of the simpler expectation "pan to be scrabbled for." And it seems certain that some ways of introducing the rat to this whole situational complex will be more favorable than will others.[8] It must be confessed, however, that, as yet, we have but little information as regards such, let us call them, "situational" laws. The necessary experiments have not been carried out. It seems certain, however, that such "situational" laws are important and will in some degree vary from individual to individual.

SUMMARY

1. The learning of rats to pull in strings to get food presents a problem for theories of learning.

2. A conditioned response type of theory applied to this case appears inadequate.

3. The writer suggests the sign-gestalt theory.

4. The sign-gestalt theory conceives learning as consisting in the formation of new sign-gestalt expectations (hypotheses).

5. A sign-gestalt expectation (hypothesis) is to be defined as an "intervening variable"—a set—in the animal whereby the latter adjusts for the fact that such and such a spatially and temporally immediately

---

[7] It is here that my doctrine differs essentially from Guthrie's [2]. According to Guthrie the essential problem for the experimenter who would induce learning is to make the required new response occur in the presence of the given stimulus. For him such repeated occurrence will be, as such, enough to produce learning. For learning, as he sees it, is merely the associationistic (conditioned) attachment of said response to said stimulus.

[8] It may be noted that this growth of the new set tended to make its appearance in the present case in a relatively sudden, saltatory fashion. In other words, the experimenter could practically always tell the particular occasion when the animal "got" the new sign-gestalt expectation. On such an occasion the animal, for the first time, seemed to seize the string directly ("and as if he knew what he was about").

present stimulus object will lead (as the result of a particular type of behavior or lack of behavior on the part of the animal himself) to such and such a spatially and temporally more distant stimulus object.

6. An analysis of the types of environmental situation in which, and relative to which, such new sign-gestalt expectations may be induced suggests the subdivision of learning into seven types, to wit: (a) substitute-stimulus learning (i.e., conditioned reflex learning proper); (b) signal learning; (c) trial and error learning; (d) trial and error plus signal learning (e) delayed-reaction learning; (f) inferential learning; and (g) inventive learning. The laws for any one of these seven subtypes may well be somewhat different from those for each of the others.

7. The present case is to be classified as one of inventive learning.

8. In this present case the new response "pulling the string" is to be brought about in the first instance as an "accidental" part of the working out of the already, initially, present sign-gestalt expectations. This new response has as its consequence, however, the presence of a further stimulus object "pan and food within reach." And it appears that eventually the rat "gets" the new sign-gestalt expectation—to wit: "behaving to the immediately present stimulus object 'string' is going to lead to the further stimulus object 'food and pan within reach.' "

9. The laws of this learning—this getting of the new expectation or set—would seem to be: (a) That the more frequently and recently the pulling response has been induced the more likely the new sign-gestalt expectation is to arise. (b) That certain types of environmental arrangements will undoubtedly be more successful than others both for initially inducing this pulling and for causing to result from it the new sign-gestalt expectation. As to the exact character of these, as we may call them, "situational" laws we can at present, however, say almost nothing.[9]

REFERENCES

1. Adams, D. K., "Weight discrimination in rats," Psychol. Bull., 30 (1933), 703.
2. Guthrie, E. R., The psychology of learning, New York: Harper, 1935.
3. Hilgard, E. R., "The nature of the conditioned response. I. The case for and against stimulus-substitution," Psychol. Rev., 43 (1936), 366–385.
4. ———, "The nature of the conditioned response. II. Alternatives to stimulus-substitution," Psychol. Rev., 43 (1936), 547–564.
5. Horton, G. P., "A quantitative study of hearing in the guinea pig (Cavia cobaya)," J. Comp. Psychol., 15 (1933), 59–73.
6. Hull, C. L., "The concept of the habit-family hierarchy and maze learning." Part I and Part II, Psychol. Rev., 41 (1935), 33–54, 134–152.

[9] Since writing this article I have had the opportunity of reading the manuscript of a forthcoming article by Harold Schlosberg entitled "The relationship between success and the laws of conditioning." If I had read Schlosberg's article first, I would have modified some of the above statements.

7. Klüver, H., *Behavior mechanisms in monkeys,* Chicago: University of Chicago Press, 1933.

8. Köhler, W., *The mentality of apes,* New York: Harcourt, 1925.

9. McDougall, W., and K. D. McDougall, "Notes on instinct and intelligence in rats and cats," *J. Comp. Psychol.,* 7 (1927), 145–175.

10. Maier, N. R. F., "The effect of cortical destruction on reasoning and learning in rats," *J. Comp. Neur.,* 54 (1932), 45–75.

11. McCulloch, T. L., "Performance preferentials of the white rat in force-resisting and spatial dimensions," *J. Comp. Psychol.,* 18 (1934), 85–111.

12. Skinner, B. F., "The generic nature of the concepts of stimulus and response," *J. Gen. Psychol.,* 12 (1934), 40–65.

13. ———, "Two types of conditioning reflex and a pseudo-type," *J. Gen. Psychol.,* 12 (1935), 66–77.

14. Tolman, E. C., *Purposive behavior in animals and men,* New York: Century, 1932.

15. ———, "Sign-gestalt or conditioned reflex," *Psychol. Rev.,* 40 (1933), 246–255.

16. ———, "The law of effect: a reply to Dr. Goodenough," *J. Exper. Psychol.,* 16 (1933), 463–470.

17. ———, "Psychology versus immediate experience," *Philos. Sci.,* 2 (1935), 356–380.

18. ———, "Theories of learning," chapter xii, in *Comparative Psychology* (F. A. Moss, ed.), New York: Prentice-Hall, 1934.

19. ———, and C. H. Honzik, *'Insight' in rats,* Univ. Calif. Publ. Psychol., 4 (1930), 215–232.

20. ———, and I. Krechevsky, "Means-end-readiness and hypothesis—a contribution to comparative psychology," *Psychol. Rev.,* 40 (1933), 60–70.

21. ———, and E. Brunswik, "The organism and the causal texture of the environment," *Psychol. Rev.,* 42 (1935), 43–77.

22. Upton, M., "The auditory sensitivity of guinea pigs," *Amer. J. Psychol.,* 41 (1929), 412–421.

23. Wever, E. G., "The upper limit of hearing in the cat," *J. Comp. Psychol.,* 10 (1930), 221–234.

13

THE DETERMINERS OF BEHAVIOR AT A CHOICE POINT

[*Psychological Review,* JANUARY, 1938]

THE QUESTION I AM going to discuss[1] is the very straightforward and specific one of "why rats turn the way they do, at a given choice point in a given maze at a given stage of learning."

The first item in the answer is fairly obvious. They turn the way they do because they have on the preceding trials met this same choice point together with such and such further objects or situations, down the one path and down the other, for such and such a number of preceding trials. Let me, however, analyze this further, with the aid of a couple cf diagrams. First, consider a diagram of a single choice point (fig. 1).

In this figure the point of choice itself is designated as O_c; the complex of stimulus objects met going down the left alley, as O_L, that met going down the right alley, as O_R; the goal at the left, as O_{GL}; and that at the right, as O_{GR}. The behavior of turning to the left is represented by the arrow B_L; and that of turning to the right, by the arrow B_R. And the point I am now making is that the relative strength of the tendency to turn, say, left (rather than right) will be, first of all, a result not only of the present presentation of O_c but also of all the previous presentations of it together with the O_L, O_{GL}, O_R, and O_{GR} consequences of having behaved by B_L and B_R on all these preceding occasions. In short, I would schematize this feature of the causal determination of the left-turning tendency by the diagram shown in figure 2.

---

[1] Presidential address delivered before the American Psychological Association, Minneapolis, September 3, 1937.

The expression $B_L/(B_L + B_R)$ at the right-hand side of figure 2 is the "dependent variable" (we may call it the behavior ratio). It is the percentage tendency at any given stage of learning for the group as a whole to turn left. And the hieroglyphic at the left-hand side of this figure is the "independent variable" which determines this behavior ratio. This hieroglyphic is to be read as meaning: the *sum of* all the preceding occasions in which O_C has, by virtue of B_L, been followed

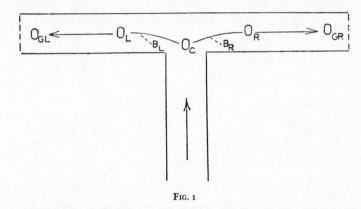

FIG. 1

by O_L and O_{GL} and by virtue of B_R been followed by O_R and O_{GR}. This diagram is thus no more than a schematic way of representing the, shall we say, (to use the term we theoretical psychologists have of late taken so violently to our bosoms) "operational" facts. The expression at the left is an "operationally defined" independent variable and that at the right, an "operationally defined" dependent variable.

For brevity's sake, I shall often substitute, however, an abbreviated symbol for the left-hand term, viz.: simply $\Sigma(OBO)$, as shown in figure 3.

One further point—the f_1 in each of these figures indicates merely the fact of the functional dependence of the dependent variable upon the independent variable. To indicate the "form" of this function we would require a more analytical diagram, such as that shown in figure 4.

But this, of course, is no more than our old friend, the learning curve. It results when we plot the independent variable along an X axis and the dependent variable along a Y axis. Nothing very new so far. It seems surprising, however, that in spite of the thousands, not to say millions, of such learning curves which have been obtained in the last four decades in American rat laboratories there are still a variety of

quite simple things about this function which we do not yet know or
with regard to which we are still in dispute.

For example, we are still in dispute, first of all, as to the relative
importance of the occurrences of the two alternative behaviors B_L and
B_R, where B_L is "wrong" and B_R is "correct." (See fig. 5.)

Thorndike [118, 119] and Lorge [69] and their co-workers, as you all
know, working with human beings in analogous, though verbal, set-ups

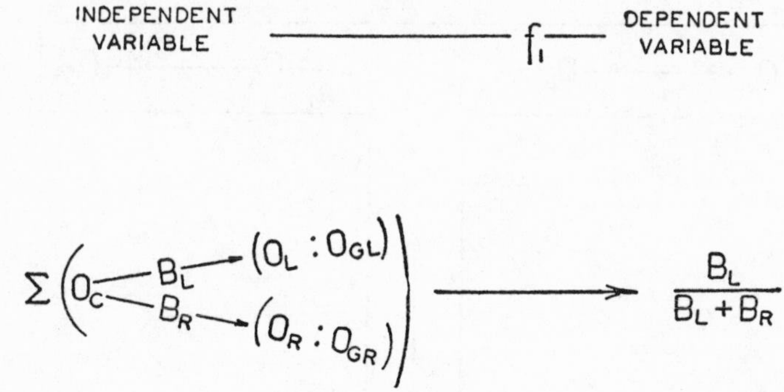

INDEPENDENT ———————————————— f_1 —— DEPENDENT
VARIABLE   VARIABLE

$$\Sigma \left(O_C \genfrac{}{}{0pt}{}{\nearrow B_L \rightarrow (O_L : O_{GL})}{\searrow B_R \rightarrow (O_R : O_{GR})} \right) \longrightarrow \frac{B_L}{B_L + B_R}$$

FIG. 2

have now concluded that the occurrence of the wrong behavior has no
such general causative effect. They find that learning appears only as a
result of the occurrences of the rewarded sequence $O_C - B_R \rightarrow (O_R : O_{GR})$.
On the other hand, still more recently, Muenzinger and Dove [95],
working with set-ups similar to Thorndike's have found that the occurrence of the wrong response $O_C - B_L \rightarrow (O_L : O_{GL})$ does weaken its tendency to reoccur. Also Carr, as a result of a series of experiments done by
his students [54, 72, 132, 135, 137] some time since in the Chicago laboratory, was finally forced to conclude that ". . . a certain number of
errors must be made and eliminated before the subject is ever able to
run the maze correctly. Correct modes of response are established in
part by learning *what not to do*" [16, p. 98, italics mine].

A second point about which we are still surprisingly ignorant is that
we do not yet know the importance of the rat's being permitted, or not
permitted, to return out of the wrong choice. In some experiments, when
the animal takes the wrong alley, he passes through a one-way gate and
is started over again. In others, he is allowed to treat it as a blind and
back out. But, so far as I know, there has been no carefully controlled
comparison between these two procedures.

Thirdly, the question of the relative effects of concentrated versus distributed repetitions has not as yet received the thoroughgoing experimental analysis that it deserves. But I understand that Professor Stone and his co-workers are now directing their attention to it and are getting some very significant findings.

Fourthly, we are ignorant concerning the difference between animals which have an initial left-hand bias and those which have an initial right-hand bias.[2] We usually lump the results for both types together in a

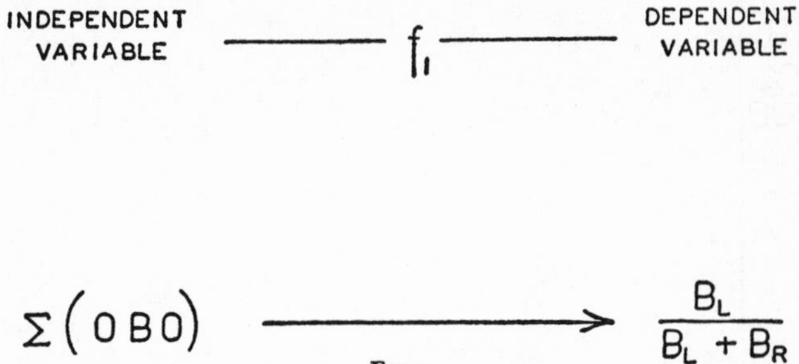

$$\text{INDEPENDENT VARIABLE} \quad \underline{\qquad\qquad} \; f_1 \; \underline{\qquad\qquad} \quad \text{DEPENDENT VARIABLE}$$

$$\Sigma \left(O\,B\,O \right) \quad \xrightarrow{\qqu\qquad\qquad} \quad \frac{B_L}{B_L + B_R}$$

Fig. 3

single curve. But we might well separate them and study them independently.

Fifthly, Brunswik [14] has recently brought to light a new point in our ignorance. He has been trying the effect of rewarding on the right and rewarding on the left different proportions of times. In other words, it was no God-given rule but apparently some merely human predilection on our part which made us heretofore tend almost invariably to make one of the alternative behaviors always rewarded and the other always punished. But other frequencies of reward and punishment are equally possible and equally deserving of study.

Sixthly, experiments by Krechevsky [59, 60, 61], seem to indicate that there may be certain general features about the content of the OBO's such, for example, as their containing variable or nonvariable paths, which are very important in determining the resultant behavior ratios and about which we need more information.

Seventhly, a further point which needs more investigation is, as Muenzinger and his co-workers [87, 88, 89, 90, 91, 92, 93] have beautifully brought out, the fact that punishment or obstacles to be overcome, *even on the correct side,* may sometimes seem to aid rather than hinder learning. [See also Tolman, 125, and Tolman, Hall, and Bretnall, 127.]

---

[2] For one of the first experiments indicating that there are such biases, see Yoshioka [149].

Eighthly, there is the question of what happens when Σ(OBO), the number of trials, has become very great. This seems to induce a special sort of result for which the term fixation has been suggested.[3] And further studies of such "fixations" are needed.

Ninthly, the problem as to the effect of temporal intervals between O_C and the resultant O_{GL} and O_{GR} are still by no means altogether completely

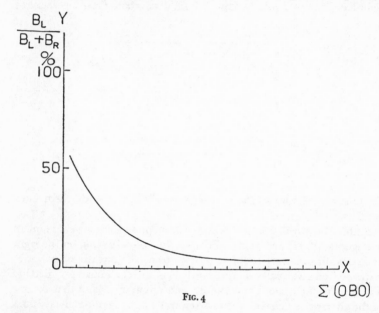

FIG. 4

worked out in spite of all the beautiful work of Hunter and his students, and others who have followed after, on the "delayed reaction" and on "double alternation."[4]

Finally, however, there is a point with regard to which we are not altogether ignorant but the importance of which we usually overlook—namely, the fact that any such function—any such learning curve, actually, is always obtained within the matrix of a larger number of other independent variables in addition to Σ(OBO). The following is a tentative list of such other variables together with Σ(OBO).

---

[3] See the original experiments on fixation by Gilhousen [31, 32], Krechevsky and Honzik [62] and Hamilton and Ellis [28, 38, 39].

[4] The literature on these matters is, of course, already enormous and I can not pretend to quote it here. It will suffice to refer to Munn's chapter on "Symbolic processes" [95, chapter vii] and to Heron's chapter on "Complex learning processes" [40].

I. Environmental Variables

        M—Maintenance schedule

        G—Appropriateness of goal object

        S—Types and modes of stimuli provided

        R—Types of motor response required

Σ(OBO)—Cumulative nature and number of trials

        P—Pattern of succeeding and succeeding maze units

II. Individual Difference Variables

        H—Heredity

        A—Age

        T—Previous training

        E—Special endocrine, drug or vitamin conditions

As you will see, I have divided such independent variables into two groups which I have called: (I) Environmental Variables, and (II) Individual Difference Variables. The *environmental variables* are M, the maintenance schedule, by which I mean time since food, water, sex, parturition, or the like, which in common parlance we would call the drive condition; G, the appropriateness of the goal object provided at the end of the maze relative to this drive; S, the specific types and modes of stimuli which the maze provides; R, the specific kinds of motor response required of the animal in the maze; Σ(OBO), the cumulative sum and manner of trials; and P, the general pattern of the maze, that is to say, the number and sorts of preceding and succeeding units. The individual difference variables are: H—heredity, A—age, T—previous training, and E—any special endocrine, drug, or vitamin conditions.

But if, now, we are to include all these independent variables together with Σ(OBO), we must have a new causal picture. I suggest the one shown in figure 6.

A main causal line has been drawn, as you see, issuing from each environmental variable. And the individual difference variables, H, A, T, and E, have been arranged as possible modifiers of each such main causal line. And what I have hereby tried to indicate is merely the actual types of experiment which we maze psychologists go in for.

I wish now, however, to pass from the above outline of experiments to a consideration of theories. But why, you may ask, can we not be satisfied with just experiments and the "facts" resulting from them?[5]

---

[5] That the facts must be obtained first of all and that we psychologists have for the most part been both extremely lazy and extremely shoddy in our pursuit of the "facts" has been eloquently pointed out by Brown [12].

I find that there are two reasons. In the first place, an entirely factual, empirical establishment of the complete functional relation, f_1, to cover the effects on $B_L/(B_L + B_R)$ of all the permutations and combinations of M, G, S, etc., etc., would be a humanly endless task. We have time in this brief mortal span to test only a relatively limited number of such permutations and combinations. So, in the first place, we are forced to propose theories in order to use such theories to extrapolate for all these combinations for which we have not time to test.

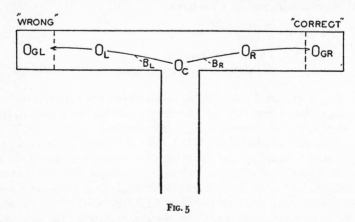

FIG. 5

But I suspect that there is also another reason for theories. Some of us, psychologically, just demand theories. Even if we had all the million and one concrete facts, we would still want theories to, as we would say, "explain" those facts. Theories just seem to be necessary to some of us to relieve our inner tensions.

But what is a theory? According to Professor Hull [49], a theory is a set of definitions and postulates proposed by the theorist (on the basis presumably of some already found facts) from which other empirically testable facts, or as he calls them, theorems, can be logically deduced. These deduced theorems will be new empirical relationships which the theorist—or more often, his research assistants—can, then and there, be set to look for.

For my own nefarious purposes, however, I wish to phrase this matter of the relationship of a theory to the empirical facts out of which it arises and to which it leads in somewhat other terms. A theory, as I shall conceive it, is a set of "intervening variables." These to-be-inserted intervening variables are "constructs" which we, the theorists, evolve as a useful way of breaking down into more manageable form the original complete f_1 function. In short, I would schematize the nature of our psychological theories by figure 7. In place of the original f_1 function, I have introduced a set of intervening variables, I_a, I_b, I_c, etc., few or many, according to the particular theory. And I have conceived a set of f_2 functions to connect these intervening variables severally to the independent variables, on the one hand, and an f_3 function to combine

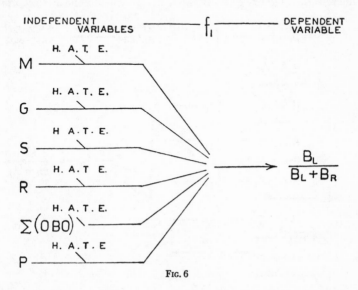

Fig. 6

them together and connect them to the final dependent variable, on the other.[6]

But turn, now, to some of the actual theories. I shall restrict myself to the discussion of three—Professor Thorndike's, Professor Hull's, and my own. This, of course, will hardly be a fair survey of the field. There are many other doctrines of learning, as, for example, Professor Guthrie's [33], and those of the other conditioned reflex psychologists [145][7] and those of the Gestalt school, [2, 45, 55, 56, 143], which are of as great importance and which have equally affected my own thinking. But I shall have to omit a discussion of them here.

Professor Thorndike's "intervening variables" are quite simple. They are "stimuli," "bonds" or "connections," and "response-tendencies."

[6] For previous presentations of this notion of "intervening variables" see Tolman [124, 126].

[7] For a superb presentation and summary of all the conditioned reflex theories of learning see Hilgard [44].

His theory I would represent, therefore, by the diagram shown in figure 8. It is Thorndike's conception of the nature of the f_2 function which seems to be the crux of his theory. Originally, his statement of this function included both a Law of Exercise and a Law of Effect. But now, as we all know, it includes a Law of Effect only, and a truncated law at that. For, as now stated, Thorndike finds that it is the repetitions of the rewarded sequence $O_c - B_R \rightarrow (O_R : O_{GR})$ which alone are important.

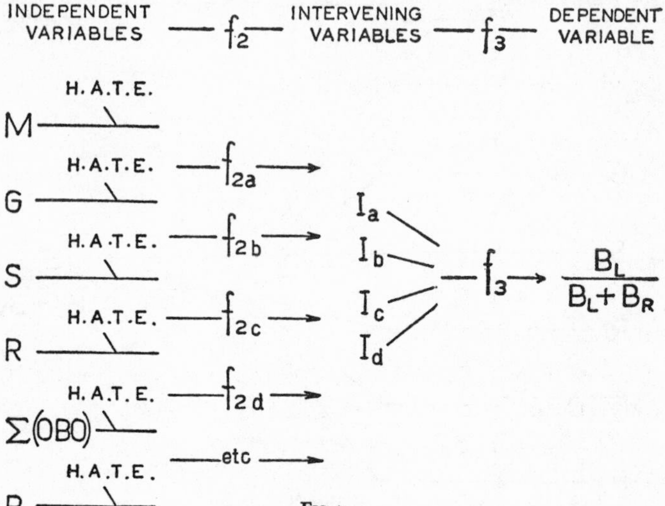

FIG. 7

These strengthen the C_R connection. The repetitions of the punished $O_c - B_L \rightarrow (O_L : O_{GL})$ sequence do not, he says, correspondingly weaken the C_L connection.

I have quite a number of quarrels with this theory. I would like to say first, however, that it seems to me that this theory of Thorndike's either in its present or in its earlier form, is *the* theory relative to which the rest of us here in America have oriented ourselves. The psychology of animal learning—not to mention that of child learning—has been and still is primarily a matter of agreeing or disagreeing with Thorndike, or trying in minor ways to improve upon him. Gestalt psychologists, conditioned reflex psychologists, sign-gestalt psychologists—all of us here in America seem to have taken Thorndike, overtly or covertly, as our starting point. And we have felt very smart and pleased with ourselves if we could show that we have, even in some very minor way, developed new little wrinkles of our own.

Let me now, nonetheless, try to present my criticisms. First, Thorndike's theory, as I see it, identifies stimuli (S's) with gross objects (O's) and identifies specific muscular responses (R's) with gross means-end behaviors (B's). And this procedure seems to me to require more justification than he gives it. It raises the problem of "equivalence of stimuli" and "equivalence of response" which Klüver [53], Waters [138], and

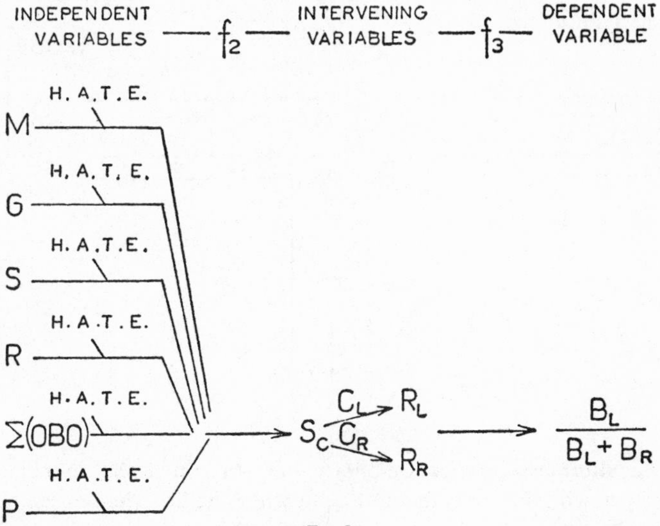

FIG. 8

others have been concerned with. It is also probably connected with the problem of perception constancy which the Gestalt psychologists and other Europeans have dealt with at such length.[8]

My second objection is that the theory as stated by Thorndike does not allow for the facts of "latent learning," of the complementary phenomenon of a sudden shoot-up in errors when a goal is removed, and of the utilization of alternative habits under different motivations. That, to allow for these facts, a distinction must be made between "learning" and "performance" has indeed already been emphasized by Lashley [63], Elliott [27], Leeper [64] and myself [122, 123]. But Thorndike's theory allows no such distinction.

Finally, my third objection is that the theory does not, for the most part, make anything of the other circumambient variables M, G, S, etc., in addition to Σ(OBO). No doubt Thorndike, if this were pointed out

---

[8] For a résumé of this work see Koffka [56, chapter vi].

to him, would try to work all these other independent variables in as further conditions tending to favor or hinder the respective strengths of C_R and C_L. But my suspicion is that he would have difficulty.

Turn, now, to Professor Hull's theory. For Hull the intervening variables are "conditionings" of the running responses to successive aggregates of exteroceptive, proprioceptive, and interoceptive stimuli. In order to explain this, first let me present another picture of the simple T-maze (fig. 9).

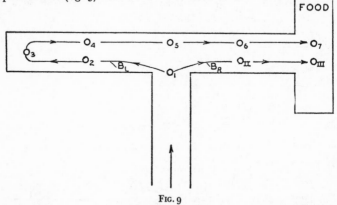

FIG. 9

Two alternative routes are shown—one in which the animal goes directly down the true path and one in which he first chooses the blind to the left. Successive points along these two paths are indicated as successively numbered O's. The true path involves three such O's, the blind alley, seven, and, to explain the tendency which develops in such a situation to go right rather than left, Hull's theory postulates the intervening variables shown in figure 10.

What I have done, as you will see, is to insert one of Hull's *own* diagrams [48, 44] in the middle and to call it his set of intervening variables. You are all familiar with such diagrams. They are very clever and can be invented, as I know to my cost, to explain practically any type of behavior, however far distant from an instance of conditioning such a behavior might at first sight appear. I have, therefore, the greatest respect for them. And, even though I argue against them, I find myself continually being intrigued and almost ready to change my mind and accept them and Hull after all.

It must be noted further, however, that there are certain other concepts besides conditioning involved in these diagrams which help to make them work. These seem to be: (1) anticipatory goal responses, i.e., the little r_G's with their little resultant proprioceptive or interoceptive s_G's whereby the character of the goal is brought back into the aggregates of conditioned stimuli at the different points along the maze; (2) the continuous drive stimulus S_D which also appears at all points and thus also becomes part of the total conditioned stimulus aggregate at each point along the maze paths; (3) the goal-gradient hypothesis whereby all conditionings are stronger the nearer they are to the goal; and (4) habit-family hierarchies whereby, if one path or route is blocked, the rat

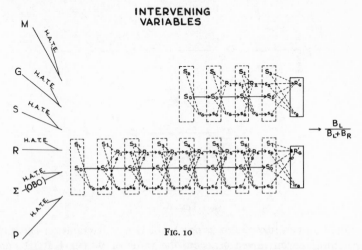

FIG. 10

readily switches over to any alternative chain of conditionings which he has at his command. By virtue of these concepts, in addition to that of conditioning *per se*, Professor Hull is able to bring into his diagram the influences not only of Σ(OBO) but also of M, maintenance schedule; G, goodness of goal; and P, maze pattern, in a rather remarkable way. He has not, on the other hand, as I see it, especially considered as yet the variables S, and R, and H, A, T, and E.

I have four rather specific criticisms of Hull's theory. First, Hull, like Thorndike, passes from O's and B's to S's and R's with no clear statement of his justification for doing so. And, again, I feel, as I did relative to Thorndike, that, if such simple S-R formulations are to have cogency, we must be told why and how the actual gross O's can be reduced to simple S's, and the actual gross means-end B's to simple R's.

My second criticism lies in the fact that I doubt that the supposed laws of conditioning are as simple and as well-known as Hull assumes. Many of the actual workers in the field, for example Loucks [70, 71], Liddell

[67], Culler [21], Schlosberg [105, 106], Hilgard [42, 43] seem to find conditioning a very variable and complicated phenomenon. To explain maze behavior by conditioning seems to me, therefore, like asking the halt to lead the blind. Or to put this another way, what Skinner [108] (see fig. 11) calls his Type I sort of conditioning (which for me is not conditioning at all) seems to be at the present stage of the game, just as well and perhaps better understood than the more classical, or what he calls his Type II, sort of conditioning.

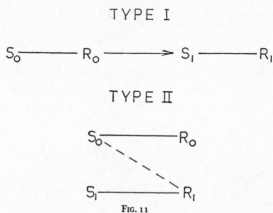

Fig. 11

Finally, when it comes to using one of Hull's diagrams for actually predicting, on any given occasion, the value of $B_L/(B_L + B_R)$ I find that the difficulty of determining the actual strengths to be assigned to the various S-R connections an almost insuperable one. But, then, perhaps an analogous sort of criticism will be raised against my diagrams. So, in conclusion, let me repeat that I have a tremendous respect for Professor Hull's theory and that I am not by any means as yet altogether certain that mine is better.

I come, now finally, to my own theory. But first, I would like to make it clear that however complicated what I am actually going to present may appear, it will be in reality an *oversimplified and incomplete* version. Partly for the sake of simplicity and partly also, I suppose, because I have not as yet completely thought the whole thing through, the diagrams I shall present will not contain as many "intervening variables" nor as complicated interfunctional relations as, I suspect, will finally actually prove necessary. They will, however, indicate the general picture.

My first diagram would be that shown in figure 12.

Note the list of *intervening variables:* "demand," "appetite," "dif-

ferentiation," "skill," "hypotheses," and "biases."[9] Such concepts are,
I am sure, irritating in that they appear subjective and not the sort to be
permitted in an honest behaviorism. Each of them is, nonetheless, I
would claim, capable of a perfectly objective definition and measurement. Thus, you will note that each is depicted as resulting from its
own correlative environmental variable plus the controlling effects of
H, A, T, and E. "Demands" result from M's; "appetites" from G's;
"differentiations" from S's; "skills" from R's; "hypotheses" from

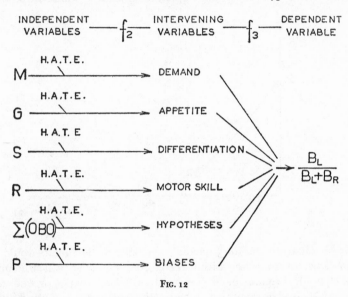

FIG. 12

Σ(OBO's); and "biases" from P's. And I am now going to assert that
each such "intervening variable" is defined by a standard experiment
in which its correlative independent environmental variable is systematically varied. Further, in each such experiment all the other independent variables are held constant while the one in question is
systematically changed. Under such conditions the resultant variations
in $B_L/(B_L + B_R)$ are, *by definition,* to be said to mirror directly the
variations in the one given intervening variable.

---

[9] In addition to these the final version of the theory would, I suspect, have to add
other intervening variables such as: "general activity," for the best discussion of this
which I know see Munn [97, chapter ii]; general attentivity or "vigilance," see Krechevsky [58]; and demand for "parsimony"—i.e., demand against "distance" and
"barriers," see, for example, Tolman [122, chapter vii], Gengerelli [30], McCulloch [84],
Tsai [133], Waters [140], Wheeler [143], and Wright [148].

For example, the intervening variable—"demand"—(say for food) shall, by definition, be measured by the variations in the behavior ratio which occur in a standard experiment when G and S and R and Σ(OBO) and P and H, and A, and T, and E, that is, all the independent variables *other than* M, are held constant at certain "standard" values, while M, itself, is systematically varied. For example, as standard values for these other variables I should probably choose: for G the regular standard living diet of the colony, for S an elevated maze in which all possible

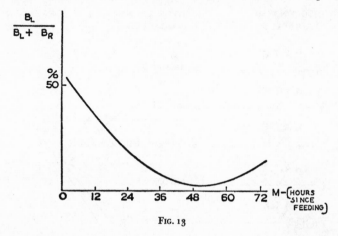

Fig. 13

visual, olfactory, auditory, tactual, and kinesthetic stimuli would be available, for R a maze which involved running rather than swimming, or climbing, or going hand over hand, or pulling strings, or what not, for Σ(OBO), that set-up which makes the left-hand side a blind and a distribution of one trial every twenty-four hours, and a number of trials which, for an average value of M, would bring the learning curve about down to the base line—say some ten trials—and for P a single-unit T with no preceding or succeeding units. With such a set-up in which all the other independent variables would thus be given these standard values and held constant, I would then vary M and study the correlated variations in $B_L/(B_L + B_R)$. And the sort of results one would get are shown in figure 13.

But the demand should really be defined as *inversely* related to this $B_L/(B_L + B_R)$ ratio, so that replotting one would have as one's final defining function that shown in figure 14. And having, thus at last, this curve—this f_2 function—between M and "demand," one would use it for defining the to-be-assumed value of the demand for any given value of M on all future occasions.

But this procedure, which I have thus outlined in some detail for demand, could also be used in analogous fashion for defining each of the other intervening variables. For each of them, also, we could set up a defining experiment in which all the independent variables other than the correlative one would be held constant while that one was systematically varied. And we would obtain in each case a resultant defining curve or table. Figure 15 schematizes the fact of such possible defining procedures.

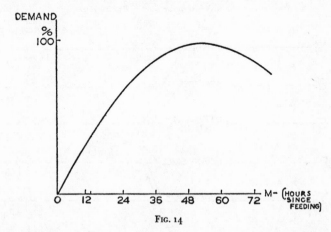

FIG. 14

A brief review of the literature would suggest that many such defining experiments have already been done. Under "demand" we think at once of Warden and his co-workers [136], and of Elliott [26]. Under the heading of "appetite" we think of Young [151, 152, 153], Elliott [25] and Bruce [13], and for an extraordinarily good summary of all the work relative to both demands and appetites we would look to Stone's chapter in Moss's *Comparative Psychology* [115]. Under the heading of "differentiation" we think of many individuals: Watson [141], Carr [17, 18, 19], Hunter [50, 51], Dennis [24], Casper [20], Lindley [68], Wolfle [147], and Honzik [46], to mention only a few. Under the heading of "motor skill" we think of Macfarlane [73]. Under that of "hypotheses" we think of practically all rat runners in the world but for the final indignity of suggesting such a term as "hypotheses" we must blame Krechevsky [57].[10] And finally, under "biases" we think of Dashiell [22], Bayroff [6], Dashiell and Bayroff [23], Schneirla [107], Yoshioka [149, 150], Ballachey

[10] See also the problems concerning this f_2-function between $\Sigma(OBO)$ and hypotheses already discussed above.

and Krechevsky [5], Spence [110], Spence and Shipley [111], Spragg [112, 113], Buel [7, 8], Ballachey and Buel [3, 4], Buel and Ballachey [10, 11], Ruch [100, 101, 102, 103], Waters [139], and Witkin and Schneirla [146]; and not even this completes the list.

Finally, turn to the f_3 function. It is by means of this f_3 function (if we but knew what it was) that we would be able to predict the final outcome for all possible values of the intervening variables. It would allow us to

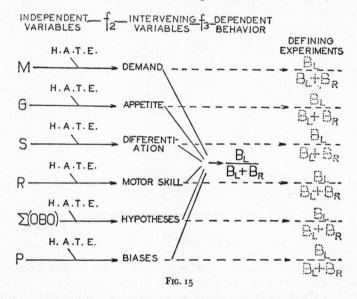

FIG. 15

predict the result of every possible strength of "demand" combined with every possible degree of "appetite," with every possible goodness of "differentiation," and so on. That is to say, the f_3 function, if we but knew it, would provide a set of rules by which to predict for all these million and one possible combinations. It would consist in some equation, geometrical picture, or what not, which would give the way of adding together the different values of these different variables. But here, alas, I confess is the feature of my doctrine about which I am, to date, haziest. I would venture, however, a few suggestions.

First I would assert that the implicit assumption of most other psychologists is to the effect that their f_3 functions are in the nature of simple algebraic summations. That is to say, these others seem to assert that a poor demand would be compensated for by a good hypothesis, a poor skill by a strong differentiation, a poor differentiation by a strong appetite, and the like. Indeed it seems to me that *all* the associationistic psychologies, whether they be of the trial and error variety or of the conditioned reflex variety really imply just such simple algebraic summations. What I have distinguished as "demands," "appetites," "differentiations," "skills," "hypotheses," and "biases" the associationistic psychologies have lumped together, one and all, as mere S-R's. If the rat be very hungry (have a strong demand) this, for them, is but an enhancement of some S-R connection; if he have a strong appetite as a result of the type of goal presented, this also is but some S-R, stronger than it otherwise would have been; if the given maze bifurcation present lots of stimuli (leads to clear differentiations) again, merely some S-R's are stronger; if the maze be constructed to require unusual motor skill from the animal, this again means merely a strengthening (or in this case probably a weakening) of some bond or other; if $\Sigma(OBO)$ has become large—if, that is to say, the hypotheses have become "developed and sure" this also means but better S-R connections; and finally, if the maze be shaped to induce, say, a strong centrifugal swing to the right or a strong forward-going tendency to the left, this, also is for them, but a matter of the strengthening of one or another S-R bond. And the final value of the resultant behavior ratio is then obtained by all such psychologies by a simple toting up of these plus and minus, strong and weak, S-R bonds. But I am very doubtful of the adequacy of any such simple type of additions.

Let me recall again the facts of "latent learning." During latent learning the rat is building up a "condition" in himself, which I have designated as a set of "hypotheses," and this condition—these hypotheses—do not then and there show in his behavior. S's are presented, but the corresponding R's do not function. It is only later, after a goal has been introduced which results in a strong appetite, that the R's, or as I would prefer to say, the B's, appropriate to these built-up hypotheses appear. So long as there is no appetite for what is found at the end of the maze, strong demands plus strong hypotheses do not add up at all. A strong hypothesis and a strong demand do not compensate for a weak appetite. And a strong demand and a strong appetite cannot in their turn overcome a weak hypothesis. And so on. The ways of combination of the intervening variables do not seem those of simple scalar addition.

Or consider, as another example, the addition of two hypotheses. And suppose that instead of the usual two-way choice point, we had one such as that shown in figure 16. In this set-up after a long series of preliminary training in which only the two side paths were open, the middle path was also opened up (I refer here to an actual experiment

devised and carried out at California by Mr. R. S. Crutchfield). As a
result of the preliminary training the two hypotheses of food to the left
and food to the right were built up. It appeared, however, in the test
runs, that these then added together in such a way as to make a very
strong resultant tendency to go straight ahead when the third central
path was opened—in short, a very much stronger tendency to go ahead
than was found to have resulted from the two hypotheses which got

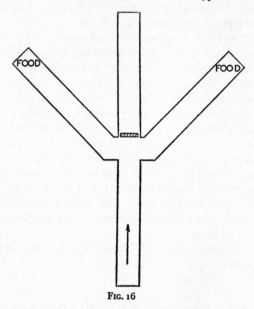

FIG. 16

built up when in another set-up the two side paths were as shown in
figure 17. The laws of the addition of hypotheses here appeared, in short,
not as scalar and algebraic, but as vectorial.

Or, again consider the facts of rat behavior which ordinarily go under
the names of "insight" and "reasoning," that is to say, such facts as have
been gathered by Honzik and myself [128, 47] and by Maier [74, 75,
76, 77].[11] These are again, as I see it, also primarily facts concerning the
addition of hypotheses. The addition here also is anything but simple
and algebraic.

And so I am brought finally to my present confession of faith—
namely, that Professor Lewin's topological and dynamic concepts [65,
66] now seem to me the best lead that I have at present for conceiving

---

[11] For a summary of most of these facts see Munn [97, chapter vii] and Heron [40].

the nature of this f_3 function. I neither understand nor approve them in their entirety. And, if I were clever enough, I should undoubtedly try in many ways to improve upon them. But nonetheless, even as they are, they seem to me by far the most stimulating and important ideas which have appeared in psychology (that is, in pure psychology, as distinct from physiology or embryology) in the past decade.

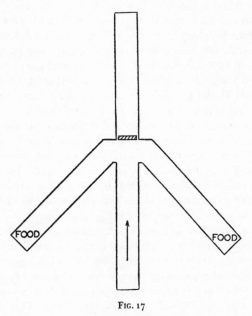

FIG. 17

One final point, concerning my thinking about the f_3 function. I am at present being openly and consciously just as anthropomorphic about it as I please. For, to be anthropomorphic is, as I see it, merely to cast one's concepts into a mold such that one can derive useful preliminary hunches from one's own human, everyday experience. These hunches may then, later, be translated into objective terms. But there seems to me every advantage in *beginning* by conceiving the situation loosely and anthropomorphically. I might never have arrived at this point of view of accepting anthropomorphism as a perfectly proper heuristic procedure all by myself. And I certainly would hardly have dared advance such a view publicly, if it had not been for the counsels of several other psychologists, especially Professors Liddell and Zener. But, in any case, I in my future work intend to go ahead imagining how, *if I were a rat, I* would behave as a result of such and such a demand combined with such and such an appetite and such and such a degree of differentiation; and so on. And then, on the basis of such imaginings, I shall try to figure out some sort of f_3 rules or equations. And then eventually I shall try to state these latter in some kind of objective and respectable sounding terms such as vectors, valences, barriers, and the like (to be borrowed for the most part from Professor Lewin).

Also, of course, I shall try to do experiments similar to those of Lewin and his students in which these intervening variables (as extrapolated from their correlative independent variables) are given such and such supposed values and then the final behavioral outcomes measured.[12]

But many of you must have been asking yourselves all this time: what about the H, A, T, and E variables? In the defining experiments I have suggested so far, which have been concerned primarily with the environmental variables, these "individual difference variables" are assumed to have been given average standard values. We rat workers have always done this, perhaps unconsciously. We have tried to keep heredity normal by using large groups, age normal by using rats between 90 and 120 days old, previous training normal by using fresh rats in each new experiment, and endocrine and nutritional conditions normal by avoiding special dosages and also again by using large groups.

But suppose, now, our interests *be* in individual differences, *per se*. What experiments do we carry out then? It seems to me that individual-difference psychologists here tend to do two sorts of things.

On the one hand, they attempt (as do we environmental psychologists) to manipulate their independent variables for whole groups of animals and to get correlated variations in $B_L/(B_L + B_R)$. Thus they vary heredity, H, as Tryon [129] and Heron [41], and Rundquist [104] have done in controlled ways for large groups, and get corresponding variations in this behavior ratio, for such groups. Or, they vary age, A, as Stone and his students have done [114], also for large groups and again get corresponding variations in the behavior ratio. Or, they vary previous training, T, that is, they study the effects of transfer—and here we have all taken pot shots—the first important experiment was, perhaps, that of Webb [142] and the last seems to be that of Bunch and Rogers [15]—and again attempt to get corresponding variations in the behavior ratio. Or, finally, they vary drugs, endocrines and vitamins, E, and get

---

[12] As a beginning in this direction we already have some rat experiments by Hall [34, 35, 36] and Hall and Ballachey [37], and a recent set of experiments by Wright [148], but the latter were done unfortunately, from my point of view, not upon rats but upon children. But analogous experiments could, I believe, be done with rats.

correlated variations in $B_L/(B_L + B_R)$. Here there are too many experiments for me to attempt to list them.[13]

Secondly, however, the individual difference psychologists have also done another *more characteristic* type of experiment. They have accepted from God, and from the accidents of miscegenation and of nursery schools, very large heterogeneous samples of rats and then they have put each such sample through a miscellaneous assortment of ex-

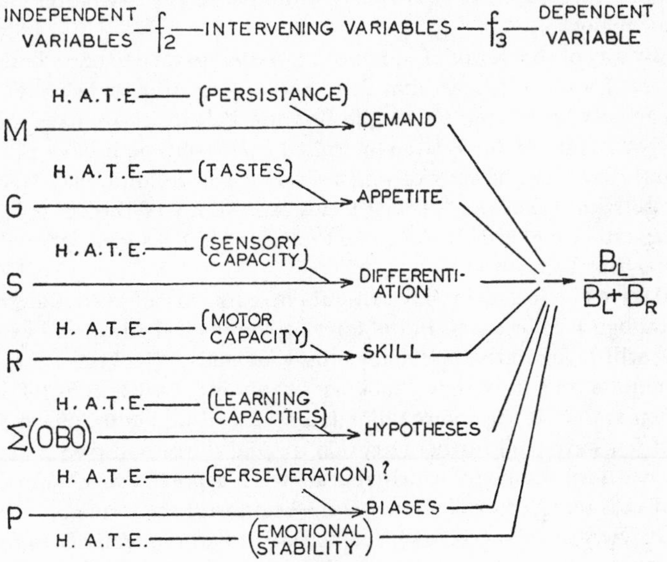

FIG. 18

periments (i.e., the different types of mazes that, in American rat culture, are required of young rats in school, and also the different types of maze, discrimination box, food, times since eating, and the like, which are required of old rats in polite society); and then they have obtained correlations and worked out factor analyses. And, finally, these individual difference psychologists have ended up with their notions concerning the number and nature of the fundamental traits or capacities— *The Vectors of Mind* [120]. These traits or capacities are, of course, but

---

[13] One of the best known early experiments was that of Anderson and Smith [1] on the effect of insufficient diets. And recent further important experiments on diet are those of Maurer [78, 79, 80], and Maurer and Tasi [82, 83], Bernhardt [7], Muenzinger and the Poes [96, 98, 99]. For recent important experiments on drugs, see Miller and Miles [85] and Williams and O'Brien [144]. Also for a summary, see Moss's own chapter in *Comparative Psychology* [86].

a new type of intervening variable and it would be nice, for me, if they fitted in neatly with the sort of intervening variables already suggested. They could then be put into my diagram as shown in figure 18. But, alas, at present the results of factor analysis do not seem to suggest any such simple or agreed-upon results. You all know how the controversy rages from Spearman's one or two factors [109] through Kelley's [52] and Thurstone's [120] three to nine factors, differing somewhat in each set-up[14] to Thorndike's [116, 117] and Tryon's [131]—God only knows how many.[15]

By way of conclusion, I want now, however, to turn to one wholly new point. I want to suggest that there also appear in maze behavior types of activity other than the simple B_L's and B_R's which we have thus far talked about. If these latter be called "achievement behaviors," then these new types of activity which I now have in mind, may be called "catalyzing behaviors." And it seems that we rat psychologists have to date rather pigheadedly (i.e., like Professor Liddell's pigs) ignored such catalyzing behaviors.

I have two instances which I would here like to call to your attention, although I believe that in the future technological advances in recording will bring to the fore many others for study. The first of these two examples consists of those "lookings or runnings back and forth" which often appear at the choice point and which all rat runners have noted, but few have paid further attention to. And the second type is that disrupted sort of activity which appears when a previously obtained goal object is removed or blocked. Let me begin with the former.

A few years ago [121; 122, chapter xiii] I had the temerity to suggest that such "lookings back and forth" might be taken as a behavioristic definition of *conscious awareness*. This was, no doubt, a silly idea. I would hardly dare propose it now. But, at any rate, such behavior is interesting and deserving of further study. Anthropomorphically speaking, it appears to be a "looking before you leap" sort of affair. Klüver [53] and Gellerman [29] have recorded it in connection with the behavior of monkeys, chimpanzees and children. And, further, I have recently learned that Professor Muenzinger and his students have also been keeping records of it in rats and that they have called it "vicarious trial and error"—or, more briefly, VTE. I shall, therefore, designate such behavior as VTE or B_{VTE} from here on.

First, let me show you some individual rat curves obtained by Dr.

<hr>

[14] I think here of Vaughn's recent important monograph [120] in which he finds eight factors governing maze behavior.

[15] For a general discussion of the problem of individual differences in animals see, also, Tryon [130].

Evelyn Gentry [94] in Muenzinger's laboratory. The one rat had a difficult discrimination—namely, to go left when a tone is sounded; the other had an easy discrimination—to go toward the white in a white-black discrimination box (fig. 19).

At the left are the error curves and at the right the VTE curves. Whenever the rat looked one or more times before making his overt

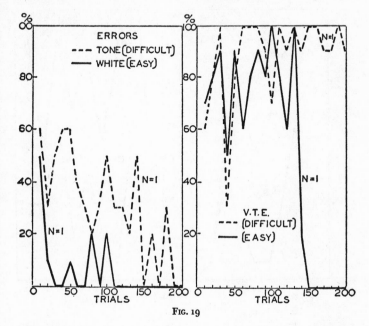

FIG. 19

choice in a given trial that trial was recorded as having involved a VTE. The points on the curves are averages for ten trials. The solid curves are for the easy discrimination and the dash curves are for the difficult discrimination. As you see, there tended to be more VTE and the latter persisted longer for the difficult discrimination than for the easy one.

Next, let me present some recent data on VTE obtained by Mr. M. F. Friedman at California on the effect of moderate amounts of cortical lesion[16] (see fig. 20). The problem was learning to turn left on a simple elevated T where one arm led to food and the other did not. The dash curves are for the brain lesion group and the solid curves are for the control group. Each point is an average of four trials. The normal ani-

<hr />

[16] The histology necessary for determining the actual amounts of these lesions has not yet been done.

mals exhibited more VTE and learned faster than did those with cerebral insults.

Next, I present some curves obtained by Honzik with an elevated discrimination set-up. The animal had to discriminate between a black and a white face-on door. There was a partition projecting out between the doors. White was the positive stimulus. One group ran over a

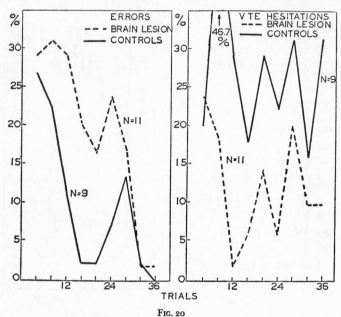

FIG. 20

continuous platform and could run back around the projecting partition if they chose the wrong door first. The other group had to jump a gap of 8½ inches to a 4-inch ledge just in front of the doors. If this jump group chose incorrectly, they had to jump back again to the starting platform and then make a second jump to the correct door. The solid curves (fig. 21) are for the jump group and the dash curves for the nonjump group. Each point represents an average of ten trials. The jumpers made more VTE's and learned faster.

Finally, let me present a set of curves also obtained by Honzik, in a similar set-up, but for two different jump groups (fig. 22). The conditions for the one-jump group were those just described. We may call them here the near-jump group. For the others, which we may call the far-jump group, the farther side of the gap was 15 inches from the to-be-discriminated doors and the taking off platform 23½ inches from these doors. Solid curves are for the near jumpers, dash curves for the far jumpers. Each point represents an average of ten trials.

The near-jump group learned faster and exhibited more VTE than did the far-jump group. It is to be noted that the far-jump group probably could not see the differences between the two doors at the place of "taking off" very well. Hence their poor error score. Further, because

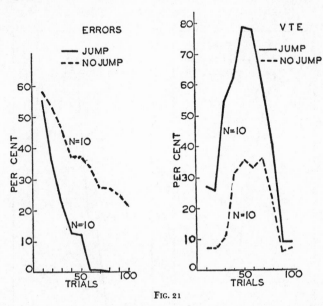

FIG. 21

they could not see very well, it did them little good to "go in for" "looking before they leapt." And, in fact, the VTE's for this far-jump group were decidedly less than for the near-jump group.

Let me briefly summarize: (1) for a difficult discrimination such as learning to turn left when a tone is sounded there was slower learning but more VTE than for an easy, white-black discrimination; (2) on a simple T, normal rats showed faster learning and exhibited more VTE than did brain lesion rats; (3) with a near jump, jump rats learned faster and showed more VTE than did nonjump rats; (4) near-jump rats learned faster and exhibited more VTE than did far-jump rats.

What, now, is to be our theoretical envisagement? Obviously, the question divides into two: (1) what effect do VTE's, when evoked, have upon learning; (2) what are the conditions of learning which favor the evoking of such VTE's?

In answer to the first question I shall postulate that VTE's always aid the learning which they accompany. In the sole case, that of the difficult discrimination, where the poorer learning was accompanied by more VTE's I believe that this learning was nonetheless faster than it would have been if it had not been for these greater VTE's. And in all the other three experiments the greater VTE's did accompany the faster learning.

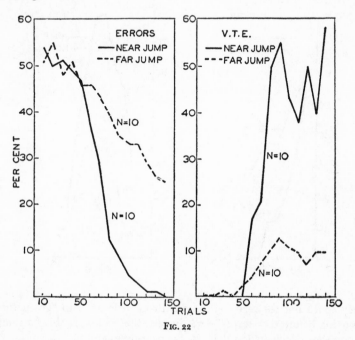

Fig. 22

Turn now, to the second question. What are the learning conditions which tend to evoke VTE's? Here I believe we are not yet ready for any general answer. I shall therefore merely reënumerate for your benefit the conditions of the four experiments. The conditions favorable to VTE's in these experiments were: (1) a difficult discrimination; (2) a normal brain; (3) a gap to be jumped which induced caution, and (4) a nearness of the jumping platform such that the extra caution exposed the animal longer to the critical stimuli.

Finally, let me by another figure suggest how I would propose to fit this catalyzing VTE behavior into my general causal diagram (fig. 23). You will note that I have shown the VTE behavior—symbolized as

B_{VTE}—as an auxiliary result of the "intervening variables." These latter are to be conceived as tending to produce their usual "achievement behavior" $B_L/(B_L + B_R)$. But, in addition, they produce more or less B_{VTE}, and the further catalyzing effect of such B_{VTE} is, I have assumed, in some way to enhance the values of one or more of the independent variables themselves—in this case especially of S and of $\Sigma(OBO)$—and thus to help induce new values of certain of the intervening variables

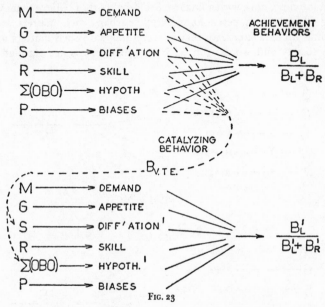

FIG. 23

and a new final value of the achievement behavior. That is to say, as shown in the figure, the achievement behavior takes some new value $B_L'/(B_L' + B_R')$.

Turn now briefly to the case of the disruption behavior which occurs when an expected goal is not obtained. I have as yet no curves or detailed data concerning either the causes or the results of such disruption behaviors. I believe, however, that they also are to be conceived as auxiliary, catalyzing sorts of affair which react back upon the independent variables and make the final values of the resultant behavior ratios different from what the latter originally would have been.

The rat's disrupted behavior is a surprised sort of hunting about and exploring. And it is my contention as shown in figure 24 that this surprised hunting and exploring brings about new values of the independent variables—especially of G and Σ(OBO),—and thus causes a different outcome in the final behavior ratio. The disrupted behavior enhances a new negative aspect in what was originally a positive goal. In short, I am assuming that because of this disrupted searching the rats are better in the next trials about not continuing to go to that side where the goal has been blocked than they would have been if this, their disrupted searching, had not appeared.

Let me close, now, with a final confession of faith. I believe that everything important in psychology (except perhaps such matters as the building up of a superego, that is everything save such matters as involve society and words) can be investigated in essence through the

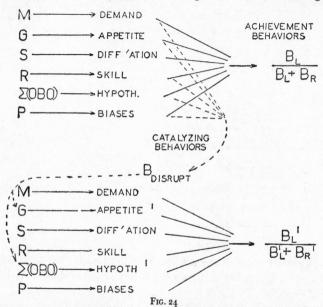

FIG. 24

continued experimental and theoretical analysis of the determiners of rat behavior at a choice point in a maze. Herein I believe I agree with Professor Hull and also with Professor Thorndike.

So in closing let me borrow a verse written by Alexander Meiklejohn in a copy of his book, as he gave it me. He wrote, and I would now repeat:

> To my ratiocinations
> I hope you will be kind
> As you follow up the wanderings
> Of my amazed mind.

REFERENCES

1. Anderson, J. E., and A. H. Smith, "The effect of quantitative and qualitative stunting upon maze learning in the white rat," *J. Comp. Psychol.*, 6 (1926), 337–361.

2. Adams, D. K., "A restatement of the problem of learning," *Brit. J. Psychol.*, 22 (1931), 150–178.

3. Ballachey, E. L., and J. Buel, "Centrifugal swing as a determinant of choice-point behavior in the maze running of the white rat," *J. Comp. Psychol.*, 17 (1934), 201–223.

4. Ballachey, E. L., and J. Buel, "Food orientation as a factor determining the distribution of errors in the maze running of the rat," *J. Genet. Psychol.*, 45 (1934), 358–370.

5. Ballachey, E. L., and I. Krechevsky, *"Specific" vs. "general" orientation factors in maze running,* Univ. Calif. Publ. Psychol., 6 (1932), 83–97.

6. Bayroff, A. G., "Direction orientation and the forward-going tendency in white rats," *J. Comp. Psychol.*, 15 (1933), 211–228.

7. Bernhardt, K. S., "The effect of vitamin B deficiency during nursing on subsequent learning in the rat," *J. Comp. Psychol.*, 17 (1934), 123–148.

8. Buel, J., "The linear maze. I. 'Choice-point expectancy,' 'correctness,' and the goal gradient," *J. Comp. Psychol.*, 17 (1934), 185–199.

9. Buel, J., "Differential errors in animal mazes," *Psychol. Bull.*, 32 (1935), 67–99.

10. Buel, J., and E. L. Ballachey, "Choice-point expectancy in the maze running of the rat," *J. Genet. Psychol.*, 45 (1934), 145–168.

11. Buel, J., and E. L. Ballachey, "Limiting factors in the effect of the reward upon the distribution of errors in mazes," *Psychol. Rev.*, 42 (1935), 28–42.

12. Brown, W., "Facing the facts." *Proc. 25th Anniv. Celebration Inaug. Grad. Stud.*, Los Angeles: University of Southern California, 1936, pp. 116–121.

13. Bruce, R. H., "A further study of the effect of variation of reward and drive upon the maze performance of rats," *J. Comp. Psychol.*, 20 (1935), 157–182.

14. Brunswik, E., "Reaction of rats to probability and danger situations" (in preparation).

15. Bunch, M. E., and M. Rogers, "The relationship between transfer and the length of the interval separating the mastery of the two problems," *J. Comp. Psychol.*, 21 (1936), 37–51.

16. Carr, H. A., *Psychology: a study of mental activity,* New York: Longmans, 1925.

17. Carr, H. A., "Maze studies with the white rat. I. Normal animals," *J. Anim. Behav.*, 7 (1917), 259–275.

18. Carr, H. A., "Maze studies with the write rat. II. Blind animals," *J. Anim. Behav.*, 7 (1917), 276–294.

19. Carr, H. A., "Maze studies with the white rat. III. Anosmic animals," *J. Anim. Behav.*, 7 (1917), 295–306.

20. Casper, B., "The normal sensory control of the perfected double-alternation spatial-maze habit of the albino rat," *J. Genet. Psychol.*, 43 (1933), 239–292.

21. Culler, E., F. Finch, E. Girden, and W. Brodgen, "Measurements of acuity by the conditioned-response technique," *J. Gen Psychol.*, 12 (1935), 223–227.

22. Dashiell, J. F., *Direction orientation in maze running by the white rat,* Comp. Psychol. Monog., 7 (1930), no. 72.

23. Dashiell, J. F., and A. G. Bayroff, "A forward-going tendency in maze running," *J. Comp. Psychol.*, 12 (1931), 77–94.

24. Dennis, W., "The sensory control of the white rat in the maze habit," *J. Genet. Psychol.*, 36 (1929), 59–90.

25. Elliott, M. H., *The effect of change of reward on the maze performance of rats,* Univ. Calif. Publ. Psychol., 4 (1928), 19–30.

26. Elliott, M. H., *The effect of appropriateness of reward and of complex incentives on maze performance,* Univ. Calif. Publ. Psychol., 4 (1929), 91–98.

27. Elliott, M. H., "Some determining factors in maze performance," *Amer. J. Psychol.,* 42 (1930), 315–317.

28. Ellis, W. D., and J. A. Hamilton, "Behavior constancy," *J. Gen. Psychol.,* 8 (1933), 421–429.

29. Gellermann, L. W., "Form discrimination in chimpanzees and two-year-old children: I. Discrimination of form per se. II. Form versus background," *J. Genet. Psychol.,* 42 (1933), 3–50.

30. Gengerelli, J. A., "The principle of maxima and minima in animal learning," *J. Comp. Psychol.,* 11 (1930), 193–236.

31. Gilhousen, H. C., "An investigation of 'insight' in rats," *Science,* 73 (1931), 711.

32. Gilhousen, H. C., "Fixation of excess distance patterns in the white rat," *J. Comp. Psychol.,* 16 (1932), 1–24.

33. Guthrie, E. R., *The psychology of learning,* New York: Harper, 1935.

34. Hall, C. S., "Emotional behavior in the rat. I. Defecation and urination as measures of individual differences in emotionality," *J. Comp. Psychol.,* 18 (1934), 385–403.

35. Hall, C. S., "Emotional behavior in the rat. II. The relationship between need and emotionality," *J. Comp. Psychol.,* 22 (1936), 61–68.

36. Hall, C. S., "Emotional behavior in the rat. III. The relationship between emotionality and ambulatory activity," *J. Comp. Psychol.,* 22 (1936), 345–352.

37. Hall, C. S., and E. L. Ballachey, *A study of the rat's behavior in a field: A contribution to method in comparative psychology,* Univ. Calif. Publ. Psychol., 6 (1932), 1–12.

38. Hamilton, J. A., and W. D. Ellis, "Behavior constancy in rats," *J. Genet. Psychol.,* 41 (1932), 120–139.

39. Hamilton, J. A., and W. D. Ellis, "Persistence and behavior constancy," *J. Genet. Psychol.,* 41 (1932), 140–153.

40. Heron, W. T., "Complex learning processes," in *Comparative Psychology* (F. A. Moss, ed.), New York: Prentice-Hall, 1934, pp. 335–366.

41. Heron, W. T., "The inheritance of maze learning ability in rats," *J. Comp. Psychol.,* 19 (1935), 77–90.

42. Hilgard, E. R., "The nature of the conditioned response: I. The case for and against stimulus substitution," *Psychol. Rev.,* 43 (1936), 366–385.

43. Hilgard, E. R., "The nature of the conditioned response: II. Alternatives to stimulus substitution," *Psychol. Rev.,* 43 (1936), 547–564.

44. Hilgard, E. R., "The relationship between the conditioned response and conventional learning experiments," *Psychol. Bull.,* 34 (1937), 61–102.

45. Holt, E. B., *Animal drive and the learning process,* Vol. I., New York: Holt, 1931, p. 151 f.

46. Honzik, C. H., *The sensory basis of maze learning in rats,* Comp. Psychol. Monog., 13 (1936), no. 64.

47. Honzik, C. H., and E. C. Tolman, "The perception of spatial relations by the rat: a type of response not easily explained by conditioning," *J. Comp. Psychol.,* 22 (1936), 287–318.

48. Hull, C. L., "The concept of the habit-family hierarchy and maze learning," Part I., *Psychol. Rev.,* 41 (1934), 33–54.

49. Hull, C. L., "Mind, mechanism, and adaptive behavior," *Psychol. Rev.,* 44 (1937), 1–32.

50. Hunter, W. S., "The sensory control of the maze habit in the white rat," *J. Genet. Psychol.,* 36 (1929), 505–537.

51. Hunter, W. S., "A further consideration of the sensory control of the maze habit in the white rat," *J. Genet. Psychol.,* 38 (1930), 3–19.

52. Kelley, T. L., *Crossroads in the mind of man,* Stanford University: Stanford University Press, 1928.

53. Klüver, H., *Behavior mechanisms in monkeys,* Chicago: University of Chicago Press, 1933.

54. Koch, H. C., *The influence of mechanical guidance upon maze learning,* Psychol. Monog., 32 (1923), no. 147.

55. Köhler, W., *Gestalt psychology,* New York: Liveright, 1929.

56. Koffka, K., *Principles of Gestalt psychology,* New York: Harcourt, 1935.

57. Krechevsky, I., " 'Hypotheses' in rats," *Psychol. Rev.,* 39 (1932), 516–532.

58. Krechevsky, I., "Brain mechanisms and brightness discrimination learning," *J. Comp. Psychol.,* 21 (1936), 405–446.

59. Krechevsky, I., "Brain mechanisms and variability. I. Variability within a means-end-readiness," *J. Comp. Psychol.,* 23 (1937), 121–138.

60. Krechevsky, I., "Brain mechanisms and variability. II. Variability where no learning is involved," *J. Comp. Psychol.,* 23 (1937), 139–163.

61. Krechevsky, I., "Brain mechanisms and variability. III. Limitations of the effect of cortical injury upon variability," *J. Comp. Psychol.,* 23 (1937), 351–364.

62. Krechevsky, I., and C. H. Honzik, *Fixation in the rat,* Univ. Calif. Publ. Psychol., 6 (1932), 13–26.

63. Lashley, K. S., "Learning: I. Nervous-mechanisms of learning," in *The Foundations of Experimental Psychology,* Worcester, Mass.: Clark University Press, 1929, pp. 524–563.

64. Leeper, R., "The rôle of motivation in learning: A study of the phenomenon of differential motivational control of the utilization of habits," *J. Genet. Psychol.,* 46 (1935), 3–40.

65. Lewin, K., *A dynamic theory of personality,* New York: McGraw-Hill, 1935.

66. Lewin, K., *Principles of topological psychology,* New York: McGraw-Hill, 1936.

67. Liddell, H. S., "The conditioned reflex," in *Comparative Psychology* (F. A. Moss, ed.), New York: Prentice-Hall, 1934, pp. 247–296.

68. Lindley, S. B., "The maze-learning ability of anosmic and blind anosmic rats," *J. Genet. Psychol.,* 37 (1930), 245–267.

69. Lorge, I., "Irrelevant rewards in animal learning," *J. Comp. Psychol.,* 21 (1936), 105–128.

70. Loucks, R. B., "An appraisal of Pavlov's systematization of behavior from the experimental standpoint," *J. Comp. Psychol.,* 15 (1933), 1–45.

71. Loucks, R. B., "Reflexology and the psychobiological approach," *Psychol. Rev.,* 44 (1937), 320–338.

72. Ludgate, K. E., *The effect of manual guidance upon maze learning,* Psychol. Monog., 33 (1923), no. 148.

73. Macfarlane, D. A., *The rôle of kinesthesis in maze learning,* Univ. Calif. Publ. Psychol., 4 (1930), 277–305.

74. Maier, N. R. F., *Reasoning in white rats,* Comp. Psychol. Monog., 6 (1929), no. 3.

75. Maier, N. R. F., "In defense of reasoning in rats," *J. Comp. Psychol.,* 19 (1935), 197–206.

76. Maier, N. R. F., "Age and intelligence in rats," *J. Comp. Psychol.,* 13 (1932), 1–16.

77. Maier, N. R. F., "The effect of cerebral destruction on reasoning and learning in rats," *J. Comp. Neur.,* 54 (1932), 45–75.

78. Maurer, S., "The effect of partial depletion of vitamin B (B¹) upon performance in rats, III," *J. Comp. Psychol.,* 20 (1935), 309–318.

79. Maurer, S., "The effect of early depletion of vitamin B₂ upon the performance in rats, IV," *J. Comp. Psychol.,* 20 (1935), 385–388.

80. Maurer, S., "The effect of acute vitamin A depletion upon performance in rats, V," *J. Comp. Psychol.,* 20 (1935), 389–392.

81. Maurer, S., "The effect of a diet of pasteurized milk upon performance in rats, VI," *J. Comp. Psychol.*, 20 (1935), 393–396.

82. Maurer, S., and L. S. Tsai, "Vitamin B deficiency and learning ability," *J. Comp. Psychol.*, 11 (1930), 51–62.

83. Maurer, S., and L. S. Tsai, "The effect of partial depletion of vitamin B complex upon learning ability in rats," *J. Nutrition*, 4 (1931), no. 4.

84. McCulloch, T. L., "Performance preferentials of the white rat in force-resisting and spatial dimension," *J. Comp. Psychol.*, 18 (1934), 85–111.

85. Miller, N. E., and W. R. Miles, "Effect of caffeine on the running speed of hungry, satiated, and frustrated rats," *J. Comp. Psychol.*, 20 (1935), 397–412.

86. Moss, F. A., "The effect of drugs and internal secretions on animal behavior," in *Comparative Psychology*, (F. A. Moss, ed.), New York: Prentice-Hall, 1934, pp. 113–148.

87. Muenzinger, K. F., "Motivation in learning. I. Electric shock for correct response in the visual discrimination habit," *J. Comp. Psychol.*, 17 (1934), 267–277.

88. Muenzinger, K. F., "Motivation in learning. II. The function of electric shock for right and wrong responses in human subjects," *J. Exper. Psychol.*, 17 (1934), 439–448.

89. Muenzinger, K. F., and H. Newcomb, "Motivation in learning. III. A bell signal compared with electric shock for right and wrong responses in the visual discrimination habit," *J. Comp. Psychol.*, 20 (1935), 85–93.

90. Muenzinger, K. F., and A. Wood, "Motivation in learning. IV. The function of punishment as determined by its temporal relation to the act of choice in the visual discrimination habit," *J. Comp. Psychol.*, 20 (1935), 95–106.

91. Muenzinger, K. F., and H. Newcomb, "Motivation in learning. V. The relative effectiveness of jumping a gap and crossing an electric grid in a visual discrimination habit," *J. Comp. Psychol.*, 21 (1936), 95–104.

92. Muenzinger, K. F., and F. M. Fletcher, "Motivation in learning. VI. Escape from electric shock compared with hunger-food tension in the visual discrimination habit," *J. Comp. Psychol.*, 22 (1936), 79–91.

93. Muenzinger, K. F., and F. M. Fletcher, "Motivation in learning. VII. The effect of an enforced delay at the point of choice in the visual discrimination habit," *J. Comp. Psychol.*, 23 (1937), 383–392.

94. Muenzinger, K. F., and E. Gentry, "Tone discrimination in white rats," *J. Comp. Psychol.*, 12 (1931), 195–206.

95. Muenzinger, K. F., and C. C. Dove, "Serial Learning: I. Gradients of uniformity and variability produced by success and failure of single responses," *J. Gen. Psychol.*, 16 (1937), 403–414.

96. Muenzinger, K. F., E. Poe, and C. F. Poe, "The effect of vitamin deficiency upon the acquisition and retention of the maze habit in the white rat. II. Vitamin B_2 (G)," *J. Comp. Psychol.*, 23 (1937), 59–66.

97. Munn, N. L., *An introduction to animal psychology, the behavior of the rat*, New York: Houghton Mifflin, 1933.

98. Poe, E., C. F. Poe, and K. F. Muenzinger, "The effect of vitamin deficiency upon the acquisition and retention of the maze habit in the white rat. I. The vitamin B complex," *J. Comp. Psychol.*, 22 (1936), 69–77.

99. Poe, E., C. F. Poe, and K. F. Muenzinger, "The effect of vitamin deficiency upon the acquisition and retention of the maze habit in the white rat. III. Vitamin B^1," *J. Comp. Psychol.*, 23 (1937), 67–76.

100. Ruch, F. L., "Goal direction orientation, generalized turning habit and goal gradient as factors in maze learning in the rat," *J. Comp. Psychol.*, 17 (1934), 225–232.

101. Ruch, F. L., "Experimental studies of the factors influencing the difficulty of blind alleys in linear mazes. I. Experiments with the maze patterns RLRLLRLR-RLRL and LRLRRLRLLRLR," *J. Comp. Psychol.*, 20 (1935), 21–34.

102. Ruch, F. L., "Experimental studies of the factors influencing the difficulty of blind alleys in linear mazes. II. Generalized-turning habits," *J. Comp. Psychol.*, 20 (1935), 35-52.

103. Ruch, F. L., "Experimental studies of the factors influencing the difficulty of blind alleys in linear mazes. III. Is there an anticipatory tendency in maze learning?," *J. Comp. Psychol.*, 20 (1935), 113-124.

104. Rundquist, E. E., "Inheritance of spontaneous activity in rats," *J. Comp. Psychol.*, 16 (1933), 415-438.

105. Schlosberg, H., "Conditioned responses in the white rat," *J. Genet. Psychol.*, 45 (1934), 303-335.

106. Schlosberg, H., "The relationship between success and the laws of conditioning," *Psychol. Rev.*, 44 (1937), 379-394.

107. Schneirla, T. C., *Learning and orientation in ants*, Comp. Psychol. Monog., 6 (1929), no. 30.

108. Skinner, B. F., "Two types of conditioned reflex and a pseudo type," *J. Gen. Psychol.*, 12 (1935), 66-77.

109. Spearman, C., *The nature of "intelligence" and the principles of cognition*, London: Macmillan, 1927.

110. Spence, K. W., "The order of eliminating blinds in maze learning by the rat," *J. Comp. Psychol.*, 14 (1932), 9-27.

111. Spence, K. W., and W. C. Shipley, "The factors determining the difficulty of blind alleys in maze learning by the white rat," *J. Comp. Psychol.*, 17 (1934), 423-436.

112. Spragg, S. D. S., "Anticipation as a factor in maze errors," *J. Comp. Psychol.*, 15 (1933), 319-329.

113. Spragg, S. D. S., "Anticipatory responses in the maze," *J. Comp. Psychol.*, 18 (1934), 51-73.

114. Stone, C. P., "The age factor in animal learning: I. Rats in the problem box and the maze. II. Rats on a multiple light discrimination box and a difficult maze," *Genet. Psychol. Monog.*, 5 (1925), 1-130; 6 (1925), 125-202.

115. Stone, C. P., "Motivation: drives and incentives," in *Comparative Psychology*, (F. A. Moss, ed.), New York: Prentice-Hall, 1934, pp. 73-112.

116. Thorndike, E. L., *Educational psychology, Vol. III.; Mental work and fatigue; Individual differences and their causes*, New York: Teachers College, Columbia University, 1923.

117. Thorndike, E. L., *The measurement of intelligence*, New York: Teachers College, Columbia University, 1927.

118. Thorndike, E. L., *The fundamentals of learning*, New York: Teachers College, Columbia University, 1932.

119. Thorndike, E. L., *Wants, interest and attitudes*, New York: Century, 1935.

120. Thurstone, L. L., *The vectors of mind*, Chicago: University of Chicago Press, 1935.

121. Tolman, E. C., "A behaviorist's definition of consciousness," *Psychol. Rev.*, 34 (1927), 433-439.

122. Tolman, E. C., *Purposive behavior in animals and men*, New York: Century, 1932, chapter xiii.

123. Tolman, E. C., "The law of effect: a reply to Dr. Goodenough," *J. Exper. Psychol.*, 16 (1933), 459-462.

124. Tolman, E. C., "Psychology vs. immediate experience," *Philos. Science*, 2 (1935), 356-380.

125. Tolman, E. C., "Distance-preferentials. A new apparatus and some results," *Psychol. Bull.*, 33 (1936), 727.

126. Tolman, E. C., "Operational behaviorism and current trends in psychology," *Proc. 25th Anniv. Celebration Inaug. Grad. Stud.*, Los Angeles: University of Southern California, 1936, pp. 89-103.

127. Tolman, E. C., C. S. Hall., and E. P. Bretnall, "A disproof of the law of effect and a substitution of the laws of emphasis, motivation and disruption," *J. Exper. Psychol.*, 15 (1932), 601–614.
128. Tolman, E. C., and C. H. Honzik, *"Insight" in rats,* Univ. Calif. Publ. Psychol., 4 (1930), 215–232.
129. Tryon, R. C., *The genetics of learning ability in rats: preliminary report,* Univ. Calif. Publ. Psychol., 4 (1929), 71–89.
130. Tryon, R. C., "Individual differences," in *Comparative Psychology,* (F. A. Moss, ed.), New York: Prentice-Hall, 1934, pp. 409–448.
131. Tryon, R. C., "A theory of psychological components—an alternative to 'mathematical factors,' " *Psychol. Rev.*, 42 (1935), 425–454.
132. Tsai, L. S., "Gradual vs. abrupt withdrawal of guidance in maze learning," *J. Comp. Psychol.*, 10 (1930), 325–332.
133. Tsai, L. S., *The laws of minimum effort and maximum satisfaction in animal behavior,* Monog. Nat. Instit. Psychol., 1932, no. 1.
134. Vaughn, C. L., *Factors in rat learning—an analysis of the intercorrelations between 34 variables,* Comp. Psychol. Monog., 14 (1937), no. 69.
135. Wang, T. L., *The influence of tuition in the acquisition of skill,* Psychol. Monog., 33 (1925), no. 154.
136. Warden, C. J., *Animal motivation: Experimental studies on the albino rat,* New York: Columbia University Press, 1931.
137. Waters, R. H., "The influence of large amounts of manual guidance upon human maze learning," *J. Gen. Psychol.*, 4 (1930), 213–228.
138. Waters, R. H., "Equivalence of response in learning," *Psychol. Bull.*, 33 (1936), 798–799.
139. Waters, R. H., "The wall-seeking tendency and maze learning in the white rat," *J. Psychol.*, 4 (1937), 23–26.
140. Waters, R. H., "The principle of least effort in learning," *J. Gen. Psychol.*, 16 (1937), 3–20.
141. Watson, J. B., *Kinaesthetic and organic sensations: Their rôle in the reactions of the white rat,* Psychol. Rev. Monog., 8 (1917), no. 2.
142. Webb, L. W., *Transfer of training and retroaction,* Psychol. Rev. Monog., 24 (1917), no. 3.
143. Wheeler, R. H., *The science of psychology,* New York: Crowell, 1929.
144. Williams, G. W., and C. O'Brien, "The effect of sodium phenobarbital on the learning behavior of white rats," *J. Comp. Psychol.*, 23 (1937), 457–474.
145. Wilson, W. R., "Principles of selection in 'trial and error' learning," *Psychol. Rev.*, 31 (1924), 150–160.
146. Witkin, H. A., and T. C. Schneirla, "Initial maze behavior as a function of maze design," *J. Comp. Psychol.*, 23 (1937), 275–304.
147. Wolfle, D. L., "The effects of continuous interchange of alley sections on the maze behavior of rats," *J. Comp. Psychol.*, 19 (1935), 91–106.
148. Wright, H. F., *The influence of barriers upon strength of motivation,* Contrib. Psychol. Theory, 1 (1937), no. 3.
149. Yoshioka, J. G., "Direction as a factor in maze solution in rats," *J. Genet. Psychol.*, 38 (1930), 307–320.
150. Yoshioka, J. G., "A study of orientation in a maze," *J. Genet. Psychol.*, 42 (1933), 167–183.
151. Young, P. T., "Preferential discrimination of the white rat for different kinds of grain," *Amer. J. Psychol.*, 40 (1928), 372–400.
152. Young, P. T., "Relative food preferences of the white rat," *J. Comp. Psychol.*, 14 (1932), 297–319.
153. Young, P. T., "Relative food preferences of the white rat, II," *J. Comp. Psychol.*, 15 (1933), 149–166.

14

PHYSIOLOGY, PSYCHOLOGY, AND SOCIOLOGY

[*Psychological Review*, MAY, 1938]

I WOULD DEFINE physiology as a study of the laws determining the *activities* of muscles and glands; I would define psychology as a study of the laws determining the *behavior* of whole organisms; and I would define sociology as the study of the laws determining the *conduct* of groups of organisms.[1]

Accepting these definitions, one's first reaction concerning the interrelations of the three sciences would be to think of physiology as the most basic, psychology as the next most basic, and sociology as the least basic— or, in other words, to conceive the facts and laws of psychology as dependent upon those of physiology and the facts and laws of sociology as dependent upon those of psychology. But the thesis that I am actually going to try to uphold here is the reverse and, at first sight, seemingly absurd one, to wit: that the facts and laws of psychology are, rather, in some part dependent upon those of sociology and that the facts and laws of physiology are similarly in some part dependent upon those of psychology.

It was the Gestalt psychologists who first brought it home to psychologists in America that even within the confines of a single science, such as psychology by itself or physics by itself, the whole can often be said to govern its parts quite as truly as the parts may be said to govern the whole. Hence what I am going to argue for is, in a sense, merely a further extension of this Gestalt doctrine to be applied to the interrelationships between the three successively larger sciences of physiology, psychology, and sociology.

[1] This respective use of the three words, "activities," "behavior," and "conduct," was suggested to me by Professors K. F. Muenzinger and R. H. Bruce.

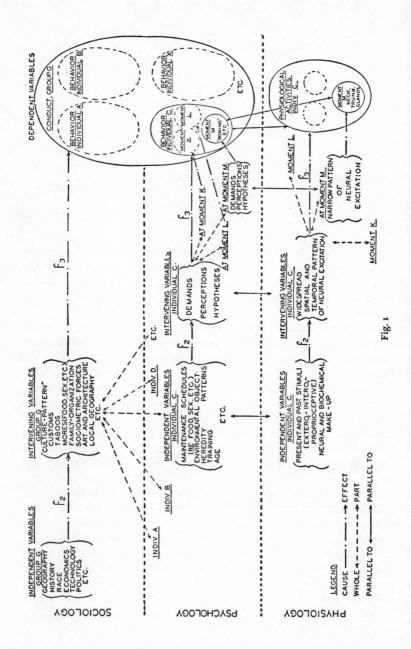

Fig. 1

But the whole argument will be made clearer perhaps by basing it on a concrete example. The situation I have chosen is relatively banal but it will, I hope, do for the purpose. As an example of *group conduct* I have taken the "carrying out of a marriage and wedding by a middle-class American social and religious group" some twenty or thirty years ago—at a date, that is, when there were such groups and when marriages and weddings were expressions of them in a way that is probably less true today. As an example of *individual behavior* within this group conduct I have picked the behavior of a certain young man C in "going to this wedding." And, finally, as examples of *physiological activity* I have chosen the parallel "muscle contractions and gland secretions" occurring in C in going to the wedding and in particular at the moment M when he encounters, on his way to the church, the family of a bridesmaid in whom he is "interested."

Let us indicate the interrelations between these three levels of performance and the explanatory concepts which I would conceive as respectively involved in them by means of a diagram.

In figure 1 physiology has been put along the bottom, psychology in the middle, and sociology at the top. Further, it has been assumed that each of these sciences operates with three classes of variable, to wit, *independent variables, intervening variables,* and *dependent variables.*

Independent variables are to be defined as those which the science in question manipulates in direct experimental (or historical) fashion and which it assumes as the ultimate causes of its phenomena. These independent variables have been put towards the left on each level of the diagram. The final *dependent variables*—i.e., the "group conduct," the "individual behavior," and the "physiological activities,"—which are ultimately to be predicted and, so far as possible, controlled, have been put at the right on each level. And, lastly, the *intervening variables* are to be conceived as further constructs which each science finds it helpful to invent and to introduce as explanatory steps between the independent variables, on the one hand, and the final dependent variables, on the other. These have been put in between on each level. Finally, it must be noted that for each science there have also been inserted two sets of functions, indicated by dash-dot arrows, viz.: f_2 functions whereby the intervening variables result from the independent variables and f_3 functions[2] whereby the final dependent variables result from the intervening variables.

---

[2] What I would designate f_1 functions (in contrast to these f_2 and f_3 functions) would be the complete functions stretching all the way from the independent variables, on the left, to the final dependent variables, on the right. If such f_1 functions were entirely known, there would be no need of the intervening variables. The latter and the f_2 and f_3 functions would be all absorbed into these f_1 functions. See Tolman [8, 10].

Look now in more detail at the right-hand side of the diagram and consider, first, both the sociological and the psychological dependent variables. The "group conduct" to be predicted is that of the whole group G in the carrying out of this marriage and wedding. This conduct I have represented by the large unbroken elliptoid figure extending over both the sociological and the psychological levels. Within this larger elliptoid I have indicated a series of smaller elliptoids. Each of these latter is to represent *a* "behavior" (relative to the wedding) of some one of the component individuals in the group. One of these, the unbroken-line elliptoid, represents the behavior of individual C. Further, it will be noted that within this total behavior of C in "going to the wedding" there are also to be mutually distinguished a number of still smaller, component behaviors represented by smaller included elliptoids. And among these smaller behaviors is that of "stopping, bowing, chatting, etc." occurring at the moment M in which C encounters the family of the bridesmaid.

Look, now, at the physiological dependent variables represented on the bottom level. It will be observed that I have assumed a parallelism between physiological activities and psychological behaviors, not the older psychophysical or psychophysiological parallelism but a simple behavior-physiological parallelism. And this parallelism I have represented by double-headed solid-line arrows. Furthermore, just as the smaller behaviors involved at moments K, L, M, etc., were to be conceived as contained within the larger, more total behavior of "going to the wedding," so the smaller complexes of physiological activities at moments K, L, M are in like fashion to be considered as comprised within that larger loose complex of physiological activities which parallels the total behavior.

Let us consider, now, some general features concerning these three types of dependent variable. First, it is to be observed that the "group conduct" is the most extensive both temporally, spatially, and interindividually. It covers all the preparations for the wedding (e.g., the sending out and receiving of invitations, the sending and receiving of wedding presents, the decoration of the church, and the like), and indeed even the original rearing and bringing together of the two young people in question, in addition to the wedding proper. It is such (spatially, temporally and interindividually) extensive group processes which the sociologist is interested in predicting and, if he be an applied sociologist, of eventually learning to control—i.e., learning to prevent, to modify, or to cause to be repeated unmodified through successive generations (in the same or other groups).

Any single "individual behavior" such as this one of C in "going to the wedding" is temporally and spatially less extensive and it inheres in but a single individual. It is one of many behaviors by one of many individuals, all of which are involved in the total group conduct. It extends over only a relatively small number of hours and a relatively small expanse of space. And, further, any such behavior can often be subdivided into a number of still smaller but distinguishable component behaviors. Each of these latter extends over minutes only. Finally, it may be either the larger more inclusive behavior or one of these smaller component behaviors which in the given case the psychologist is interested in predicting.[3]

Turning to the "physiological activities," we note that there is no single complex of physiological activities to be coördinated with the total group conduct. Physiological activities *per se* are expressions of individual organisms. There is no physiology for a group as such. Within the individual organisms there do seem to be, however, more and less extensive, more and less enduring, arrays of muscle contractions and gland secretions—parallel, respectively, to the more inclusive and the less inclusive "behaviors." Thus it may be either the larger or one of the smaller physiological complexes which the physiologist is interested in predicting and controlling. Actually, however, it is my guess that (in the present state of our knowledge) it is usually only one of the smaller complexes which a physiologist in any given case is attempting to predict and control.

Let us consider, now, the independent and the intervening variables at each of the three levels.

Sociology.—Turn to the upper left-hand corner. Here I have put what I conceive to be the independent variables for sociology.[4] They are the geographical, historical, racial,[5] economic, technological and political factors which underlie and condition Group G and its conduct. They are the ultimate determiners of this group and of such particular conducts carried out by it as that of the present marriage and wedding. It is these geographical, historical, racial, economic, technological, and

---

[3] This problem of superordinate and subordinate behaviors—i.e., of means-end hierarchies—is one requiring more study and attention than it has yet received. For a previous attempt at discussing it, see Tolman [7, chapter vi].

[4] It will be obvious to any *bona fide* social scientist that my notions as to the specific concepts of the social sciences are relatively naïve. I venture to hope, however, that my conclusions as to the interrelations of them to the other two sciences will nonetheless still hold.

[5] I am using "racial" here in a loose sense to refer to the hereditary biological constitution of a group (due to inbreeding or what not) in so far as this heredity makes this group different, if it does, from other groups. See Linton [4, chapter ii].

political causes which would have to be changed if Group G were to be other than it is and if it were not to "go in for" this present marriage and wedding.

In attempting, however, to work out the functional connection between these ultimate determiners and any final group conduct, the social scientist is led to construct certain hypothetical "intervening variables." That is to say, instead of attempting to state at once the complete (f_1)[6] functional connections between any given conduct (such as the present wedding), and such geographical, historical, racial, economic, technological, and political causes, a sociologist today seems to find it more feasible merely to trace such conducts back, first (f_3 function), to a set of "intervening variables" such as the customs, taboos, religious and sex mores, types of family-organization, "statuses,"[7] "sociometric forces,"[8] art and architecture, local geography, etc., of the given group. A most useful single term to cover these intervening variables would seem to be that of the "culture pattern" suggested by Benedict [1]. Only after having invented this intervening variable of the culture pattern, does the sociologist attempt to find a further set of laws or functions (f_2) to connect such a culture pattern to the final independent variables of geography, history, genetics, economics, technology, and politics. The social sciences break up the total relation into two successive steps—the f_2 laws and the f_3 laws. The f_3 laws as now stated seem to be relatively simple. They are hardly more than descriptive exemplifications of the culture patterns. The f_2 laws, on the other hand, are hardly known at all. Anthropologists and sociologists are apparently as yet finding great difficulty in saying much of anything with regard to the f_2's.[9]

Psychology.—Turn now to psychology. The sort of independent variables, which, as psychologists, we assume as determinative of the behavior of individual C, I have located in the diagram directly under the sociological intervening variables for the group as a whole. These psychological independent variables are: "maintenance schedules" (*re* food, sex, sleep, etc.), "environmental object-patterns," "heredity," "training," and "age," etc. And I have drawn a double-headed dash arrow between these psychological independent variables for C and the sociological in-

---

[6] See footnote 2.

[7] See Linton [4, chapter viii].

[8] See Moreno [6].

[9] As an example of an attempt to discover such f_2 laws, see the studies edited by Margaret Mead [5]. This survey of thirteen primitive cultures sought for general laws (i.e., f_2 laws) which would connect the relative strengths of the customs of "coöperation," "competition" and "individualism" to such independent variables as economic and technological factors. But it did not succeed in finding any clear-cut relationships of this sort. The only important f_2 law that anthropologists have as yet uncovered seems to be merely the very general one of "historical diffusion."

tervening variables above them. Also, I have drawn other double-headed dash arrows to suggest similar part-whole relationships between the psychological independent variables for each of the other individuals in the group and the sociological variables for the whole group. In short, the culture pattern of the group appears to be a whole which is made up of the maintenance schedules, the environmental object patterns, the heredities, the previous trainings, the ages, etc. of all the various individuals within the group. But, if this be correct, then it appears that the psychologist's independent variables are not in any final sense independent and absolute. They are always immersed in a "field" constituted by the "culture pattern" of the whole group. They cannot be manipulated wholly independently of this field.

Further, it is to be stressed that such a field—such a culture pattern—is a relatively interconnected whole. Hence any experimental variation that the psychologist attempts to make in any one independent variable is almost surely bound to produce at the same time uncontrolled and unwanted changes in others of the independent variables also acting upon the given individual. Or, in short, psychology here comes up against two sorts of difficulty:

First, psychologists cannot study the f_2 function issuing from some one independent variable—for example, sex maintenance schedule—for some one individual without danger of at the same time affecting, even though only in some slight degree, the sex *mores* of the whole group. And such a change in group *mores* will react back upon and affect all the other independent variables (e.g., the environmental object pattern of persons and things) also acting upon this same individual. Any one independent variable for any one individual is, in short, always part of a whole interconnected sociological field. And the laws found for any one such independent variable will always thus be colored by the latter's interconnections with all the other variables in this field.

And, secondly, even if psychology surmounts, to some extent, the above difficulty and tears the effects of the separate independent variables apart, it will still remain true that the laws for individual behavior which psychology finally arrives at will be laws holding, so far as we can be certain, only within the given culture in which they have been found. Only by studying psychology within many cultures would it eventually be possible to arrive at a pure psychology—a psychology which one could feel certain would hold for all cultures.[10]

---

[10] And such a universal pure psychology might well turn out in the end to be restricted to but relatively simple and biologically conditioned facts. And, further, it may well be that this field of a pure biological (noncultural) psychology is after all best investigated with animals [10].

And thus we come to the first part of our original thesis—namely, that sociology is in some considerable measure ancillary to psychology.

Let us assume, however, that in spite of the above we do not give up but proceed to prosecute psychology as best we may. Let us look next at the "intervening variables" as listed for psychology. I have designated them as "demands, perceptions, and hypotheses."[11] These "demands," "hypotheses," and "perceptions" lead to C's behavior of "going to the wedding." They would be: for example, the demand to win favor with the particular bridesmaid, the demand to make a good impression on her family, the demand for party food,—i.e., sweets, liquor, etc.—hypotheses as to the direction and distance of the church, hypotheses as to the probability of meeting the bridesmaid's family, perceptions of the concrete objects and persons involved in getting dressed, going to the church, and so on. These demands, hypotheses and perceptions[12] would combine together according to some f_3 function (not as yet sufficiently known by psychologists) to produce the final behavior of "going to the wedding."

We note next, however, that such a larger set of demands, hypotheses and perceptions leading to the total behavior of "going to the wedding" must be conceived as comprising a number of component sets of smaller demands, perceptions and hypotheses. That is to say, just as the total behavior of "going to the wedding" was conceived as containing within itself separable moments such as: "getting dressed in such and such a fashion," "starting at the correct time," "stopping, bowing, talking," etc., so now the general more inclusive set of demands, perceptions and hypotheses is to be conceived as containing within itself corresponding subordinate sets of smaller demands, perceptions, and hypotheses.

The relationship of each of these minor sets to the more inclusive one, I have indicated by double-headed dash arrows. The relationship is again one of parts to whole. That is to say, in attempting to vary for experimental study any one such minor set of demands, perceptions and hypotheses occurring at some single moment such as M, we will thereby tend to change, at least in some degree, the larger more inclusive set. This latter will act as a "field" within which the minor ones are enmeshed.

Or, in other words, we meet here again an analogous difficulty to that for the study of the behavior of single human individuals always immersed as we saw in larger cultural wholes. The intervening variables for the large behavior comprise and determine those for the smaller be-

---

[11] For the defense of such intervening variables for psychology, see Tolman [8, 9, 10].

[12] It is, of course, understood that these demands, hypotheses and perceptions are behavioristically, not introspectively, defined affairs [8].

haviors just as truly as conversely those for the smaller, included behaviors also constitute and determine those for the total behavior.[13]
We cannot study the small behaviors without knowing also the laws of
the larger including behaviors.

Physiology.—But turn now to the physiological level. Its relation to
the psychological (behavioral) level above it is one of parallelism. This
parallelism is to be conceived as present and is indicated by double-
headed unbroken-line arrows for the independent and the intervening
variables as well as for the dependent variables.

Consider, first, the independent variables. Corresponding and parallel
to the independent variables as identified by the psychologist, the physiologist finds patterns of present and past *stimuli* (exteroceptive, interoceptive, and proprioceptive) plus such and such neural and biochemical
make-ups. That is to say, stimuli and neural and biochemical make-ups
are to be conceived as being the same events and processes which the
psychologist calls maintenance schedules, past and present environmental object patterns, heredity, training, age, and the like. The
difference is one of language and size of descriptive unit. But any "operational" change made in the one set of entities will always be accompanied by some corresponding change in the other parallel set of entities.

Look, next, at the intervening variables. Here also we find a parallelism. For the physiologist the intervening variables are spatially, temporally, electrically, and perhaps also chemically, identifiable excitations
within the nervous system.[14] But these can be considered as parallel to
the psychologist's "intervening variables" of demands, perceptions, and
hypotheses. Further, just as the larger demands, perceptions, and hypotheses, which are determinative of the total behavior of "going to the
wedding" are to be conceived as containing within themselves subordinate demands, perceptions, and hypotheses occurring at moments K, L,
M, etc., so here at the physiological level the larger set of neural excitations must be supposed to contain within themselves distinguishable
narrower more momentary patterns of excitation.

What the above means is that before studying the laws governing any
relatively small group of physiological activities (muscle contractions
and gland secretions) such as those at moment M, we have to note, first,
that such a minor group of physiological processes occurs only within
some larger matrix of processes. Hence the laws which we, as physiolo-

---

[13] Again it must be emphasized that this problem of the interrelationship between
the superordinate and subordinate behaviors requires much more analysis and study
than anyone has as yet given it.

[14] Here again, as was the case with sociology, I feel myself treading upon relatively
uncertain ground.

gists, discover for the minor process probably only hold within the specific larger matrices in which they have been studied. And this limitation the physiologist (or at least the psychologist who poses as a physiologist) is apt to forget.

Furthermore, and this is the main practical burden of the argument, it seems it is just here that the psychologist is probably at present in the more strategic position. For the larger, controlling set of circumambient events (intervening variables) can today, it would seem, often be better identified and controlled in the psychologist's terms of demands, perceptions and hypotheses than in the parallel physiological ones of widespread (and not easily get-at-able) neural patterns of excitation. The physiologist who seeks to predict and control some narrow, neural phenomenon such as that leading to the specific muscle contractions and gland secretions at moment M can, I believe, do it today only by defining the circumambient and controlling matrix *psychologically rather than physiologically*.

And so we come to the second half of our original thesis—namely, that (at any rate, today, *in the present stage of the two sciences*) psychology tends to be in large part ancillary to physiology.[15]

In conclusion, let me briefly recapitulate:

1. *Sociology versus psychology.*—It has appeared that we cannot (at least in the case of society-forming animals such as human beings) study psychology—i.e., the *behavior* of individuals—save within larger sociological wholes. The intervening factors determining the *group conduct* act as a "field"[16] determinative of the independent variables acting upon the individuals within the group. And this makes for two kinds of difficulty or limitation for psychology:

a. The field presented by the social group tends to cause interfunctional relations between the psychologist's independent variables.

b. Even if it prove in some measure possible to get around this first difficulty, there is still a second difficulty in that (having studied the f_2 and f_3 functions within merely one social group) we shall still have to study them over again within other different types of social group. For in such other types of group the independent variables of "maintenance-

---

[15] This of course *does not mean* that, therefore, the physiologist and physiological psychologist should not persist in continuing a very rigorous pursuance of the physiological facts *per se*. It may be that before long this present practical situation as between psychology and physiology may become reversed. *Note added January, 1951:* The use of "ancillary" here and later seems not to have been altogether happy. What was meant was that an adequate sociology is a precondition to a complete psychology and an adequate psychology is a precondition to a complete physiology.

[16] For the general importance of the methodological concept of the field, see Lewin [3] and Brown [2].

schedule," "environmental pattern," etc. may take on quite other and wholly new values, the effects of which cannot be extrapolated from the findings for the first type of group.

In a word, we are forced to conclude that sociology is to a surprising degree ancillary to psychology.

2. *Psychology versus physiology.* Psychology and physiology are parallel sciences—(i.e., a behavior-physiological parallelism, not a psychophysical parallelism). From a purely theoretical point of view neither, therefore, would seem ancillary to the other. We note further, however, that for both sciences there appeared to be the difficulty that any relatively limited behavior (or correlated set of physiological activities) is practically always immersed in a "field" constituted by a larger behavior (or larger set of correlated physiological activities). And this presents a difficulty analogous to that as between psychology and sociology. For it appears that to study any small behavior we have to know the larger behavior that this smaller one is immersed in; and, similarly, to study any smaller group of physiological activities we have to know the larger surrounding group of physiological activities.

And it also appears, further, that psychology is, today at any rate, here in perhaps the better position. For today it seems easier and more feasible to identify and control the larger circumambient processes in psychological rather than in physiological terms.

Hence we must conclude that (*practically speaking*) psychology today is also in some considerable degree ancillary to physiology.

REFERENCES

1. Benedict, R., *Patterns of culture,* New York: Houghton Mifflin, 1934.
2. Brown, J. F., *Psychology and the social order,* New York: McGraw-Hill, 1936.
3. Lewin, K., *A dynamic theory of personality,* New York: McGraw-Hill, 1935.
4. Linton, R., *The study of man: an introduction,* New York: Appleton-Century, 1936.
5. Mead, M. (editor), *Cooperation and competition among primitive peoples,* New York: McGraw-Hill, 1937.
6. Moreno, J. L., *Who shall survive? A new approach to the problem of human interrelations,* Washington, D.C.: Nervous and Mental Disease Publishing Co., 1934.
7. Tolman, E. C., *Purposive behavior in animals and men,* New York: Century Company, 1932.
8. ———, "Psychology vs. immediate experience," *Philos. Science,* 2 (1935), 356–380.
9. ———, "Operational behaviorism and current trends in psychology," *Proc. 25th Anniv. Celebration Inaug. Grad. Studies,* Los Angeles, University of Southern California, 1936, pp. 89–103.
10. ———, "The determiners of behavior at a choice point," *Psychol. Rev.,* 45 (1938), 1–41.

15

PREDICTION OF VICARIOUS TRIAL AND ERROR BY MEANS OF THE SCHEMATIC SOWBUG

[Psychological Review, JULY, 1939]

THE PRESENT REPORT[1] consists of two parts: first, the presentation of some experimental results; and second, the presentation of a theoretical schema for the interpretation of those results.

THE EXPERIMENT

The experiment was a white-black and white-gray discrimination experiment but the interest was not simply in the relative ease with which the subjects (rats) learned to differentiate between the correct and incorrect stimulus objects but also in the relative amounts of "looking back and forth" or, to use Muenzinger's term, "vicarious trial and error" (or "VTE") which they exhibited in the course of acquiring these differentiations.[2] In short, our experiment will be concerned not only with learning scores but also with VTE scores.

Three groups of rats with pigmented eyes (all approximately five months old at the beginning of the experiment) were run in a modified Lashley discrimination set-up. (See fig. 1.) For all these groups the correct door was white, but for one the incorrect door was black, for another it was medium gray, and for the third it was a very light gray. The group

---

[1] Read, in part, before the American Psychological Association, September 7, 1938.

[2] For a discussion and summary of most of what is known to date about vicarious trial and error, much of it obtained in the Colorado laboratory, see Muenzinger's recent splendid report [7]. See also Tolman [9; 10, chapter xiii; 11] and Dennis and Russell [5].

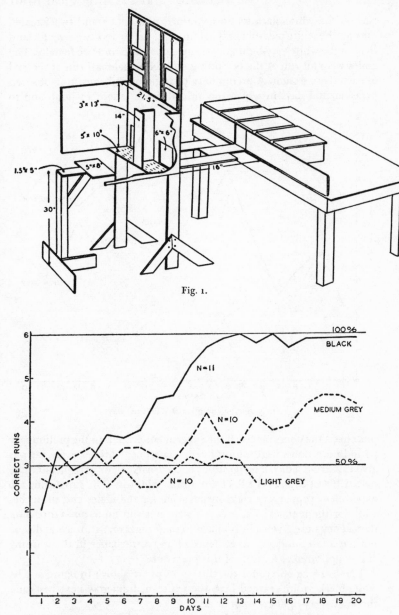

Fig. 1.

Fig. 2. Learning curves. Average number of correct runs per day.

run on the white-black set-up contained nine males and two females, that on the white-medium-gray set-up eight males and two females, and that on the white-very-light-gray set-up eight males and two females. The males were all run at the beginning and the females all run at the end of each day's session. A preliminary training period consisting of seven experimental days in which the animals were taught to jump and to

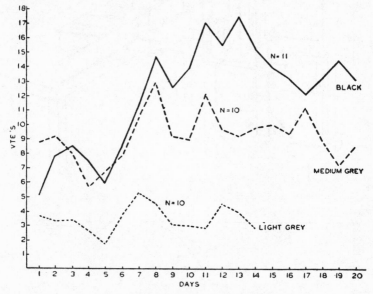

FIG. 3. Average number of VTE's per day.

push open the doors preceded the experiment proper. In the preliminary period both doors were white. In the experiment proper every rat was given six trials a day. The positions of the correct door were on alternate days, LRRLLR and RLLRRL for all three groups. The gap during the experiment proper was eight inches wide for the males and six inches wide for the females. The animals were not run on Saturdays or Sundays. They were given a heavy meal in their cages on Saturdays and were not fed at all Sundays. No evidence of any disturbance in the learning curves appeared as a result of this procedure.

The learning curves for the three groups are shown in figure 2. The white-black group learned best, the white-medium-gray next best, and the white-very-light-gray not at all.

Each look by a rat at one door, which was followed by a look at (or a final taking-off-toward) the other door, was counted as one "vicarious trial and error"—one VTE. For each group the average VTE's per rat in the six trials of each day are shown in figure 3. The white-black group exhibited the most, the white-medium-gray group the next most, and the white-very-light-gray group the fewest VTE's.

Figure 4 presents the time curves. These are the times from the instant

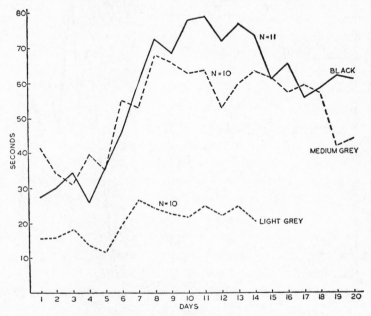

FIG. 4. Time curves. Average number of seconds before jumping.

the animal was put on the stand until he first took off either to the correct or to the incorrect door. It will be observed that these time curves are quite similar to the VTE curves.

Finally, in order further to emphasize the picture, curves for a couple of single individuals are presented.

Figure 5 shows the curves for an individual in the white-black group. This animal exhibited a complete and unvarying left-going position habit for the first seven days. He averaged only a second or two before taking off to the left, irrespective of whether this was correct or incorrect. On the third trial of the eighth day, however, he slowed up, made one VTE, took 16 seconds, and then jumped to the right-hand side, and this was correct. From then on he began making more and more VTE's and averaging more correct jumps even when they were to his previously avoided right-hand side.

Figure 6 shows the same three curves, for an individual in the white-medium-gray group. It will be observed that the learning did not become so complete and the VTE's and the longer times did not begin so soon

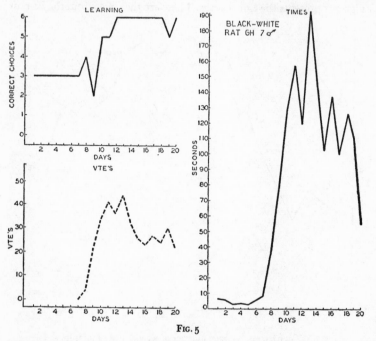

FIG. 5

and did not begin to come down again with any such certainty as was the case for the rat in the white-black group.[8]

So much for the facts; let us turn now to the theory.

THE THEORY

The theory (which in its present stage should not be taken too seriously) consists in the assumption that all higher organisms are in a certain *underlying* sense tropistic. This, not literally but figuratively speaking, tropistic or taxic character of higher organisms provides, I believe, the necessary model for stating how in this experiment with rats different

---

[8] These two animals were selected since they were deemed "typical." It must be admitted, however, that there was considerable overlapping between the two groups. In particular, it is to be noted that there were one or two rats in the white-black group who never made many VTE's and yet learned quickly. Their VTE's, what there were of them, did, however, go up just before learning and then come down again.

strengths of hunger, different goodnesses of perceptual differentiations, and different degrees of learning, combine to produce the actual amounts of correct choosing and of VTE-ing that they do. Or, to put it another way (see fig. 7), the schematic sowbug is my present conception of what I have elsewhere [11] merely labelled as the f_3 function. The name

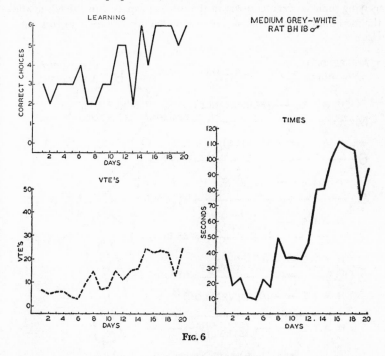

FIG. 6

"schematic sowbug" is, of course, merely a would-be picturesque term for this essentially tropistic character which I have introduced into my f_3 function.

Blum [1, 2, 3, 4], working with simple actually tropistic animals, discovered that many of the apparent deviations from the forced-movement type of behavior to be predicted from Loeb's theory could be explained by assuming that progression velocity (forward or backward) may vary independently of orientation velocity. I have taken over this distinction between orientation and progression for my bug and then I have assumed, further, that any set of qualities, which form a discriminable dimension for the given species, can be represented conceptually as lying at different angles around the nose of such a bug. Thus, if two qualities in such a dimension are relatively near together, they will be represented as lying in the sowbug's schematic space with a narrow angle between them; but, if the two qualities are discriminably far apart, they will be represented as having a wider angle between them. The white and the black in the present experiment I would represent, for example, as lying some 90 degrees apart in the sowbug's space, but the white and the medium gray as lying, say, only some 60 degrees apart in this same space.

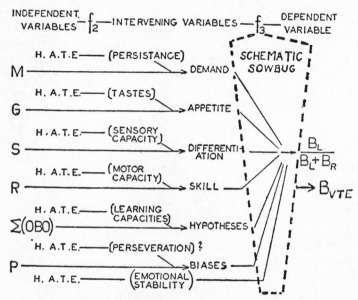

FIG. 7. The Schematic Sowbug as the f_3 function.

Figure 8 presents a first diagram of the bug. It is shown as lying at an angle to the parallel rays from a single stimulus source, say, white. It is bilaterally symmetrical. It has symmetrically placed pairs of motor appendages. These latter, however, are represented by vector arrows rather than as actual motor organs. The pair with small white rectangles on them, at the front just behind the head, are the orientation vectors, the pair with the plus marks on them at the rear are the progression vectors.

The curve with small rectangles labelled "orientation distribution" indicates the relative intensities of perceptual stimulation of the successive receptor points. These strengths of excitation are to be conceived as determined by the angles at which the rays hit plus the angular distances of the receptor points in question from the animal's median plane. The more perpendicularly a ray hits and the nearer the receptor point, which it hits, is to the nose (i.e., the median plane), the stronger the excitation. When all the rays come (as in this case) from the left, the distribution is skewed and its mode lies to the left of the median plane.

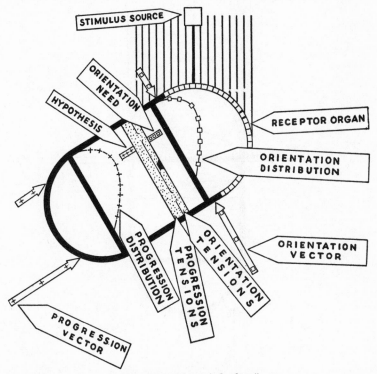

FIG. 8. The "Schematic Sowbug."

But when the rays come straight on, the orientation distribution becomes symmetrical. It is also to be assumed, following Loeb, that the right-hand motor appendages are activated by the left-hand receptors, and the left-hand motor appendages by the right-hand receptors. (I am assuming, that is, a positively taxic bug.) In other words, the area under the orientation distribution which is to the left of the median plane determines the length of the right-hand orientation vector, and the area under this curve which is to the right of the median plane determines the length of the left-hand orientation vector.

Further, it must be noted that although the shape of the orientation distribution is determined by the angular direction of the rays, its height is determined, rather, by a specific "orientation need" relative to the given quality. This specific need is indicated by the little column with rectangles in it which is shown as rising up out of the upper stippled

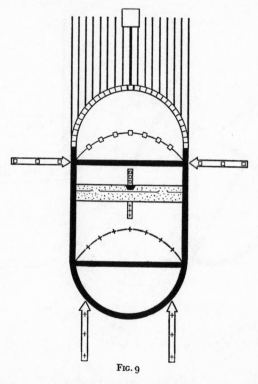

Fig. 9

area, which latter represents the general orientation readiness or tension. This way of representing the tension or readiness as a stippled area inside the organism, the degree of stippling corresponding to the degree of the demand (derived in this case from hunger), I have adapted from Lewin [6]. Further, it is also to be assumed that once the bug has looked directly at a given stimulus source the specific need relative to this specific quality and the corresponding resultant orientation distribution both temporarily sink.

The rear curve with the plus signs—the progression distribution—is to be conceived as following as to shape the orientation distribution.

That is to say, its mode will shift following that of the orientation distribution when and if the animal turns. The height of this progression distribution is to be conceived, however, as determined by the strength of the specific hypothesis—represented by the lower column with the plus signs on it—which hypothesis, in this case, is to the effect that the given stimulus source is good. This hypothesis in its turn is a product of the

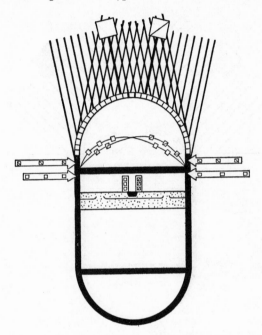

FIG. 10. Difficult discrimination.

general progression tension—represented by the lower stippled area—plus specific past experience relative to this specific type of stimulus source. It is such past experience which makes such a plus hypothesis ready to erupt. Note, further, that it is the right-hand and left-hand areas under the progression distribution which determine the relative lengths of the two progression vectors.

It is obvious that as here indicated the bug is in unstable equilibrium and will turn left until, as shown in figure 9, it will face the stimulus, where its orientation and progression distributions will be symmetrical and, if nothing else happens, it will proceed to progress forward directly towards the stimulus source.

Now let us turn to the case of two competing stimuli, for this is the situation represented in our experiments, and the one in which VTE-ing occurs. The next two figures show the relative sizes of the orientation vectors, first for a difficult discrimination (fig. 10) between the two stimuli (represented in the figure by a white rectangle and a white rectangle with a diagonal line) and second for an easy discrimination (fig. 11)

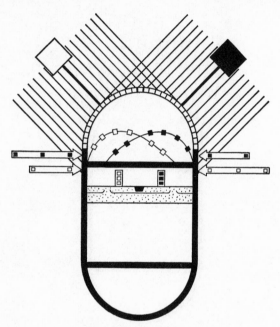

FIG. 11. Easy discrimination.

between the two stimuli (represented in the figure by a white rectangle and a black rectangle). It is obvious that in this latter case the imbalance of the orientation vectors is relatively great. Both figures, however, show the animal in the doldrums. In both cases he is like Buridan's ass between the two equidistant bundles of hay. Suppose, however, that he has just looked directly at one of the two stimuli, then our assumption is that his orientation need for that one, say white, will have become temporarily depressed. His white-orientation distribution will have become lower and his white-orientation vectors will have both become relatively short and he will swing over toward the right. But thereupon his orientation need with regard to the right-hand stimulus will, we assume, also become temporarily weaker while the one for the left-hand stimulus will recover and so he will swing back again. In short, he will VTE.

Why, however, does this tendency for VTE-ing appear sooner for the white and black choice than for the white and gray choices? As was said earlier, all the animals tended to start with initial position habits—that is to say, initial irrelevant hypotheses. But an already established hypothesis will tend as such to interfere with VTE-ing. For, if this hypoth-

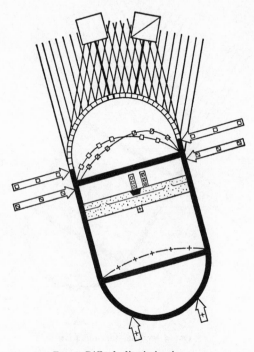

FIG. 12. Difficult discrimination.

esis is strong enough, the animal will simply progress toward the given side and the imbalance in the orientation vectors relative to the brightness value of two qualities will not have a chance to get in its effects.

The next three figures indicate the relative heights of such already established initial hypotheses which would be big enough thus to *prevent* VTE-ing. First, for a difficult discrimination (fig. 12). It will be seen that here only a small initial irrelevant hypothesis in favor of the one side will be enough thus to prevent VTE-ing from occurring. Next consider a mediumly difficult discrimination (fig. 13). Here a stronger initial irrelevant hypothesis would be necessary to prevent VTE-ing. And, finally, for a still easier discrimination (fig. 14) a still stronger initial hypothesis would be necessary to prevent VTE-ing. Hence VTE-ing starts more readily for the white and black easy discrimination than for the more difficult white and medium-gray discrimination and still more readily than for the white and very-light-gray very difficult discrimina-

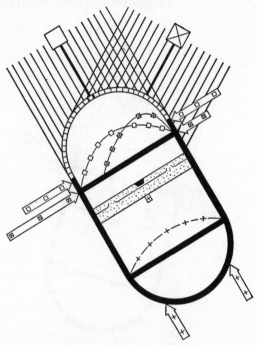

FIG. 13. Medium discrimination.

tion. The initial irrelevant hypotheses are less likely to be strong enough to prevent VTE-ing in the case of the easier discriminations.

Finally, let us consider the course of learning. Figure 15 shows the situation, as I conceive it, early in learning for a white vs. medium-gray discrimination. The initial irrelevant hypothesis has through lack of success been displaced and correct hypotheses have through the repetitions of success and failure begun to be set up. That is to say, a plus progression curve has started for the plus (white) stimulus source and a minus progression has started for the minus (gray) stimulus source. There are plus forward-*pushing* vectors and minus backward-*pulling* vectors. These resultant progression vectors both plus and minus are, however, still relatively small, and VTE-ing still occurs.

But such VTE's, as soon as they appear, are, I shall assume, a help. I shall suppose, in short, that each time the rat VTE's and looks at one or the other door there is some slight tendency for the effect of the correct hypotheses already forming to be reinforced. And since VTE-ing

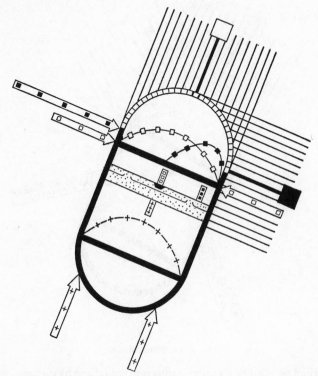

FIG. 14. Easy discrimination.

occurs more readily for the white-black group, this means that the white-black learning tends to be faster than this white-medium-gray learning. Figure 16 shows the situation later in learning. Here the positive and negative vectors have become very strong. They have overcome the imbalance of the orientation vectors. There is practically no VTE-ing, and the bug now progresses directly towards the positive (i.e., white) stimulus.

Another point about both figures 15 and 16 is very important. It will be noted that along the lower membrane of the progression tension I have tried to indicate the fact of increased permeabilities to the hypotheses which are being acquired. That is to say, as learning progresses the right-hand side of this membrane is conceived as becoming more and more permeable to the negative hypothesis and the left-hand side of the membrane as becoming more and more permeable to the positive hy-

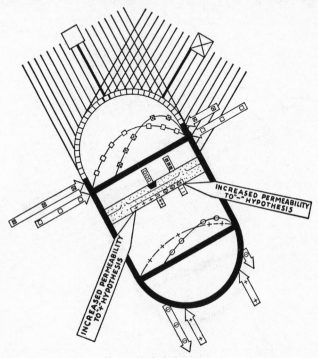

FIG. 15. Early in learning.

pothesis. The effect of learning is thus conceptualized by increases in the respective permeabilities to the two hypotheses.[4]

One last word. This schematic sowbug, however bizarre and silly it may appear, is of course in no important sense original. All its more essential characteristics have been proposed by others. I conceive it to

---

[4] Another and possibly better way to have conceived the bug might have been to have called the permeabilities the hypotheses and then to have called the resultant projecting columns not hypotheses, but progression needs. The height of the progression needs would then have been said to result from (a) the intensities of the general progression tension together with (b) the strengths of the corresponding hypotheses (i.e., the specific degrees of permeability, respectively, to plus progressions and to minus progressions).

be patterned very much after Lewin's psychological "person" as he draws such a person in a "life space" [6]. What I have done is to add to Lewin's diagram a nose and a tail and more specific receptor and motor mechanisms; I have also added the notion of spatially representing discriminable arrays of qualities as different angles in the "life space." And, of course, as I have already pointed out, it was from Loeb and Blum that I borrowed the notion of the manner of interconnection of these

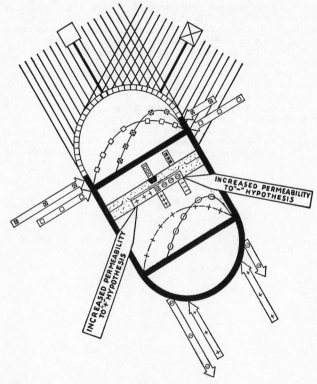

FIG. 16. Late in learning.

sensory and motor mechanisms according to the forced movement doctrine of tropisms. Again, it was from Spence [8]—though he may not like it—that the notion of the orientation and progression curves was taken. I have merely adapted Spence's generalization curves and put them inside my bug.

Finally, I wish to express my very great indebtedness to Mr. Clarke W.

Crannell for his help in designing some of the actual details of the bug and for making the photographs from which the above figures have been copied.

REFERENCES

1. Blum, H. F., E. J. Hyman, and P. Burdon, *Studies of oriented movements of animals in light fields.* Univ. Calif. Publ. Physiol., 8 (1936), 107–118.

2. Blum, H. F., "L'orientation du copépode 'Harpacticus Fulvus' sous l'influence de la lumière," *Archives Internationales de Physiologie,* 38 (1934), 1–8.

3. Blum, H. F., "Le mecanisme d'orientation de la larve de *Homarus vulgaris* sous l'influence de la lumière," *Bull. de L'institut Oceanographique,* 1934, no. 660.

4. Blum, H. F., "An analysis of oriented movements of animals in light fields." *Cold Springs Harbor Symposia on Quantitative Biology,* 3 (1935), 210–223.

5. Dennis, W., and R. W. Russell, Comments on recent studies of *VTE. J. Genet. Psychol.,* 54 (1939), 217–221.

6. Lewin, K., *A dynamic theory of personality.* New York: McGraw-Hill, 1935.

7. Muenzinger, K. F., "Vicarious trial and error at a point of choice: I. A general survey of its relation to learning efficiency," *J. Genet. Psychol.,* 53 (1938), 75–86.

8. Spence, K. W., "The differential response in animals to stimuli varying within a single dimension," *Psychol. Rev.,* 44 (1937), 430–444.

9. Tolman, E. C., "A behavioristic theory of ideas," *Psychol. Rev.,* 33 (1926), 352–369.

10. ———, *Purposive behavior in animals and men.* New York: Century, 1932.

11. ———, "The determiners of behavior at a choice point," *Psychol. Rev.,* 45 (1938), 1–41.

16

PSYCHOLOGICAL MAN

[*The Journal of Social Psychology*, FEBRUARY, 1941]

THERE HAS COME a frenzy in the tides of men. Social forces whose power we have not understood or, if we have understood, we have been helpless to control, have sucked us into a dark whirlpool. What, as psychologists, ought, or can, we say at such a time? The concepts of motivation, attitude, personality—these seem about all that we psychologists have to offer. And it must be confessed they do sound awfully barren, jejune, and too much a matter of mere individual behavior to be very heartening in the face of the all-powerful social currents which are sweeping us today. Yet we psychologists still have, I believe, the task and duty of seeing how far just such concepts can help us.

I

Consider the motives leading to war. Human beings both like war and hate and recoil from it. Under some conditions they do more of the former and under others more of the latter. Psychology and the other social sciences proceed to record these facts. And at first consideration it would seem that this is all that as mere sciences they can do. Thus, the Good, the *Summum Bonum,* to the psychologist, or to other social scientists, would seem to be merely that which the majority of the people want. And war is something which people both want and don't want or—perhaps better put—something which, at a given time, some individuals and some groups want and which at the same time, or at other times, other individuals and other groups hate. A psychologist can, it would seem, merely count noses, and, if in the long run, more noses seem to

Address of the Chairman, Society for the Psychological Study of Social Issues, September, 1940.

love the stench of war, it would seem that he can but conclude that wars always will be and must be.

But my contention is going to be that psychology as a study of motivation and personality structure does not really have to end with a mere counting of noses. Motivation is not so simple and atomistic an affair as is thus implied. We do not love and hate war as mere individuals but as components of larger groups with whom we have identified. Any analysis of war or of other large-scale social phenomena requires, then, an investigation of this matter of the individual's relation to a group and the motives emphasized by that group.

To adopt, then, this sociological point of view, human motives can and must, I believe, be reëvaluated into four different types of socially oriented subclasses, which, for lack of better names, I shall call respectively: the *id wants,* the *ego wants,* the *superego wants,* and the *enlarged ego wants.* Let me hasten to add, however, that I am not here proposing these terms *id, ego* and *superego* in precisely their original psychoanalytical meanings. The psychoanalytical meanings will however, I hope, help to suggest my meanings.

Consider, first, the *id wants.* Here I would group all the fundamental biological demands such as those for food, water, air, shelter, absence of pain, and sex. These are to be conceived as going off relatively independently of one another and as constituting by themselves a mere congeries of simultaneous or successive demands.

Consider, next, the *ego wants.* These I would conceive, in contrast, as built up through early training, and by virtue of the social mores to which the individual is subjected, upon the id wants. They differ from the id wants in that they are directed towards the self as a persisting whole. They are the prestige wants, the wants for personal strength and ability, and for personal domination. And normally they are ancillary to the id wants, for it is obvious that these goals of prestige, ability, and dominance will, generally speaking and in the long run, serve as means towards the better achievement of the id goals. That is, normally—in say, the young child—prestige, ability, and dominance seems to be primarily ways of obtaining better id goals. The child who stands out from his mates and who has especial strength and ability is one who tends to be better treated both by siblings and parents and hence gets better food and more love and less pain. It must be noted, however, that such a greater consummation of the id wants, at least in adults, need not always result from the attainment of the ego goals. Sometimes an "abnormal" social set-up may develop such that the ego goals of prestige and dominance result, not in the fulfillment, but in the crucifying of the id wants. The prestige of the religieux of the middle ages required sexual abstinence, fasting and, in general, the denial of the flesh rather than any enhanced satisfaction of the flesh.

Consider, next, the *superego wants*. These are, in a sense, just the opposite of the ego wants. A strongly developed superego demands that the individual submerge himself in the group—the family, the school, the political party, the gang, the economic class, the nation, the entire human race, or whatever it may be—with which he has identified. The superego wants are the selfless wants. But nevertheless, here, as also in the case of the ego wants, the normal result is an attainment of a greater satisfaction of the id wants. The superego, normally is thus also ancillary to the id. The child who develops a strong set of superego demands, who always tends to submerge his own prestige and dominance and his id satisfactions in those of the group, is also a child who may tend in the long run to be protected and secure—one whose fundamental id needs will tend to be looked after by its parents or in later life by parent-surrogates. But again, in some social set-ups this consummation of id wants as a result of the attainment of the superego goals does not result. In some social situations as, for example, in war the "good" individual— the "good" private in the ranks—is brought thereby not to the satisfaction of his id wants but to their wholesale crucifixion. The result as far as the id is concerned is not more life but death.

Further, it must again be stressed that not only the superego wants and the ego wants tend thus, on occasion, to conflict with the id wants out of which they both arise and relative to which they are normally both ancillary but they also almost invariably and inevitably conflict one with the other. The ego wants demand that the individual have prestige, that he stand out from the group. The superego wants demand just the opposite—that the individual submerge himself in the group and renounce his individual prestige.

Finally, let us turn to what I am calling the *enlarged ego wants*. By the enlarged ego I refer to a further feature involved in an individual's adherence to and identification with a group. He who identifies with a group not only tends to develop a strong superego in the sense of being ready to sacrifice many of his id wants and his primary ego wants for the welfare of that group, but also acquires a compensating enlarged ego. This enlarged ego he equates with the group. The successes and failures of the latter become *his* successes and failures. And when there are successes these come in large measure to compensate for and assuage the privations demanded of his primary ego and of his id. Thus, for example, we are told that the feudal serf compensated vicariously not only in the glory and prestige of his lord but also in the latter's superior food, drink, and shelter.

Let me sum up, now, this account of the four classes of wants and their interrelationships by eight statements, as follows:

1) A congeries of biologically determined id wants is fundamental and the original source of all wants. (2) The primary ego wants, i.e., those for prestige and dominance of the self, are built up upon the id wants and tend in a "normal" childhood and in a "healthy" social order to lead to increased satisfaction of the id wants. (3) In some set-ups, however, this may not occur. In some social orders the achievement of the ego satisfaction may actually lead to the denial, rather than to the fulfillment, of the id wants and yet the ego wants may continue in control to a surprising degree. (4) The superego wants for submission to, and the approval of, the group also are originally built up upon the id wants. The subservient child or party member or patriot is in a normal and "healthy" family or political party or nation rewarded therefor. (5) But here again such an outcome does not always materialize. In some set-ups of the social order the achievement of the superego wants of submission and docility may result in the sacrifice of most or, in the extreme case, even of all of the id satisfactions; and yet these superego wants continue in control. (6) It appears, further, that not only may the ego wants and the superego wants conflict with the id wants to which they are normally ancillary but they may also, and almost inevitably do, conflict with one another. For, obviously, not all the members of the group can simultaneously belong to the élite. If one is to submit to the group, one cannot usually also dominate the group. (7) Further, there develops through the identification with the group an expanded or enlarged ego. This enlarged ego has as its goal the prestige and success of the group with which the individual has identified. (8) Finally, such satisfactions of the enlarged ego can often come to compensate in large measure for the deprivation of most of the primary ego wants and of many of the id wants.

II

My thesis from here on is going to be that the above classification of motives becomes a practical and useful frame of reference not only for describing and comparing the motivational structures of different individuals but also for comparing the motivational structures of different social orders.

And as a fundamental step in the application of the above analysis to social orders I shall invoke the descriptive evaluations of Western society presented by Drucker in an article in *Harpers* and in a recent book, both entitled *The End of Economic Man* [1, 2].

Drucker contends that since Christianity, western Europe has been dominated successively by some three or four "ideas" or concepts as to the best way in which individual happiness and welfare can be obtained. Each of these concepts, which I shall call myths, has held up a certain type of man—a certain way of life—as the ideal and has assumed that, if this ideal can be achieved, individual happiness and welfare will result. One of the last of these myths—the one which has just begun to lose its force for the masses in this country and which has already, according to Drucker, lost practically all of its force for the masses in Europe (except in Russia)—is the myth of the Economic Man. It is the myth which is held by both capitalists and socialists. It is the myth that the economic satisfactions are the only important ones and that, if these can be universally achieved, either through free competition as predicated by the protagonists of capitalism or through social ownership of the tools of production as predicated by the protagonists of socialism, then all the other good things of human life—that is, human welfare and human happiness in general—will also inevitably result. To quote:

Every organized society is built upon a concept of the nature of man and of his function and place in society. Whatever its truth as a picture of human nature, this concept always gives a true picture of the nature of the society which recognizes and identifies itself with it. It symbolizes the fundamental tenets and beliefs of society by showing the sphere of human activity which it regards as socially decisive and supreme. The concept of man as an "economic animal" is the true symbol of the societies of bourgeois capitalism and of Marxist socialism, which see in the free exercise of man's economic activity the means toward the realization of their aims. Economic satisfactions alone appear socially important and relevant. Economic position, economic privileges, and economic rights are those for which man works. For these he wages war, and for these he is prepared to die. All others seem mere hypocrisy, snobbism, or romantic nonsense [2, p. 45].

But prior to this myth of Economic Man there have dominated since Christianity two other concepts which Drucker designates, respectively, as the idea, i.e., the myth, of Spiritual Man, and the idea or myth of Intellectual Man. And, finally, there is now just appearing or there has already appeared in the fascist countries the myth of Heroic Man.

My thesis is, now, that each of these successive myths is really equivalent to a set of propositions concerning the relative importance to be allotted to the satisfaction of id wants, ego wants, superego wants, and enlarged ego wants.

Consider, first, the myth of Spiritual Man and the Christian era which attempted to live by it. This, I hold, was a myth and an era in which the primary importance of the superego values was predicated. Christianity was a society which officially and for the average man preached the prime importance of loyalty and self-sacrifice. But these are the superego values. If each person obeyed the Golden Rule, turned the other cheek, and loved his neighbor as himself, and submerged himself for the glory of God, then individual happiness and welfare, it was asserted, must accrue to all.

But such a truly Christian society could not be maintained indefinitely. The attempt to make such a way of life the rule for all produced a type of social order which was necessarily unstable. For it meant the constant suppression of id wants and of primary ego wants. Also it was inevitable that in the élite the primary ego wants should expand at the expense of the publicly preached superego wants. But any society in which some wants are too suppressed and in which the élite obviously lead a different psychological life from that constantly preached by them to the masses is bound sooner or later to break down. The impingment of any new technological or external social force which suggests some new way, some new possibility, of life will lead to the myth's downfall. In late Christian society the masses were continually tempted to indulge, and the leaders actually did indulge, the sins of gluttony and self-indulgence, on the one hand, and those of personal pride, vainglory, on the other. That is, they constantly fell into the temptation of satisfying their ids and their primary egos. Hence with the fall of Constantinople and the spread of the wisdom of the ancients, Christian society was all ready to accept a new way of life. The ego demands could be gainsaid no longer and the intelligentsia and the upper classes grasped at the new possibilities for satisfying their primary egos.

Philosophy and the arts once again flourished. The Renaissance and Reformation came and with them a new myth—that of Intellectual Man. This new myth was that of the prime importance of ego wants. But once again the resulting society was unstable. For the fulfillment of the ego wants was possible only among the intellectually and artistically favored and the economically secure. It was not a way of life which could be experienced by all classes; and so the Renaissance in its turn was ready to fall as soon as internal or external forces suggested still another possibility of life.

And in this case the new way came from within. For, in the course of the Renaissance, Intellectual Man gave birth to science and laid the beginnings of the industrial revolution. And the industrial revolution brought it about that a relatively widespread and deepened satisfaction of id wants was made possible. The id no longer had to be sacrificed either to the superego as in Christianity or to the ego as in the Renaissance and the Reformation, but could at last come into it own and with this coming into its own there appeared the new myth of Economic Man. Industry, thrift, private investment could now, it was felt, bring material welfare to all. That is, the myth declared that as soon as all should have enough food, shelter, and sex and each man obeyed his own "enlightened self-interest"—that is, as soon as the id was not abandoned but it and the primary ego worked together—then all would live happily forever after. Whether it was that the prince would marry the beggar maid and thus make possible the satisfaction of her id wants, or the noble lord would marry the daughter of an American industrialist and make possible once again the satisfaction of his lordship's id wants, or whether you and I and the next man would all join in a Socialist Utopia by sleeping in a joint house, eating from a joint kitchen and giving free rein to our love for the other sex, freed from distorting notions of property rights, the myth was the same. It was the myth that the id wants and the primary ego wants built upon them are enough.

But, as Drucker has argued, this myth is one which has now also already lost its force or is fast losing it. But why? Its goals are now technologically possible. Enough material production could now, at least in America, be achieved so that, if goods were properly distributed, beggar maids could all become, or better, be born, princesses, noble lords could all find rich wives, and all of us could communistically share food, drink, and sex, flatter our respective egos and have plenty left to go around.

But western Europe has abandoned or is abandoning this goal just as the last steps towards its final consummation seemed about to be realized. There must, then, have been some fundamental weakness inherent in this myth also. And that weakness was, as I see it, that in modern society the attempt to satisfy the id wants and the primary ego wants left the superego wants and the enlarged ego wants almost wholly neglected. The ruling classes because of their strong primary and restricted class egos would not give up their perquisites so that the ids and primary egos of the masses could be equally satisfied. The two hundred families put their own interests first as did also the French labor leaders, and France went under at the first blow of foreign invasion. Id wants and primary ego wants had been preached so strongly at the expense of the superego goals of loyalty and self-sacrifice that cooperative action became impossible. And human beings crave to be loyal and to perform self-sacrifices just as much as they crave food, drink, sex, and individual prestige.

Democratic Italy and Germany, and after them, Spain, Norway, Holland, Belgium, and France all collapsed for fundamentally the same reasons. All were ready for the appearance of strong men—dictators, i.e., father surrogates—relative to whom the superego wants could again find satisfaction. The myth of Heroic Man came into its own. This myth differs from that of Economic Man in that it reinstates once again the importance of self-sacrifice, submission to the group. The id satisfactions are not, however, completely denied (as they were in early Christianity) largely, of course, because of our present greater technological sufficiency. They are, however, to be kept at a low level. The common man will have a job and security even though his level of subsistence will be reduced. But, more importantly, he is once again assured that his sacrifices are for the sake of some larger whole. Once again he that loseth all is promised all. Furthermore, this time he is promised it not in some merely future life, as in Christianity, but here and now in the success, the glory, and the prestige of his earthly group. His enlarged ego as well as his superego is to be rewarded superabundantly. He is to be an integral part of some all-conquering super race which shall gloriously survive on this earth. This, of course, is a horrible doctrine to those of us who are outside the conquering group, but it is a glorious and heartening one to those who are among the chosen.

III

What, then, of the future? Will the myth of Heroic Man also go under? Yes, I assert that it will.[1] It cannot persist for two reasons: The first reason is that it requires ever-continuing group successes. The private in the ranks will not continually forego most of his id satisfactions and all of his primary ego satisfactions unless he be continually compensated by the ever-renewed success of the larger group—i.e., unless the satisfactions of his enlarged ego continuously make up to him for the deprivations of his id and of his primary ego. Hence when the group as a whole fails of new successes, either because the other opposing groups do not finally go under or they do go under and hence there are no new fields to conquer, there is bound to be internal collapse. The frustration of their ids and of their primary egos suffered by the masses will lead to aggression against the élite who have deprived them.

And the second reason why this myth of the Heroic Man cannot

---

[1] Drucker himself emphasizes that the myth of Heroic Man is but a straw at which the masses have grasped while waiting for some new and more abundant myth to appear.

persist forever is that in this case also the élite do not, and in fact cannot, practice what they preach. They do not and cannot suffer the same id deprivations and primary ego deprivations which they impose upon the masses. Neither do they, or can they, practice quite the same intensity of subordination to the group—i.e., quite the same intensity of superego satisfactions which they preach to the masses. Perhaps the original leaders—the Hitlers and the Mussolinis—do and can work permanently for the success of the group. The Hitlers and the Mussolinis are, however, peculiar. They are driven by childhood and adolescent inferiorities. They can compensate only by the successes of the groups with which they have identified. But the second generation of leaders, who are now being trained, will not be so driven. They will not have started from nothing. They will have been early adopted into the élite. And the greater primary id satisfactions and primary ego satisfactions possible to the élite will sooner or later corrupt them. They will come to think not in terms of the group but in terms solely of their primary selves and of their narrow class.

Granted then that Fascism will sooner or later break down—that the myth of Heroic Man is doomed—can we predict what the new myth, which will follow it, must be? Perhaps we cannot. Perhaps there *is* nothing in the bare logic of events to tell us what shall and must succeed. Two relatively immediate possibilities seem to me, however, possible. On the one hand, all we may perhaps expect is another Dark Ages—a complete breakdown in civilization as thus far known—a future some such as that depicted in H. G. Wells' *Things to Come*. On the other hand, there is a second possibility which, if certain forces which we can now descry in our midst are strong enough, can and will come. I wish to suggest this latter possibility.

IV

The forces which, as I see it, will bring this second result are the forces resulting this time, not from an industrial revolution, but from a psychological revolution—the revolution in which Freud is the outstanding name. If these forces are strong enough, then the new myth will be that of Harmonious Man or, if I dare say it, of Psychological Man.

The social order which adopted this myth of Psychological Man would be one in which all four sets of wants—the id wants, the primary ego wants, the superego wants, and the enlarged ego wants—would all be brought into harmony with one another and all granted reasonable amounts of satisfaction in both the masses and the élite. Both the common man and the leader would be consciously aware of all their needs.

Particularly the leaders would be made conscious of what it was all about. They, the more intelligent, the more trainable, would be taught to be constantly on the lookout that their primary ego wants and their enlarged ego wants did not run away with their superego needs. They would be taught always and in some measure to submerge and sacrifice themselves for the good of the group.

The id demands of all could be satisfied because of modern technology. In fact, even one of the most economically conservative among us admitted it would now be possible to provide a car in every garage and a chicken in every pot. The difficulty to date has been that of distribution. But this difficulty, as I believe and as Drucker suggests, will disappear when we no longer have the myth that the id wants and the primary ego wants are solely important. These latter will tend to be rewarded once we have become less focused upon them. If the leaders but shift their emphasis from the id to the rational and coöperative whole—if we can but imbue our children, not with the goal of getting rich, but with that of being rational and internally and externally coöperative human beings—the problem of the distribution of material goods will no longer be a problem but a straightforward task upon which leaders and led will naturally coöperate.

The primary ego satisfactions of the masses will also have to be satisfied. That is, each common man, however humble his abilities, must be given some feeling of his own individual success and some degree of resulting primary prestige. But this, I believe, will be possible with the development and spread of the modern psychology of abilities and traits. Clinics, vocational guidance centers, schools, even institutions for the feeble-minded are already accomplishing wonders in this direction. Pleasure, success, prestige in doing some task well is, I am confident, a possible goal for everyone. When we no longer preach that the individual must be better than everybody else in all things, but preach, rather, the goal of internal coöperation of his own wants and abilities, then prestige will come to each not from being better than all others but in being the very best that he himself can be.

The superego satisfactions of sacrifice also will be provided for both the masses and the élite by all sorts of vocational groups and place groups in which the individual can immerse himself and relative to which he will be willing to give up some of his primary ego demands. But, and here we come back again to the question of war, these larger groups must (and will) finally stop not at a nation, a class, a race, whose final and all-consuming competition is with the other nations, classes, races, but with the idea of humanity as a whole with which the individual must identify.

That is, our enlarged ego satisfactions will also have to be satisfied, but these satisfactions will have to come primarily in our identification with humanity and not from our identification solely with mere narrower groups as such. We must not preach American against Germans, against Europeans, against Asiatics, against Africans, but all humanity against nature, against disease and misery and ignorance—against battle, murder, and sudden death. Our violent aggressions—our wars—will then occur not between one group and another but between the whole of humanity and hostile nature.

v

But you will ask, finally, how are we to implement any such Utopia? How are we, as social psychologists, to make our desire for it actually bring it about, I know but one answer—*education*. And by education I mean what goes on in the nursery school and in the home, in secondary schools and in colleges, in trades unions and in chambers of commerce, in *CCC* camps and in our selective military training camps, in our churches and in the market place, in pressure groups and in Congress. In all these institutions we must have everlasting teaching and propaganda always in the direction of the harmonious balancing in all classes of the id satisfactions, the ego satisfactions, the superego satisfactions, and the enlarged ego satisfactions.

Our present society is going under. The myth of Economic Man has disappeared or is just disappearing. The myth of Heroic Man has come. But it also is going to disappear. And we here in America have perhaps still time to combat this myth of Heroic Man, not through adopting it ourselves—that will be our ever-constant danger—but only, if (now that technology has been solved), we see to it that this technology be used not merely in the name of America and the American way of life but in the name of a human, a psychologically informed, way of life. Then our aggressions which we shall still have and shall still enjoy will take themselves out not against our fellow men but against disease and starvation and maladjustment. We shall fight primarily not against the Nazis and the Hitlers abroad but always and simultaneously here at home against the myth which they symbolize.

Aggression, which is a combination of id and ego drives, will not disappear. But the sort of aggression which ends in violence (and which, as Professor Stratton has pointed out,[2] is the only sort of aggression which we really want to get rid of) will disappear because, whatever our narrower groups, we will also all be members of a larger total human com-

---

[2] George M. Stratton. *Science News Letter*, July 27, 1940, pp. 54 f.

munity and the enemy of that latter group will be nature and not other human beings.

Finally, it is obvious that if this education for the new order, that is, for Psychological Man, is really ever going to prevail, it can do so only if there also appears some corresponding new emotional dynamic behind it—some new religion to push and to force it. And this new religion will have to be as strong as the religion of simple nationalism that is behind the myth of Heroic Man or the simple Protestant religion of enlightened self-interest and direct communication with God that was behind the early myth of Economic Man. But where is such a new religion—such a new set of symbols and slogans to be found—that will emotionally put across our education for Psychological Man? I confess that I do not at present clearly descry any such a religion. I feel, however, that it will have to be some combination and balancing and adding together of the old religions. It must be a nationalism, but a nationalism which declares that one's own nation is better when other nations are also strong. It must be a religion of individual salvation, but one in which the salvation of the other fellow is just as necessary as one's own salvation. It must be a religion of self-sacrifice, but one in which self-sacrifice brings butter and guns (if the latter must be) not merely to ourselves but to others also.

VI

This would be my Utopia, and the sermon I would try to preach, though Utopias and sermons are, I realize, inexcusable in such a company as this. But our fellow human beings today all over the world are giving up their lives in the name of new loyalties. And, if we psychologists here in America don't preach our own sermons, we shall be caught by theirs. If we don't say our say, not merely as to how to detect and measure and tabulate social change, but as to what good social changes would be, then we shall deserve no better fate than the one which otherwise undoubtedly lies in store for us. America will have to be not only a surviving America, but also a New America. For, if it be not a New America, it will not survive.

REFERENCES

1. Drucker, P. F., "The end of economic man in Europe," *Harp. Mo.*, 178 (1939), 561–570.
2. ———, *The end of economic man*, New York: Day, 1939.

17

A DRIVE-CONVERSION DIAGRAM

[*Psychological Review*, SEPTEMBER, 1943]

THE PRESENT PAPER[1] is an attempt to schematize the interconnections between the basic biological drives, the derived social techniques and also between these and certain types of final behavior-propensity. Such interconnections I shall call "conversion channels." That is to say, I shall conceive that the original energy from the basic biological drives gets "converted" (when these biological drives are frustrated) first into the auxiliary social techniques and, finally (if these latter be also frustrated), into other still more derived behavior propensities.

The scheme here to be presented was developed originally in an attempt to analyze the motivational causes of *war*.[2] For that reason the discussion is somewhat limited as to range. Nevertheless, the general principles evolved have, I believe, some general validity—that, in fact, they throw some new light upon the whole problem of motivation.

Table 1 shows the list of biological drives which I would assume. Practically every item in this list can be identified in terms of some well-known animal experiment (or field observation). Further, the items have been grouped under the two headings: the *appetites* and the *aversions*. The appetites are to be conceived as set going primarily by internal metabolic conditions and as ended by the reaching of positive

---

[1] This paper was written to be presented as part of a Round Table on Recent Advances in Motivation under the auspices of the National Institute of Psychology at the meetings of the American Psychological Association, September 3, 1942, but because of the war emergency these meetings had to be cancelled.

[2] Cf. E. C. Tolman, *Drives toward war*. New York: Appleton-Century, 1942. The writer wishes to acknowledge his indebtedness to the D. Appleton-Century Company for permission to reprint the tables and figures presented here.

goal objects; whereas the aversions are conceived as set going primarily by actual or potential environmental presences and ended by the avoidance of such presences. It may also be noted, in passing, that (perhaps

TABLE 1
THE BIOLOGICAL DRIVES

A. *The Appetites*
    Hunger drive
    Thirst drive
    Sex drive
    Maternal (suckling of young) drive
    Nurturance (giving aid and protection) drive
    Infantile-dependence drive
    Nest-building and nest-using drive
    General-activity drive
    General-exploratory or curiosity drive
    Rest-and-sleep drive
    Elimination drive (urination and defecation in specific types of locale)
    Play and aesthetic drives

B. *The Aversions*
    Fright (injury avoidance)
    Aggression (obstruction avoidance)
    Gregariousness (isolation avoidance)

somewhat unorthodoxly) I have included the "play" and "aesthetic" drives among the basic appetites and simple gregariousness (i.e., the avoidance of isolation from the group) among the basic aversions.

Table 2 presents a list of what I would call the principal derived social drives (or social techniques). I prefer the term techniques to that of drives because I wish to emphasize the essentially instrumental or ancillary character of these social propensities. Their primary function is to be instrumental to the more basic biological drives. And they are

TABLE 2
THE SOCIAL DRIVES OR TECHNIQUES

A. *Self-Assertive Techniques*
    Establishing dominance status
    Competitive acquisition
    Demanding and soliciting food
    Succorance (demanding aid and protection)

B. *Collective Techniques*
    Imitation
    Mutual assistance (grooming)
    Coöperative work

C. *Self-Abasive Techniques*
    Submitting (accepting nondominance status and withdrawing from competition)
    Giving (in response to solicitation)

D. *Collective Assertive Techniques*
    Loyalty to group (attack on enemies of group)

undoubtedly more a result of experience and of learning than are the biological drives. Again all the individual items in the list can be spotted in terms of well-known animal field observations or experiments—this time, primarily observations or experiments upon monkeys or chimpanzees. Further, it is to be noted that the items have been grouped under the four headings of: (*A*) *Self-Assertive Techniques,* (*B*) *Collective Techniques,* (*C*) *Self-Abasive Techniques* and (*D*) *Collective Assertive Techniques.* This grouping corresponds, I believe, to certain real internal coherencies. That is to say, each subgroup of techniques tends, I would believe, to hang together in a considerable degree and to become strong or weak as a whole for given individuals in given situations.

Turn, now, to figure 1. This figure indicates the position and character of the routes or "conversion-channels" through which, as I conceive it, the energy from the basic biological drives gets converted (when these biological drives are frustrated) first into the social techniques and ultimately, if these latter be frustrated, into various other still more derived behavior propensities. That is to say, the arrows in the figure represent such channels. And the words enclosed in the dashed rectangles mounted on these arrows indicate those psychological mechanisms which I would conceive to be causatively operative in producing such channels. These mechanisms consist of "instrumental learning" and of various ones of the Freudian dynamisms.

Examining the details, we observe that, when the biological drives are frustrated, what I conceive as first happening is that the energy from these biological drives gets converted into either self-assertive techniques or into collective techniques—sometimes more into the one and sometimes more into the other. In both types of conversion the mechanisms which are causative in determining the channels are those of *learning* and of *fixation*. That is to say, the frustrated child or chimpanzee *learns* either to be self-assertive or to be collective because, in the given situation, the one or the other type of technique proves to be the more helpful in removing his biological frustrations. And then, secondly, the dynamism of *fixation* tends to come into play and to cause the particular conversion channel to become relatively rigid and enduring. That is to say, the child or chimpanzee tends to persist in being self-assertive, or in being collective, even in new situations in which such respective techniques are no longer appropriate. This would be Allport's "functional autonomy."

If we look now at the left-hand side of the figure. we see indicated there that, when the self-assertive techniques are themselves frustrated, their energy may get further converted, through *identification with*

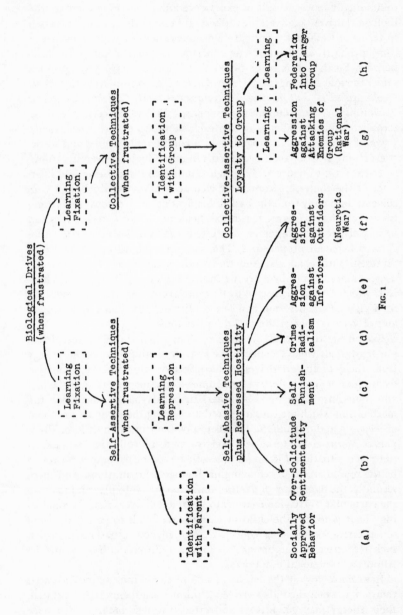

FIG. 1

the parent into *a,* the final behavior propensity of socially acceptable behaviors, or through *instrumental learning* accompanied by *repression* into the self-abasive techniques. Let us consider this latter possibility further. These self-abasive techniques are conceived as achieved only by an accompanying repression of the hostility against the frustrating parents or other dominating agents. But this repressed hostility then tends to come out, in its turn, in a variety of *indirect* ways such as *b* to *f* listed along the bottom of the figure, that is to say, in ways such as: *b,* oversolicitude and sentimentality; *c,* self-punishment; *d,* crime and radicalism; *e,* aggression against inferiors; and *f,* aggression against outsiders. These different behavior propensities each occurs, however, only as a result of its own special conversion channel. And each such conversion channel is to be conceived as determined in its turn by a specific dynamism or dynamisms. There was not room, however, in figure 1 to indicate the character of these latter.

Figure 2 presents, therefore, an enlargement of that area of the scheme projecting downward from self-abasement and the accompanying repressed hostility. We see now that it is the dynamism of *reaction formation* which I assume to be responsible for the channel whereby the repressed hostility gets converted into *b,* oversolicitude or sentimentality. And it is the dynamism of *introjection* which I conceive to be responsible for the conversion channel leading to *c,* self-punishment. Similarly, it is the dynamism of *symbolization* which is conceived as mostly responsible for the channel leading to *d,* hostility against parent surrogates, that is to say, to crime and what we may call *neurotic* radicalism. Further, it is the dynamism of *displacement* which is conceived as mostly responsible for the conversion channel leading to *e,* aggression against inferiors. And, finally, it is the two dynamisms of *identification with the group* and of *projection* which are conceived to be primarily responsible for the channel leading to *f,* aggressions against outsiders; i.e., to *neurotically* motivated war. It is not to be supposed, however, that the actions of these dynamisms are necessarily mutually exclusive. Thus the dynamism of symbolization is probably also involved to some extent in all of the five different conversion channels and not merely in that which leads to crime and radicalism. And so, no doubt, some of the other dynamisms, such as displacement, may be said to be involved in all of the conversion channels.

Let us return now to figure 1, and observe the right-hand side of the diagram. Here is indicated what I suppose to happen when, and insofar as, the energy from the frustrated biological drives gets converted, not into the self-assertive techniques, but into the collective techniques. The

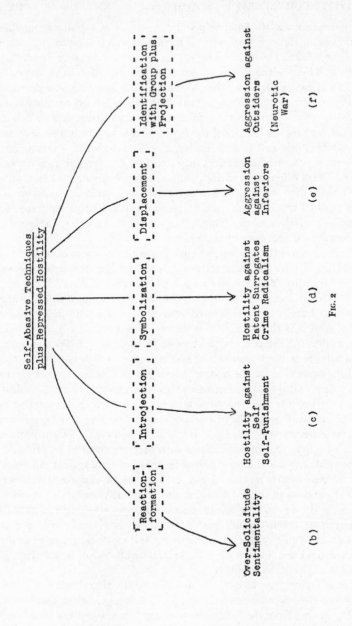

Fig. 2

diagram indicates, that is, that when the collective techniques them-selves are interfered with, or frustrated, then the dynamism of *identifica-tion with the group* may be expected to come into play and to provide a conversion channel through which the energy from the frustrated collective techniques gets converted into the collective assertive tech-niques (namely, into loyalty to the group). But, further, this loyalty to the group may then through *learning* come to express itself, *g,* in planned attacks against interfering outsiders; i.e., in *war*. But, in this case, the war can be deemed relatively rational by contrast to that listed over *f,* which was, as we saw, merely an outlet (through *projection* and *group identification*) for repressed hostilities. Or, secondly, this loyalty to the group may also, I believe (although here I may be leaving the role of the psychologist for that of the preacher), come through *learning* to be converted into: *h,* the behavior of federating with the opposing groups, thus producing some still larger group within which the original oppositions can be resolved. That is to say, such a new conversion channel leading to the behavior of federating will, I assert, be established as soon as mankind discovers, i.e., *learns,* that wars are a surprisingly inefficient way of preserving the continued existence of group life—even the group life of the victors.

Summing up, there are certain general points to be made. First, I should like to emphasize that even though this drive-conversion diagram may be both somewhat superficial and incorrect as to detail and even though its resultant explanation of the two types of motive for war may be wrong, I do believe that it provides a useful and essentially correct way of conceiving the interdependence between the more basic and the more derived motives. The basic energy comes from the biological drives. The social drives or techniques are secondary motives which are derived from the biological ones—partly through innate endowment and partly as a result of instrumental learning. And such social drives or techniques are to be conceived as themselves interconnected in various ways as a result of learning and of the dynamisms. And from these social techniques (when these in their turn are frustrated) there are derived such further behavior propensities as are listed at the bottom of the diagram.

Secondly, the particular outcomes shown are but a few examples of the possible directions of conversion which might occur. If, for example, I had started out with an interest not in war but in, say, the activity of "getting ahead" in America, the channels leading from the self-assertive techniques would have to have been multiplied many times to indicate all the specific varieties of getting ahead, which tend to get set up in different individuals in our society.

Thirdly, I should like to point out that, in treating the biological drives as a unit and the self-assertive techniques as another unit and the self-abasive, the collective, and the collective-assertive techniques as still other units, I have undoubtedly oversimplified and blurred the concrete facts. Thus, for example, whether self-assertion or collectivity gets learned may well depend in some part upon which particular biological drive it is which has been frustrated. And, again, whether self-abasement or *identification with parent* follows (in the case of frustrated self-assertion) may also depend in part upon which specific expression of self-assertion it was which was frustrated. And, similarly, the particular indirect expression of frustrated hostility which comes out may also depend in part on the particular subvariety of self-abasement which was involved. And so on. In other words, the point I am making here is that the conversion channels should be conceived as running more from specific to specific and less from biological drives in general, to self-assertive drives in general, etc. Certainly the Freudian discussions suggest that the libido cathexes are relatively specific affairs. Nevertheless, I still believe that in some sense my grouping of all biological drives into one unit (of course Freud himself did this with the id), all self-assertive techniques into another unit, all collective techniques into another, and all collective assertive techniques into still another, has some real social and psychological validity.

A fourth point, which needs more elaboration than I have given it, concerns the nature of the conversion channel itself. A conversion channel, as I am conceiving it, is really a two-sided affair. (1) On the one hand, it is, as I have already emphasized, a route for the converting of energy, or tension, or libido, or drive force (or whatever you want to call it) from the original drive or behavior propensity (when the latter is frustrated) to some other dependent drive or behavior propensity. But (2), on the other hand, a conversion channel is also in the nature of a "belief" by the organism to the effect that the carrying out of the derived drive, or behavior-propensity, is a "means" toward the achievement of the goals of the original drive or propensity. It is now, no doubt, this latter, or "belief" side, of the conversion channel against which *your* repressed (or maybe unrepressed) hostilities will be mostly directed. In support, however, of *my* belief that such a "belief" quality is in truth to be ascribed to conversion channels, let me cite the fact that new behavior propensities tend to be abandoned when they do not prove to contribute to the original goals. Conversion channels are, that is to say, to a considerable extent "docile" and adjustive relative to the ultimate outcomes. There is, to be sure, only a tendency towards such docility. Particularly is this property of docility only a tendency when the conversion channel is a result of a dynamism rather than of learning. Thus, for example, the "taking it out on inferiors" (as a way of getting even with one's parents) tends to persist even though not really successful. You may feel, in short, that the interconnection between the original "getting even" and this derived "taking it out on inferiors" is not properly to be called a belief at all. Yet the psychoanalysts would tell us that, when they analyze such individuals, there is some sense in which the unconscious of the patient does contain just such childish beliefs. The dynamisms do seem, in short, to be expressions of childish modes of thinking (i.e., believing). Furthermore, insofar as a conversion channel is to be conceived as a belief it has the two accompanying properties of (1) being more or less correct and (2) of being more or less "docile" and susceptible to correction as a result of changes in the actual environmental realities.

To sum it all up, then, as regards the conversion channel. The latter is, as I conceive it: (1) a route or channel through which energy or tension or libido gets transmitted from one drive or behavior propensity to another. It is also (2) a belief, that the consummation of the derived behavior propensity will contribute to the reaching of the goal of the original behavior propensity. (3) This belief may be relatively true or false. And (4) it may be more or less docile and ready to change, if it be false. If a conversion channel is primarily a result of learning, it will be relatively docile and reasonable; whereas, if it is primarily a result of a dynamism, it will be relatively insensitive and childlike.

Finally, it must be noted that I have left practically untouched the fundamental problem of why in a particular instance learning, or particular dynamisms, do or do not appear. Why, say, does one individual go in for "introjection" and resulting self-punishment whereas another (with the same repressed hostilities) goes in for "displacement" and taking it out on inferiors? Or, again, what are the conditions which determine the learning of self-assertiveness in the one case and the learning of collectivity in the other? And what are the factors, internal and external—i.e., of nature and of nurture—which favor (or prevent) easy identification with parents? And so on. Neither the Freudians nor anybody else can, as yet, give us adequate answers. Nobody really knows in detail how (or how much) heredity works, nor how (or how much) different types of environmental condition are active in producing learning or in favoring the operation of particular dynamisms.

As a last word, then, I would state frankly that such a drive-conversion diagram, as that presented, would still be (even if it were correct and final—which obviously it is not) a scheme more for the asking of important questions than for the presenting of final answers.

18

A STIMULUS-EXPECTANCY NEED-CATHEXIS
PSYCHOLOGY

[*Science,* FEBRUARY 16, 1945]

AT THE TIME I sent in the peculiar title of this paper[1] obviously I was
suffering from mental obfuscation. However, in the intervening four or
five months my mind has had time, I hope, to clear. In fact, I now seem
actually to have discovered what the paper is to be about and to have
invented a quite normal title for it, to wit: "The Contribution of Rats
to Human Psychology."

In other words, what I really want to talk about is the simple, though
somewhat hackneyed, subject of the contribution of rat experiments to
the understanding of human behavior. It would seem that the ultimate
goal of all psychologists (even of rat psychologists) is the explanation of
the behavior of human beings. It appears further, however, that those
of you, among us, who have concentrated primarily on human beings
have become increasingly aware (as the psychologists of thirty or even
twenty years ago were not) that human behavior takes place only in
social contexts. You human-oriented psychologists have begun reading
(and perhaps even *inventing*) bits of anthropology and sociology. As a
result, you have finally become convinced that men are not born, like
Athena, full-grown and all-armored but, rather, as naked babes who
begin acquiring their armor at their mothers' breasts, in the alarms and
excursions of toilet training and in the give and take of sibling rivalries.

Now this has produced a real revolution in all our thinking—even in
that of us rat psychologists. But, unfortunately, it seems also to have led

---

[1] Address of the vice-president of Section I, American Association for the Advance-
ment of Science, Cleveland, Ohio, September 12, 1944.

to some tendency (or perhaps I am merely oversensitive) on the part of you human psychologists now to look down, or rather up, your noses at us poor animal psychologists whom you seem to descry as still left hanging uncomfortably out on the limb—that is, on the good old philogenetic limb. And we animal psychologists (being very suggestible) actually begin to feel quite hang-dog about it all ourselves and we too begin trying to look snootily down (or up) our own noses at our own selves hanging by our own tails out on that same good old limb. But this I, for one, am finding a very uncomfortable position. Hence, the main purpose of this paper is to try to justify that limb to myself and to try to get myself right side up on it as rapidly, and with as much circumspection, as possible.

To return, now, to the new insight that human behavior is always behavior in a social, or culture, context, what have we animal psychologists left to do? The primates (that is, the chimpanzees and monkeys among us) have not been too hard hit. They have rapidly shifted their attention from problems of learning and insight to such problems as social dominance and submission; coöperation in work activities; a pair of chimpanzees mutually picking off one another's fleas; the sexual cycle of the female ape and how the different stages of her genital swelling affect the food generosity or the food stinginess of her accompanying male; chimpanzees raised by human parents, and human babies raised by chimpanzee parents. Oh, no, I forgot. This last has not yet been tried. But it undoubtedly will be (although the folklore seems to prefer the she-wolf as the mother image) by intention, or by default, if the world continues killing off human mothers at its present rate.

So much, then, for the primate psychologists; but what are we poor rodents to do? What can we contribute to the problems of human behavior, always enmeshed (as the latter is now so clearly seen to be) in the situations set by specific cultures and by specific social groupings? Our only comeback would seem to be that, whereas rats must be admitted to have very little social life and absolutely no culture, there are certain basic laws and principles which can still be studied more conveniently and with just as much validity in rats as in men.

But, first, let us consider further the nature of the new insights as to human behavior. Basically, these are merely the realization that every adequate description and every quantified rating of any aspect of human behavior must always involve and refer to a particular cultural milieu. For example, psychologists no longer conceive of I.Q.'s *per se* and abstracted from given cultural set-ups. Rather, they now realize that any given intelligence rating is always derived from performance with re-

spect to the particular goals of a particular culture—goals with respect
to which the individual in question has been reared and relative to
which he now has to perform. Similarly, psychologists no longer think
(or so I hope) of motivation *per se* but always of motivation with respect
to those particular types of means-end layout provided by a particular
society. Or, to take a final example, psychologists no longer consider
emotional stability or its inverse emotional instability as something
purely biological but rather as an entity which has final meaning only
when defined by the norms and values of a going social group. For a
man is emotionally stable or unstable not in a vacuum but by reference
to the specific values which his culture prescribes. Thus, to have
catalepticlike trances was (we are told by Ruth Benedict) highly *de
rigeur* on the part of women who would become shamans among the
Shasta Indians in California. By having such seizures they then become
counsellors of great power and importance. To quote: "It is clear that,
far from regarding cataleptic seizures as blots upon the family escutcheon
and as evidences of dreaded disease, cultural approval had seized upon
them and made them the pathway to authority over one's fellows. They
were the outstanding characteristic of the most respected social type, the
type which functioned with most honor and reward in the community."[2]
But though cataleptic trances were thus highly approved among the
Shasta Indians, obviously they would be rated as signs of emotional instability today in Cambridge, Mass. (Or would they?)

But does this line of reasoning mean that we are now left with nothing
but relativity? Do the words intelligence, motivation, and emotional instability, taken apart from specific culture contexts, have no meaning?
No, I do not intend to go as far as that. I would submit that there do still
remain certain generalized and useful formal meanings for these terms.
For, even though the actual material content and the accompanying
quantified ratings of intelligence, motivation and emotional stability
will not necessarily carry over from one culture to another—for example,
from California to Boston, to the Trobriand Islands or to Cleveland—it
will still be true that these terms are useful and necessary as generalized
frames of reference. They are frames whereby we can compare behaviors
of different cultures and the behaviors of different individuals in any
one culture. Thus, as such formal frames of reference, what we mean by
intelligence is probability of success in reaching goals: by motivation,
probability of persistence in striving towards goals; and by emotional
stability, probable tendencies not to exhibit unacceptable divagations in
the pursuance of such goals. Intelligence is tendency to succeed, motiva-

---

[2] Ruth Benedict, *Patterns of culture*, Boston: Houghton Mifflin, 1934, p. 267.

tion is tendency to persist, and emotional stability is tendency not to exhibit unacceptable divagations.

On the other hand, it still remains true that we can not meaningfully rate the actual intelligence, the actual motivation, or the actual stability of an individual raised in one culture, say, a Trobriand Islander, if set down in another culture, say, in New York (and having to react to a New Yorker's goals) or, similarly, those of a New Yorker set down in the Trobriand Islands (and having to react to the Trobiand Islander's goals). And there is still the further question as to how far a New Yorker's intelligence, motivation, and emotional stability, as rated in reaching one New York goal, will really carry over to, and are the same as, his intelligence, motivation, and emotional stability in reaching other New York goals.

Let us consider this latter question further and let us begin with intelligence. Our first answer may be drawn from the dictates of common sense. Common sense undoubtedly would point out that some New Yorkers seem to be generally bright (successful) *re* all things New Yorkian, whereas others seem to be generally dumb (unsuccessful) *re* most things New Yorkian. This common-sense observation tends to lead, then, further, to the notion of a single entity to be called "intelligence" or at any rate New York intelligence. And Spearman, as we all know, entertained this notion and sought to give it statistical validity in London and ended up with g.[3] However, as has already been argued, it is quite obvious that this London (or New York) g would not carry over, as such, to the Trobriand Islands. The man of high general intelligence in New York (or London) might well prove astonishingly dumb on the Trobriand Islands and, *vice versa,* the man generally dumb in New York (or London)—witness the Admirable Crichton—might prove surprisingly bright (that is, successful) on the Trobriand Islands. And so we return again to our original question. Is New York intelligence or London intelligence really unitary as Spearman supposed?

As a next step in the argument let us now shift our attention, from New York or London to Chicago. For in Chicago, as we all know, much brilliant statistical analysis has gone into showing that, at least along the shores of Lake Michigan, there are some seven, or is it nine, major subvarieties of intelligence. That is, Thurstone[4] and his students have demonstrated that Chicago intelligence seems to have at least the following major, and mutually independent, components: intelligence in

[3] C. E. Spearman, *The abilities of man,* London: Macmillan, 1927.

[4] L. L. Thurstone, *Primary mental abilities,* Chicago: University of Chicago Press, 1938.

words, in numbers, in spatial relations, in quickly perceiving visual or verbal meanings, in remembering relatively rote material, in inducing a general principle from presented particular data and in deducing particulars from presented general principles. That is, it has been found in Chicago that there are few interconnections between successes in reaching goals lying in the seven different directions of words, numbers, space, perceptually presented particulars, remembered particulars, induced relations and deduced particulars. Thus, for a man to be good (or poor) verbally does not mean any necessary concomitant tendency for him to be good (or poor) numerically, or spatially, or the rest. But, if he is good in reaching one goal in primarily verbal terms, he will also have a tendency to be good in reaching other goals which also lie primarily in the verbal direction (provided, of course, all the problems continue to be couched in good Chicagoese.).

Is this, then, our conclusion? Are there seven or perhaps nine basic kinds of intelligence capable of being universally generalized? At first sight, it might seem so. For it takes no great stretch of the imagination to suppose that what Thurstone found for Chicago would also hold for New York, London, for Cleveland or even (though I hate to admit it) for San Francisco. But consider again the Trobriand Islands. If Trobriand Islanders were raised in Chicago (and especially if they went to the University of Chicago) obviously there would be found the same outcome with them. But would we find these same seven "vectors of the mind" in the Trobriand Islands themselves? One doubts it. If a factor analysis were made of abilities on those islands, one might well find not seven but three or ten or fifteen dimensions of intelligence among which there might well prove to be some, to us, quite funny ones—such, say, as an ability to influence others by sorcery, which would correspond to no basic factor to be discovered in Chicago, Cleveland, London, or San Francisco, though such a factor or ability might, perhaps, be found in Los Angeles.

My belief is, then, that that which Thurstone and his students have found are not seven biologically laid-down aspects of intelligence but rather certain major directions of success prescribed by our Western culture complex. We learn to perceive, to use words, to use numbers, to deal with certain types of spatial relations, to memorize nonsense materials (such as telephone numbers), to induce and to deduce. And each of these major learnings, whatever it may be based upon in the way of innate abilities, gets developed by the arrangements and accidents of our Western bringing up, more or less independently of each of the others. I do not pretend that such a hypothesis has really been proven, or that I have grounded it in actual data. I present it, however, as an *a priori* possibility and one which is, at least, worthy of examination. Moreover, it also makes sense when we return now, at long last, to rats.

For, it has been found that in all the intelligence problems which have been tried with rats there are extraordinarily small correlations between tendencies to succeed in any two different problems. One maze tends to correlate but little with another and mazes do not correlate at all with discrimination boxes, or with puzzle boxes, and the rest.[5] It appears, in short, that where culture does not operate (as in rats, thank God, it does not) intelligences (i.e., tendencies to succeed) turn out to be very specific and almost unrelated to one another. This appears both in intercorrelation studies and from the further tests which, I understand, have been made on the Tryon and the Heron bright and dull strains.[6, 7] In short, I shall take very great biological specificity as my basic assumption. This notion I originally learned from Tryon.[8] I now believe with him (unless he has changed his mind in the meantime) that the biological and hereditary bases of intelligence are multitudinous, relatively narrow, and very specific. Assortative mating, as it occurs in human societies, plus the coercive effects of our educational systems, have, however, the tendency to weld these multitudinous possibilities into a finite number (Thurstone's seven) of culturally defined directions. The advantages (or disadvanges) of our systems of mating and of education tend to produce some human individuals who are good in most of the seven directions and others who are poor in most of them. But they also produce individuals who are good in some of the seven though poor in others. But again, I wish to contend that the particular seven categories, that we find, are not so many genetically segregating units but the product of a given culture. For once again, I would assert that the Trobriand Islander living on his islands might well be found by Thurstone to have not seven but say, fifteen or perhaps only three "vectors of the mind." And few, if any, of these fifteen or three might be found to coincide with the seven found in Chicago.

So much for intelligence. Consider now the second of our three sample variables—motivation. No good factor analyses have yet, so far as I know, been made of human motivation in this country, although Spearman did claim to find in London a single generalized motivation factor, w.[9]

---

[5] C. L. Vaughn, *Factors in rat learning,* Comp. Psychol. Monogr., 14 (1937), no. 3.

[6] R. C. Tryon, *39th Yearbook, National Society for the Study of Education,* 1940, Part I, 111–119.

[7] W. T. Heron, *J. Comp. Psychol.,* 19 (1935), 77–89.

[8] R. C. Tryon, *J. Comp. Psychol.,* 30 (1940), 283–336.

[9] *Op. cit.*

However, though we do not have good correlation matrices for motivation, in human beings, we do have one for rats. E. E. Anderson[10] measured the motivation of fifty-one male albino rats in a variety of exploratory-driven, hunger-driven, thirst-driven, and sex-driven problems. What did he find? First, there were no correlations from one drive to another. Secondly, in cases of the hunger and the thirst drives, he also found little or no correlations between the different measures of each of these drives by itself. That is, the rat who performed well as compared with the others, when all were under the influence of hunger, in one getting-to-food test did not necessarily perform well as compared with the others, when all were again under the influence of hunger, in another getting-to-food test. And a similar lack of intercorrelations was found between different measures of the thirst drive. Thirdly, in the cases of the exploratory and the sex drives, however, he did find evidences of something which carried over from one test to another. The rats who were highly exploratory in one apparatus (which encouraged exploration) did show some tendency also to be the ones who were highly exploratory in other apparatuses, which likewise encouraged exploration. Similarly, he found intercorrelations between different measures of the sex drive. The rats who copulated most frequently when a receptive female was present also tended to be the ones who dug most rapidly through sand to get to such a female; and the like. In short, some motivations, such as hunger and thirst, when measured (as in rats) outside the grouping effects of a culture appeared very specific and contingent upon the features of the particular situation. Others, however, such as exploration and sex, appeared more general and less tied to specific situations.

When now we turn to human beings, although the corresponding studies have not been made with them, it seems probable that much evidence of generalized and more culturally determined drives would also be found. Thus, for example, some men in our culture would appear to be highly motivated in the whole area of scholarly pursuits but poorly motivated in those of sports or business. Others would appear to find great motivation in the general area of being good husbands and fathers while others would show but little of that generalized drive and would exhibit, rather, strong drives for writing poetry, painting pictures, or for an exaggerated night life. But here, again, though we might well find such an appearance of "vectors of motivation," it would seem obvious that as in the case of the "vectors of intelligence," they would be mostly the products of a particular civilization and not of human biol-

---

[10] E. E. Anderson, *The interrelationship of drives in the male albino rat*, Comp. Psychol. Monogr., 14 (1938), no. 6.

ogy. There are certain major goals which our culture sets up. And, growing up in this culture, some of us, due no doubt in part to our special inheritances but probably much more as a result of the accidents of early training and experience, tend to pick up some of these goals and others of us tend to pick up others of them. If, to use the vernacular, an individual has been "raised right," he may acquire most of them, but, if he has not been "raised right," he may acquire but few—or only those of lesser repute. And an individual raised in a totally different culture might well acquire almost none of our major motivations. Again the doctrine I am contending for is that of an as yet perhaps unknown set of basic biological drives upon which given cultures then build their own smaller or greater number of culturally defined and specified motivational directions.

In fact, it would seem that Freudian psychology and its offshoots and derivatives considered not as therapy but as explanatory principles are no more and no less than some stimulating hypotheses as to how a given culture, working through the early family set-up and the early training procedures characteristic of the family and of the larger culture in which the family is immersed, may operate to emphasize in given individuals certain of the major motivational directions of the given society and in other individuals, others of those major directions.

Finally, turn to the last of our three variables which I have suggested—merely by way of example—that of emotional stability. This is, undoubtedly, the as yet least clearly conceived of the three. I defined it above as the tendency of the individual not to exhibit irrelevant and unacceptable divagations in the pursuance of a given goal. Let us turn now once again to rats. Let us consider Hall's pioneer studies.[11] You will remember that his rats were deposited one by one in an open field and records were kept of how much they moved about, how much they defecated and how much they urinated. And he found that the individuals who defecated and urinated most also tended to be the ones who did the least moving about. Such animals tended to freeze in one spot. Furthermore, he and his students have also found that two different strains can be bred—one a strain high in defecation, urination, and immobility and one a strain low in these propensities.

The question which arises next is then, how general (or how specific) is this complex of responses? I confess to not being too clear on the point. But, for the sake of argument and to bring the discussion in line with what I have contended for the other two variables, I shall again adopt a similar position. I shall assert that these tendencies, which Hall and

---

[11] C. S. Hall, *Psychol. Bull.*, 38 (1941), 909–943.

his students have bred for, constitute a relatively specific biological entity. And I shall contend further than these tendencies to defecate, urinate, and freeze into immobility, taken by themselves, can not, as such, be evaluated as either emotionally stable or unstable. They are biological substrata upon which a culture may or may not build. If the rats themselves had a culture, they might either disdain or promote to the status of seers and prophets the individuals who showed such propensities. In the first case, such propensities would be said to be symptoms of instability; in the second case, symptoms of genius and of greatness. I suspect, however, that rats, if they had a culture, would, like men, be more apt to find such propensities bad. They might well feel about them as we feel about bed wetting beyond a certain age. Though in a strictly neutral sense bed wetting may, for all I know, be a nice outlet for certain deep-lying motivational conflicts.

In short, my argument is that emotional stability, like intelligence and motivation, is, in the last analysis, an evaluative and cultural concept. It depends upon the rules of the given culture which behaviors are to be defined as unacceptable divagations and which are to be designated, rather, as incidental, colorful (and perhaps desirable) accompaniments of the carrying out of prescribed goals. Holding to this point of view, all I now wish to emphasize about such researches as those of Hall and his students is that they are important contributions to the problem of the uniqueness and the inheritability of certain funny types of propensity which cultures may then either utilize (or condemn) and weld into either what they call stability or into what they call instability.

This concludes my purely descriptive evaluation of the three basic psychological concepts—intelligence, motivation, and emotional stability. I have emphasized that I believe all three to be *von Grund aus* cultural concepts. They can not be given specific contents divorced from the particular cultures in which they operate. And the significance of the work with rats was that it proved in each case that the inherited bases may be relatively specific and may have no simple one-to-one relationships with the finally molded culturally defined variable.

Finally, however, there is one further point which I, as a rat psychologist, must raise. For if, as I have been arguing, there are no unitary intelligence, motivation, or stability functions necessarily common to all men in all cultures and still less common to men (who operate in cultures) and to rats (who operate outside of cultures), what, it may be asked, is the significance of most of our rat studies other than those on heredity? What about the thousands of studies on learning and on motivation and the smaller but pioneer number of studies on conflicts in rats? My answer would be to assert that, although rats have no culture, still the formal laws about the causation and development of intelligence, motivation and instability are universal in character and can be examined in rats just as well as, and far more conveniently than, in men.

And this brings me back once again to my original abortive title—"A Stimulus-expectancy Need-cathexis Psychology." And now I must add still a third neologism, namely, conflict instability, so the complete title would read: "A Stimulus-expectancy, Need-cathexis, Conflict-instability Psychology." In other words, there are, I believe, three basic types of causal determiner (to wit, stimuli, needs, and conflicts) which may be thought to be the respective primary causes of our three variables. And the equations involving these determiners and other factors such as numbers of repetitions, primacy, recency and the like, which connect these determiners to the final three variables, can be better studied in rats than in men.

The basic laws of intelligence concern the fact that successive re-presentations of arrays of environmental stimuli arouse in an organism "sign-gestalt expectations" (as I originally called them) or what Hilgard and Marquis[12] have called, more simply, "expectancies." I am grateful for and shall accept their shorter term (although it is possible that I may use it in ways they didn't intend). Thus an intelligence functioning (that is, a success functioning in the reaching of a goal) is, as I see it, an expectancy on the part of the organism, aroused by that part of the stimulus layout which is immediately presented, to the effect that such and such performances or behaviors (if carried out) would be successful in reaching such and such a goal. These expectancies fundamentally are merely sets in the nervous system aroused by environmental stimuli. In the case of human beings such neurally based expectancies are (as we know) often accompanied by consciousness; but they need not be. And, in any case, their definition does not involve the question as to whether or not they are conscious. It is pointer-reading behaviors which operationally define them. To sum up, the total causal factors underlying such expectancies are, as I see it: (1) the presented environmental stimuli; (2) the hereditary determinants of ability, whatever they finally turn out to be; and (3) the laws of learning (i.e., sign-gestalt, or expectancy, formations). And the operation of all these basic factors and laws can be as well studied in rats as in men—even though (as I have insisted, probably by this time *ad nauseam*) the particular expectancies which get built up in men are determined and guided by particular cultural set-

[12] Hilgard, E. R., and D. G. Marquis, *Conditioning and learning*, New York: Appleton-Century, 1940.

ups and even though, also, the amounts and kinds of repeated presentations (and the span of environmental entities, offered in any one presentation) are likewise, in the case of men, also culturally determined. The basic shape and equations of the learning curve can still be determined by the study of rats, and far more conveniently than by the study of men.

Turn, next, to motivation. The basic problems of motivation I have tried to epitomize by the hyphenation—need-cathexis. That is, motivations are derived basically from the arousal of needs plus the added fact that (through heredity and/or through training) certain types of goal objects get cathected by a given need. Such cathected goal objects, when reached, relieve the need. It now appears, further, that the basic laws concerning the arousal of needs—especially in the case of the simple viscerogenic needs—may likewise be successfully studied in rats. And the basic laws of cathexis whereby particular goal objects get cathected by particular needs can also be studied in rats. Some important beginnings have, in fact, already been made by P. T. Young in his studies of food preferences.[13] But the further (and humanly more interesting) problem of how, on the basis of the simple viscerogenic needs, the more complicated psychogenic ones (to use Murray's dichotomy)[14] get built up, probably can not (I must admit) be studied in rats—although it probably can be, and in large part is being, studied in chimpanzees. But problems such as the list of major psychogenic needs and of the concrete types of goal which get cathected by them has obviously to be investigated separately in each culture. In other words, although possibly we can study in chimpanzees the basic laws of what I have elsewhere called "drive conversions,"[15] that is, the conversion of the libido of the viscerogenic needs into the libido of various psychogenic needs, we can not, I fear, approach the study of the actual goal aims of the psychogenic needs of men in various actual cultures except by studies within those cultures.

Turn now, finally, to our third sample variable—emotional stability. Here we have as yet very few general principles (whether in rats or in men). But, as I have already indicated, I believe the appropriate neologism would be "conflict-instability." That is, I am supposing that it is conflicts between two or more needs which are the basic causal determiner of those kinds of behavior which a given culture will declare to be symptoms of emotional instability. Those particular irrelevances and divagations (such, for example, as bed wetting, nail biting, stammering,

[13] P. T. Young, *J. Comp. Psychol.*, 14 (1932), 297–319; *J. Comp. Psychol.*, 15 (1933), 149–165.

[14] H. A. Murray, *Explorations in personality*, New York: Oxford University Press, 1938.

[15] E. C. Tolman, *Drives toward war*, New York: Appleton-Century, 1942.

flushing, cataleptic trances, visions, and hallucinations) which a given culture may either disdain or capitalize upon, result primarily when two needs conflict with one another. Alongside of some major overt need some second covert need is at work and interferes with the attaining of the major goal. The individual is having to handle two (or it may be more) needs at once and it is this which causes the "funny" behaviors. Hall's rats would seem, for example, to have been interrupted in their exploring by their coincident fear. But as to the basic laws which made some of the individual rats more susceptible to such interference than others we as yet know practically nothing. We do not know whether Hall's more stable rats (in calling them more stable we are, of course, evaluating them as if they were human beings living in our culture) were so because they had inherited little fear or because they had inherited better "inner walls" for keeping their different need compartments separated (to borrow Lewin's figure).[16] And, if we did know this for rats, we certainly do not know it for men. Is the emotionally stable man in our culture one who has no conflicting needs or is he rather one whose tough compartmentalized make-up keeps his competing needs from interfering? Or is he perhaps, quite oppositely, one whose needs do interfere but in such a way that the culture considers him a leader or a genius? We do not know. In any case, however, it is clear that, while it will be desirable to work out more of the basic principles of need conflict with rats, it also has to be confessed that special studies with men in their own actual cultural set-ups likewise will be necessary. For, again let me emphasize that the "funny" behaviors which are termed instability in one culture may be called genius or at least a peculiar delightfulness and richness of coloring in another.

But enough. What, by way of summary, can we now say as to the contributions of us rodent psychologists to human behavior? What is it that we rat runners still have to contribute to the understanding of the deeds and the misdeeds, the absurdities and the tragedies of our friend, and our enemy—*homo sapiens*? The answer is that, whereas man's successes, persistences, and socially unacceptable divagations—that is, his intelligences, his motivations, and his instabilities—are all ultimately shaped and materialized by specific cultures, it is still true that most of the formal underlying laws of intelligence, motivation, and instability can still be studied in rats as well as, and more easily than, in men.

And, as a final peroration, let it be noted that rats live in cages; they do not go on binges the night before one has planned an experiment; they do not kill each other off in wars; they do not invent engines of

---

[16] K. Lewin, *A dynamic theory of personality*, New York: McGraw-Hill, 1935.

destruction, and, if they did, they would not be so inept about control-ling such engines; they do not go in for either class conflicts or race conflicts; they avoid politics, economics, and papers on psychology. They are marvelous, pure, and delightful. And, as soon as I possibly can, I am going to climb back again out on that good old philogenetic limb and sit there, this time right side up and unashamed, wiggling my whiskers at all the silly, yet at the same time far too complicated, specimens of *homo sapiens,* whom I shall see strutting and fighting and messing things up, down there on the ground below me.

19

COGNITIVE MAPS IN RATS AND MEN

[*Psychological Review*, JULY, 1948]

I SHALL DEVOTE the body of this paper[1] to a description of experiments with rats. But I shall also attempt in a few words at the close to indicate the significance of these findings on rats for the clinical behavior of men. Most of the rat investigations, which I shall report, were carried out in the Berkeley laboratory. But I shall also include, occasionally, accounts of the behavior of non-Berkeley rats who obviously have mis-spent their lives in out-of-state laboratories. Furthermore, in reporting our Berkeley experiments I shall have to omit a very great many. The ones I *shall* talk about were carried out by graduate students (or under-paid research assistants) who, supposedly, got some of their ideas from me. And a few, though a very few, were even carried out by me myself.

Let me begin by presenting diagrams for a couple of typical mazes, an alley maze and an elevated maze. In the typical experiment a hungry rat is put at the entrance of the maze (alley or elevated), and wanders about through the various true path segments and blind alleys until he finally comes to the food box and eats. This is repeated (again in the typical experiment) one trial every 24 hours and the animal tends to make fewer and fewer errors (that is, blind-alley entrances) and to take less and less time between start and goal box until finally he is entering no blinds at all and running in a very few seconds from start to goal. The results are usually presented in the form of average curves of blind entrances, or of seconds from start to finish, for groups of rats.

[1] Thirty-fourth Annual Faculty Research Lecture, delivered at the University of California, Berkeley, March 17, 1947. Presented also on March 26, 1947, as one in a series of lectures in dynamic psychology sponsored by the division of psychology of Western Reserve University, Cleveland, Ohio.

All students agree as to the facts. They disagree, however, on theory and explanation.

1. First, there is a school of animal psychologists which believes that the maze behavior of rats is a matter of mere simple stimulus-response connections. Learning, according to them, consists in the strengthening

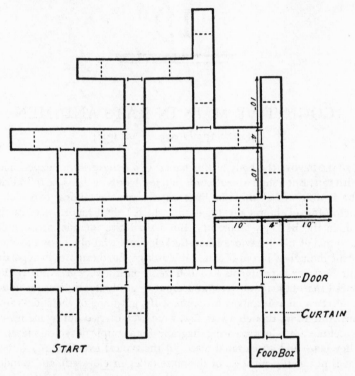

FIG. 1. Plan of maze: fourteen-unit T-alley maze. From M. H. Elliott, *The effect of chance or reward on the maze performance of rats,* Univ. Calif. Publ. Psychol., 4 (1928), 20.

of some of these connections and in the weakening of others. According to this "stimulus-response" school the rat in progressing down the maze is helplessly responding to a succession of external stimuli—sights, sounds, smells, pressures, etc., impinging upon his external sense organs—plus internal stimuli coming from the viscera and from the skeletal muscles. These external and internal stimuli call out the walkings, runnings, turnings, retracings, smellings, rearings, and the like which appear. The rat's central nervous system, according to this view, may be likened to a complicated telephone switchboard. There are the incoming calls from sense organs and there are the outgoing messages to muscles. Before the learning of a specific maze, the connecting switches (synapses according to the physiologist) are closed in one set of ways and produce the primarily exploratory responses which appear in the early trials. *Learning*, according to this view, consists in the respective strengthening and weakening of various of these connections; those connections which result in the animal's going down the true path become relatively more open to the passage of nervous impulses, whereas those which lead him into the blinds become relatively less open.

It must be noted in addition, however, that this stimulus-response school divides further into two subgroups.

a. There is a subgroup which holds that the mere mechanics involved in the running of a maze is such that the crucial stimuli from the maze get presented simultaneously with the correct responses more frequently than they do with any of the incorrect responses. Hence, just on a basis of this greater frequency, the neural connections between the crucial stimuli and the correct responses will tend, it is said, to get strengthened at the expense of the incorrect connections.

b. There is a second subgroup in this stimulus-response school which holds that the reason the appropriate connections get strengthened relatively to the inappropriate ones is, rather, the fact that the responses resulting from the correct connections are followed more closely in time by need reductions. Thus a hungry rat in a maze tends to get to food and have his hunger reduced *sooner* as a result of the true path responses than as a result of the blind-alley responses. And such immediately following need reductions or, to use another term, such "positive reinforcements" tend somehow, it is said, to strengthen the connections which have most closely preceded them. Thus it is as if—although this is certainly not the way this subgroup would themselves state it—the satisfaction-receiving part of the rat telephoned back to central and said to the girl: "Hold that connection; it was good; and see to it that you blankety-blank well use it again the next time these same stimuli come in." These theorists also assume (at least some of them do some of the time) that, if bad results—"annoyances," "negative reinforcements"—follow, then this same satisfaction-and-annoyance-receiving part of the rat will telephone back and say, "Break that connection and don't you dare use it next time either."

So much for a brief summary of the two subvarieties of the "stimulus-response," or telephone-switchboard school.

2. Let us turn now to the second main school. This group (and I

belong to them) may be called the field theorists. We believe that in the course of learning something like a field map of the environment gets established in the rat's brain. We agree with the other school that the rat in running a maze is exposed to stimuli and is finally led as a result of these stimuli to the responses which actually occur. We feel, however, that the intervening brain processes are more complicated,

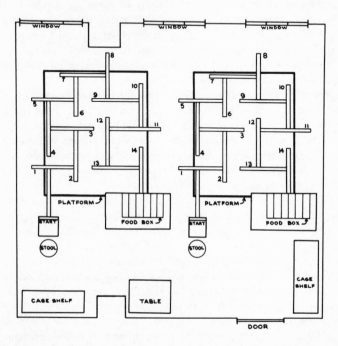

FIG. 2. Fourteen-unit T-elevated mazes. From C. H. Honzik, *The sensory basis of maze learning in rats*, Comp. Psychol. Monog., 13 (1936), no. 4, p. 4. These were two identical mazes placed side by side in the same room.

more patterned and often, pragmatically speaking, more autonomous than do the stimulus-response psychologists. Although we admit that the rat is bombarded by stimuli, we hold that his nervous system is surprisingly selective as to which of these stimuli it will let in at any given time.

Secondly, we assert that the central office itself is far more like a map control room than it is like an old-fashioned telephone exchange. The stimuli, which are allowed in, are not connected by just simple one-to-one switches to the outgoing responses. Rather, the incoming impulses are usually worked over and elaborated in the central control room into a tentative, cognitivelike map of the environment. And it is this tentative map, indicating routes and paths and environmental relationships, which finally determines what responses, if any, the animal will finally release.

Finally, I, personally, would hold further that it is also important to discover how far these maps are relatively narrow and striplike or relatively broad and comprehensive. Both strip maps and comprehensive

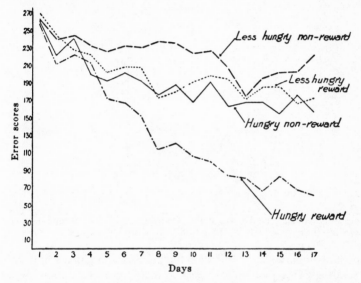

FIG. 3. Error curves for four groups, 36 rats per group. From E. C. Tolman and C. H. Honzik, *Degrees of hunger, reward and nonreward, and maze learning in rats,* Univ. Calif. Publ. Psychol., 4 (1930), 246. A maze identical with the alley maze shown in fig. 1 was used.

maps may be either correct or incorrect in the sense that they may (or may not), when acted upon, lead successfully to the animal's goal. The differences between such strip maps and such comprehensive maps will appear only when the rat is later presented with some change within the given environment. Then, the narrower and more striplike the original map, the less will it carry over successfully to the new problem; whereas, the wider and the more comprehensive it was, the more adequately it will serve in the new set-up. In a strip map the given position of the animal is connected by only a relatively simple and single path to the position of the goal. In a comprehensive map a wider arc of the environment is represented, so that, if the starting position of the animal be changed or variations in the specific routes be introduced, this wider map will allow the animal still to behave relatively correctly and to choose the appropriate new route.

But let us turn, now, to the actual experiments. The ones, out of many, which I have selected to report are simply ones which seem

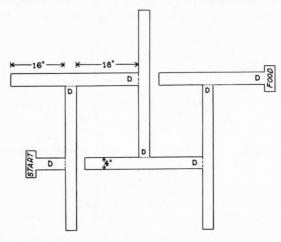

FIG. 4. Six-unit alley T-maze. From H. C. Blodgett, *The effect of the introduction of reward upon the maze performance of rats*, Univ. Calif. Publ. Psychol., 4 (1929), 117.

especially important in reinforcing the theoretical position I have been presenting. This position, I repeat, contains two assumptions: First, that learning consists not in stimulus-response connections but in the building up in the nervous system of sets which function like cognitive maps, and second, that such cognitive maps may be usefully character-ized as varying from a narrow strip variety to a broader comprehensive variety.

The experiments fall under five heads: (1) "latent learning," (2) "vi-carious trial and error" or "VTE," (3) "searching for the stimulus," (4) "hypotheses" and (5) "spatial orientation."

1. *"Latent-learning" experiments.*—The first of the latent-learning experiments was performed at Berkeley by Blodgett. It was published in 1929. Blodgett not only performed the experiments, he also origi-nated the concept. He ran three groups of rats through a six-unit alley maze, shown in figure 4. He had a control group and two experimental groups. The error curves for these groups appear in figure 5. The solid

line shows the error curve for group I, the control group. These animals were run in orthodox fashion. That is, they were run one trial a day and found food in the goal box at the end of each trial. Groups II and III were the experimental groups. The animals of group II, the dash line, were not fed in the maze for the first six days but only in their home cages some two hours later. On the seventh day (indicated by the

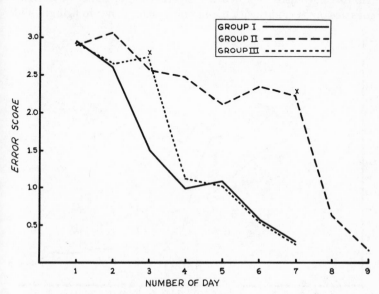

FIG. 5. From Blodgett, *op. cit.*, p. 120.

small cross) the rats found food at the end of the maze for the first time and continued to find it on subsequent days. The animals of group III were treated similarly except that they first found food at the end of the maze on the third day and continued to find it there on subsequent days. It will be observed that the experimental groups as long as they were not finding food did not appear to learn much. (Their error curves did not drop.) But on the days immediately succeeding their first finding of the food their error curves did drop astoundingly. It appeared, in short, that during the nonrewarded trials these animals had been learning much more than they had exhibited. This learning, which did not manifest itself until after the food had been introduced, Blodgett called "latent learning." Interpreting these results anthropomorphically, we would say that as long as the animals were not getting any food at the

end of the maze they continued to take their time in going through it—
they continued to enter many blinds. Once, however, they knew they
were to get food, they demonstrated that during these preceding nonrewarded trials they had learned where many of the blinds were. They
had been building up a "map," and could utilize the latter as soon as
they were motivated to do so.

Honzik and myself repeated the experiments (or rather he did and
I got some of the credit) with the 14-unit T-mazes shown in figure 1, and

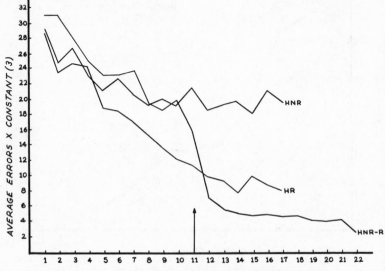

Fig. 6. Error curves for HR, HNR, and HNR–R. From Tolman
and Honzik, *op. cit.*, p. 267.

with larger groups of animals, and got similar results. The resulting
curves are shown in figure 6. We used two control groups—one that
never found food in the maze (HNR) and one that found it throughout
(HR). The experimental group (HNR–R) found food at the end of the
maze from the eleventh day on and showed the same sort of a sudden
drop.

But probably the best experiment demonstrating latent learning was,
unfortunately, done not in Berkeley but at the University of Iowa, by
Spence and Lippitt. Only an abstract of this experiment has as yet been
published. However, Spence has sent a preliminary manuscript from
which the following account is summarized. A simple Y-maze (see figure 7) with two goal boxes was used. Water was at the end of the right

arm of the Y and food at the end of the left arm. During the training period the rats were run neither hungry nor thirsty. They were satiated for both food and water before each day's trials. However, they were willing to run because after each run they were taken out of whichever end box they had got to and put into a living cage, with other animals

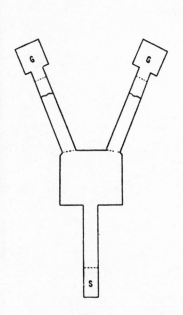

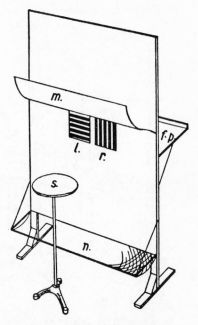

FIG. 7. Ground plan of the apparatus. From K. W. Spence and R. Lippitt, "An experimental test of the sign-gestalt theory of trial and error learning," *J. Exper. Psychol.*, 36 (1946), 494. In this article they were describing another experiment but used the same maze.

FIG. 8. Apparatus used for testing discrimination of visual patterns. From K. S. Lashley, "The mechanism of vision: I. A method for rapid analyses of pattern-vision in the rat," *J. Genet. Psychol.*, 37 (1930), 454.

in it. They were given four trials a day in this fashion for seven days, two trials to the right and two to the left.

In the crucial test the animals were divided into two subgroups, one made solely hungry and one solely thirsty. It was then found that on the first trial the hungry group went at once to the left, where the food had been, statistically more frequently than to the right; and the thirsty group went to the right, where the water had been, statistically more frequently than to the left. These results indicated that under the previous nondifferential and very mild rewarding conditions of merely being returned to the home cages the animals had nevertheless been learning where the water was and where the food was. In short, they had acquired a cognitive map to the effect that food was to the left and water to the right, although during the acquisition of this map they had not exhibited any stimulus-response propensities to go more to the side which became later the side of the appropriate goal.

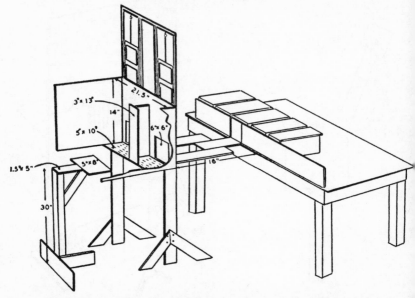

Fig. 9. From E. C. Tolman, "Prediction of vicarious trial and error by means of the schematic sowbug," *Psychol. Rev.*, 46 (1939), 319.

There have been numerous other latent-learning experiments done in the Berkeley laboratory and elsewhere. In general, they have for the most part all confirmed the above sort of findings.

Let us turn now to the second group of experiments.

2. *"Vicarious trial and error" or "VTE."* The term vicarious trial and error (abbreviated as VTE) was invented by Prof. Muenzinger at Colorado[2] to designate the hesitating, looking-back-and-forth, sort of behavior which rats can often be observed to indulge in at a choice point before actually going one way or the other.

Quite a number of experiments upon VTEing have been carried out

[2] K. F. Muenzinger, "Vicarious trial and error at a point of choice: I. A general survey of its relation to learning efficiency," *J. Genet. Psychol.*, 53 (1938), 75–86.

in our laboratory. I shall report only a few. In most of them what is called a discrimination set-up has been used. In one characteristic type of visual discrimination apparatus designed by Lashley (shown in figure 8) the animal is put on a jumping stand and faced with two doors which differ in some visual property say, as here shown, vertical stripes vs. horizontal stripes.

One of each such pair of visual stimuli is made always correct and the other wrong; and the two are interchanged from side to side in random

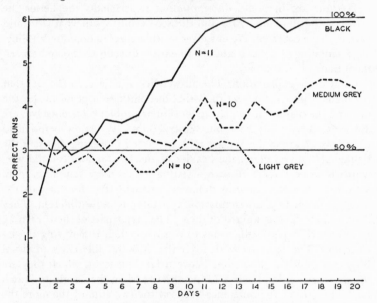

FIG. 10. Learning curves. Average number of correct runs per day.
From Tolman, *op. cit.*, p. 319.

fashion. The animal is required to learn, say, that the vertically striped door is always the correct one. If he jumps to it, the door falls open and he gets to food on a platform behind. If, on the other hand, he jumps incorrectly, he finds the door locked and falls into a net some two feet below from which he is picked up and started over again.

Using a similar set-up (see figure 9), but with landing platforms in front of the doors so that if the rat chose incorrectly he could jump back again and start over, I found that when the choice was an easy one, say between a white door and a black door, the animals not only learned sooner but also did more VTEing than when the choice was difficult, say between a white door and a gray door (see figure 10). It appeared further (see figure 11) that the VTEing began to appear just as (or just before) the rats began to learn. After the learning had become established, however, the VTE's began to go down. Further, in a study of individual differences by myself, Geier and Levin[3] (actually done by Geier and Levin) using this same visual discrimination apparatus, it was found that with one and the same difficulty of problem the smarter animal did the more VTEing.

To sum up, in *visual discrimination* experiments the better the learning, the more the VTE's. But this seems contrary to what we would perhaps have expected. We ourselves would expect to do more VTEing, more sampling of the two stimuli, when it is difficult to choose between them than when it is easy.

What is the explanation? The answer lies, I believe, in the fact that the manner in which we set the visual discrimination problems for the rats and the manner in which we set similar problems for ourselves are different. *We* already have our "instructions." We know beforehand what it is we are to do. We are told, or we tell ourselves, that it is the lighter of the two grays, the heavier of the two weights, or the like, which is to be chosen. In such a setting we do more sampling, more VTEing, when the stimulus difference is small. But for the rats the usual problem in a discrimination apparatus is quite different. They do not know what is wanted of them. The major part of their learning in most such experiments seems to consist in their discovering the instructions. The rats have to discover that it is the differences in visual brightness, not the differences between left and right, which they are to pay attention to. Their VTEing appears when they begin to "catch on." The greater the difference between the two stimuli the more the animals are attracted by this difference. Hence the sooner they catch on, and during this catching on, the more they VTE.

That this is a reasonable interpretation appeared further, from an experiment by myself and Minium (the actual work done, of course, by Minium) in which a group of six rats was first taught a white vs. black discrimination, then two successively more difficult gray vs. black discriminations (fig. 12). For each difficulty the rats were given a series of further trials beyond the points at which they had learned. Comparing the beginning of each of these three difficulties the results were that the rats did more VTEing for the easy discriminations than for the more

[3] Geier, F. M., M. Levin, and E. C. Tolman, *Individual differences in emotionality, hypothesis formation, vicarious trial and error and visual discrimination learning in rats,* Comp. Psychol. Monogr., 17 (1941), no. 3.

difficult ones. When, however, it came to a comparison of amounts of VTEing during the final performance after each learning had reached a plateau, the opposite results were obtained. In other words, after the rats had finally divined their instructions, then they, like human beings, did more VTEing, more sampling, the more difficult the discrimination.

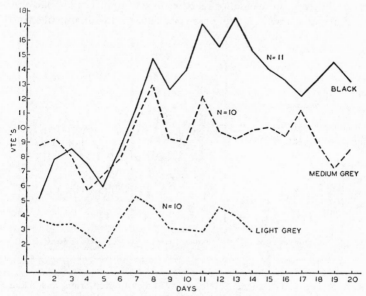

Fig. 11. Average number of VTE's per day. From Tolman, *op. cit.*, p. 320.

Finally, now let us note that it was also found at Berkeley by Jackson[4] that in a maze the difficult maze units produce more VTEing and also that the more stupid rats do the more VTEing. The explanation, as I see it, is that, in the case of mazes, rats know their instructions. For them it is natural to expect that the same spatial path will always lead to the same outcome. Rats in mazes don't have to be told.

But what, now, is the final significance of all this VTEing? How do these facts about VTEing affect our theoretical argument? My answer is that these facts lend further support to the doctrine of a building up of maps. VTEing, as I see it, is evidence that in the critical stages— whether in the first picking up of the instructions or in the later making sure of which stimulus is which—the animal's activity is not just one of responding passively to discrete stimuli, but rather one of the active

[4] L. L. Jackson, "V. T. E. on an elevated maze," *J. Comp. Psychol.*, 36 (1943), 99–107.

selecting and comparing of stimuli. This brings me then to the third type of experiment.

3. *"Searching for the stimulus."*—I refer to a recent, and it seems to me extremely important experiment, done for a Ph.D. dissertation by Hudson. Hudson was first interested in the question of whether or not rats could learn an avoidance reaction in one trial. His animals were tested one at a time in a living cage (see figure 13) with a small striped

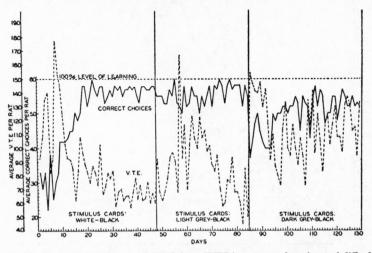

FIG. 12. From E. C. Tolman and E. Minium, "VTE in rats: overlearning and difficulty of discrimination," *J. Comp. Psychol.*, 34 (1942), 303.

visual pattern at the end, on which was mounted a food cup. The hungry rat approached this food cup and ate. An electrical arrangement was provided so that when the rat touched the cup he could be given an electric shock. And one such shock did appear to be enough. For when the rat was replaced in this same cage days or even weeks afterwards, he usually demonstrated immediately strong avoidance reactions to the visual pattern. The animal withdrew from that end of the cage, or piled up sawdust and covered the pattern, or showed various other amusing responses all of which were in the nature of withdrawing from the pattern or making it disappear.

But the particular finding which I am interested in now appeared as a result of a modification of this standard procedure. Hudson noticed that the animals, anthropomorphically speaking, often seemed to look around *after* the shock to see what it was that had hit them. Hence it occurred to him that, if the pattern were made to disappear the instant the shock occurred, the rats might not establish the association. And this indeed is what happened in the case of many individuals. Hudson added further electrical connections so that when the shock was received during the eating, the lights went out, the pattern and the food cup dropped out of sight, and the lights came on again all within the matter of a second. When such animals were again put in the cage twenty-four

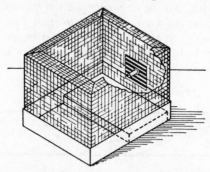

Fig. 13. From Bradford Hudson, *One trial learning: a study of the avoidance behavior of the rat,* Ph.D. thesis, University of California, Berkeley, California.

hours later, a large percentage showed no avoidance of the pattern. Or to quote Hudson's own words:

Learning what object to avoid . . . may occur exclusively during the period *after* the shock. For if the object from which the shock was actually received is removed at the moment of the shock, a significant number of animals fail to learn to avoid it, some selecting other features in the environment for avoidance, and others avoiding nothing.

In other words, I feel that this experiment reinforces the notion of the largely active selective character in the rat's building up of his cognitive map. He often has to look actively for the significant stimuli in order to form his map and does not merely passively receive and react to all the stimuli which are physically present.

Turn now to the fourth type of experiment.

4. *The "hypothesis" experiments.*—Both the notion of hypotheses in rats and the design of the experiments to demonstrate such hypotheses are to be credited to Krech. Krech used a four-compartment discrimination box. In such a four-choice box the correct door at each choice point may be determined by the experimenter in terms of its being lighted or dark, left or right, or various combinations of these. If all possibilities are randomized for the forty choices made in ten runs of each day's test, the problem could be made insoluble. (See figure 14.)

When this was done, Krech found that the individual rat went through a succession of systematic choices. That is, the individual animal might perhaps begin by choosing practically all right-hand doors, then he might give this up for choosing practically all left-hand doors, and then, for choosing all dark doors, and so on. These relatively persistent, and well-above-chance systematic types of choice Krech called "hypotheses." In using this term he obviously did not mean to imply verbal processes in the rat but merely referred to what I have been calling cognitive maps which, it appears from his experiments, get set up in a tentative fashion to be tried out first one and then another until, if possible, one is found which works.

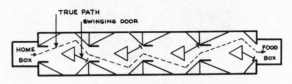

FIG. 14. From I. Krechevsky [now D. Krech], *The genesis of "hypotheses" in rats,* Univ. Calif. Publ. Psychol., 6 (1932), 46.

Finally, it is to be noted that these hypothesis experiments, like the latent-learning, VTE, and "looking for the stimulus" experiments, do not, as such, throw light upon the widths of the maps which are picked up but do indicate the generally maplike and self-initiated character of learning.

For the beginning of an attack upon the problem of the width of the maps let me turn to the last group of experiments.

5. *"Spatial-orientation" experiments.*—As early as 1929, Lashley reported incidentally the case of a couple of his rats who, after having learned an alley maze, pushed back the cover near the starting box, climbed out and ran directly across the top to the goal box where they climbed down in again and ate. Other investigators have reported related findings. All such observations suggest that rats really develop wider spatial maps which include more than the mere trained-on specific paths. In the experiments now to be reported this possibility has been subjected to further examination.

In the first experiment, Tolman, Ritchie, and Kalish (actually Ritchie and Kalish) used the set-up shown in figure 15.

This was an elevated maze. The animals ran from A across the open circular table through CD (which had alley walls) and finally to G, the food box. H was a light which shone directly down the path from G to

F. After four nights, three trials per night, in which the rats learned to run directly and without hesitation from A to G, the apparatus was changed to the sun burst shown in figure 16. The starting path and the table remaining the same but a series of radiating paths was added.

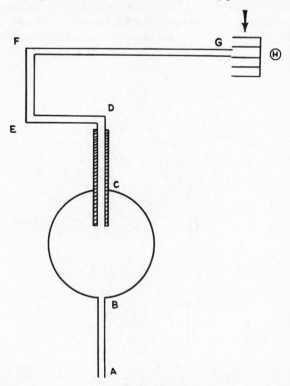

FIG. 15. Apparatus used in preliminary training. From E. C. Tolman, B. F. Ritchie, and D. Kalish, "Studies in spatial learning. I: Orientation and the short-cut," *J. Exper. Psychol.*, 36 (1946), 16.

The animals were again started at A and ran across the circular table into the alley and found themselves blocked. They then returned onto the table and began exploring practically all the radiating paths. After going out a few inches only on any one path, each rat finally chose to run all the way out on one. The percentages of rats finally choosing each of the long paths from 1 to 12 are shown in figure 17. It appears that there was a preponderant tendency to choose path 6 which ran to a point some four inches in front of where the entrance to the food box had been. The only other path chosen with any appreciable frequency was 1—that is, the path which pointed perpendicularly to the food-side of the room.

These results seem to indicate that the rats in this experiment had learned not only to run rapidly down the original roundabout route but also, when this was blocked and radiating paths presented, to select one pointing rather directly towards the point where the food had been

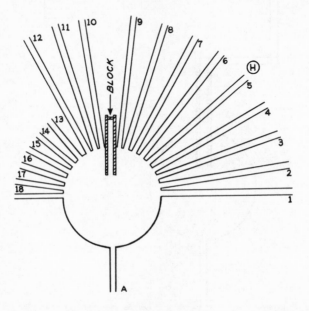

FIG. 16. Apparatus used in the test trial. From Tolman, Ritchie, and Kalish, *op. cit.*, p. 17.

or else at least to select a path running perpendicularly to the food side of the room.

As a result of their original training, the rats had, it would seem, acquired not merely a strip map to the effect that the original specifically trained-on path led to food but, rather, a wider comprehensive map to the effect that food was located in such and such a direction in the room.

Consider now a further experiment done by Ritchie alone. This experiment tested still further the breadth of the spatial map which is acquired. In this further experiment the rats were again run across the table—this time to the arms of a simple T. (See figure 18.)

Twenty-five animals were trained for seven days, twenty trials in all, to find food at F_1; and twenty-five animals were trained to find it at F_2. The L's in the diagram indicate lights. On the eighth day the starting path and table top were rotated through 180 degrees so that they were now in the position shown in figure 19. The dotted lines represent the old position. And a series of radiating paths was added. What happened? Again the rats ran across the table into the central alley. When, how-

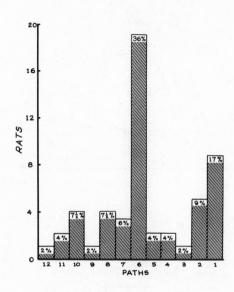

FIG. 17. Numbers of rats which chose each of the paths.
From Tolman, Ritchie, and Kalish, *op. cit.*, p. 19.

ever, they found themselves blocked, they turned back onto the table and this time also spent many seconds touching and trying out for only a few steps practically all the paths. Finally, however, within seven minutes, 42 of the 50 rats chose one path and ran all the way out on it. The paths finally chosen by the 19 of these animals that had been fed at F_1 and by the 23 that had been fed at F_2 are shown in figure 20.

This time the rats tended to choose, not the paths which pointed directly to the spots where the food had been, but rather paths which ran perpendicularly to the corresponding sides of the room. The spatial maps of these rats, when the animals were started from the opposite side of the room, were thus not completely adequate to the precise goal positions but were adequate as to the correct sides of the room. The maps of these animals were, in short, not altogether striplike and narrow.

This completes my report of experiments. There were the *latent-learning experiments,* the *VTE experiments,* the *searching-for-the-*

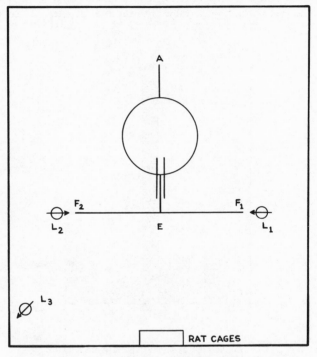

FIG. 18. From B. F. Ritchie, *Spatial learning in rats,* Ph.D thesis, University of California, Berkeley, California.

stimulus experiment, the *hypothesis experiments,* and these last *spatial-orientation experiments.*

And now, at last, I come to the humanly significant and exciting problem: namely, what are the conditions which favor narrow strip maps and what are those which tend to favor broad comprehensive maps not only in rats but also in men?

There is considerable evidence scattered throughout the literature bearing on this question both for rats and for men. Some of this evidence was obtained in Berkeley and some of it elsewhere. I have not time to present it in any detail. I can merely summarize it by saying that narrow strip maps rather than broad comprehensive maps seem to be induced: (1) by a damaged brain, (2) by an inadequate array of environmentally presented cues, (3) by an overdose of repetitions on the original trained-on path, and (4) by the presence of too strongly motivational or of too strongly frustrating conditions.

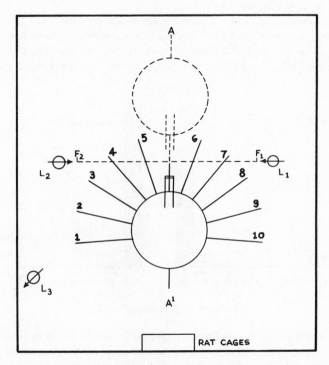

FIG. 19. From B. F. Ritchie, *op. cit.*

It is this fourth factor which I wish to elaborate upon briefly in my concluding remarks. For it is going to be my contention that some, at least, of the so-called "psychological mechanisms" which the clinical psychologists and the other students of personality have uncovered as the devils underlying many of our individual and social maladjustments can be interpreted as narrowings of our cognitive maps due to too strong motivations or to too intense frustration.

My argument will be brief, cavalier, and dogmatic. For I am not my-self a clinician or a social psychologist. What I am going to say must be considered, therefore, simply as in the nature of a *rat* psychologist's *rat*iocinations offered free.

By way of illustration, let me suggest that at least the three dynamisms called, respectively, "regression," "fixation," and "displacement of aggression onto outgroups" are expressions of cognitive maps which are too narrow and which get built up in us as a result of too violent motivation or of too intense frustration.

a. Consider *regression*. This is the term used for those cases in which an individual, in the face of too difficult a problem, returns to earlier more childish ways of behaving. Thus, to take an example, the overprotected middle-aged woman (reported a couple of years ago in *Time*)

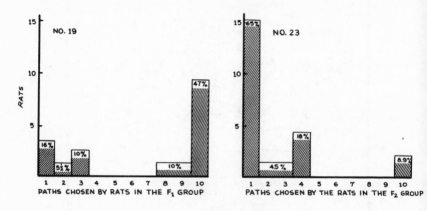

FIG. 20. From B. F. Ritchie, *op. cit.*

who, after losing her husband, regressed (much to the distress of her growing daughters) into dressing in too youthful a fashion and into competing for their beaux and then finally into behaving like a child requiring continuous care, would be an illustration of regression. I would not wish you to put too much confidence in the reportorial accuracy of *Time,* but such an extreme case is not too different from many actually to be found in our mental hospitals or even sometimes in ourselves. In all such instances my argument would be (1) that such regression results from too strong a present emotional situation and (2) that it consists in going back to too narrow an earlier map, itself due to too much frustration or motivation in early childhood. *Time*'s middle-aged woman was presented by too frustrating an emotional situation at her husband's death and she regressed, I would wager, to too narrow adolescent and childhood maps since these latter had been originally excessively impressed because of overstressful experiences at the time she was growing up.

b. Consider *fixation*. Regression and fixation tend to go hand in hand. For another way of stating the fact of the undue persistence of early maps is to say that they were fixated. This has even been demonstrated in rats. If rats are too strongly motivated in their original learning, they find it very difficult to relearn when the original path is no longer correct. Also after they have relearned, if they are given an electric shock they, like *Time*'s woman, tend to regress back again to choosing the earlier path.

c. Finally, consider the *"displacement of aggressions onto outgroups."* Adherence to one's own group is an ever-present tendency among primates. It is found in chimpanzees and monkeys as strongly as in men. We primates operate in groups. And each individual in such a group tends to identify with his whole group in the sense that the group's goals become his goals, the group's life and immortality, his life and immortality. Furthermore, each individual soon learns that, when as an individual he is frustrated, he must not take out his aggressions on the other members of his own group. He learns instead to displace his aggressions onto outgroups. Such a displacement of aggression I would claim is also a narrowing of the cognitive map. The individual comes no longer to distinguish the true locus of the cause of his frustration. The poor Southern whites, who take it out on the Negroes, are displacing their aggressions from the landlords, the southern economic system, the northern capitalists, or wherever the true cause of their frustration may lie, onto a mere convenient outgroup. The physicists on the faculty who criticize the humanities, or we psychologists who criticize all the other departments, or the university as a whole which criticizes the secondary school system or, vice versa, the secondary school system which criticizes the university—or, on a still larger and far more dangerous scene—we Americans who criticize the Russians and the Russians who criticize us, are also engaging, at least in part, in nothing more than such irrational displacements of our aggressions onto outgroups.

I do not mean to imply that there may not be some true interferences by the one group with the goals of the other and hence that the aggressions of the members of the one group against the members of the other are necessarily *wholly* and *merely* displaced aggressions. But I do assert that often and in large part they are such mere displacements.

Over and over again men are blinded by too violent motivations and too intense frustrations into blind and unintelligent, and in the end desperately dangerous, hates of outsiders. And the expression of these, their displaced hates, ranges all the way from discrimination against minorities to world conflagrations.

What in the name of Heaven and Psychology can we do about it? My only answer is to preach again the virtues of reason—of, that is, broad cognitive maps. And to suggest that the child trainers and the world planners of the future can only, if at all, bring about the presence of the required rationality (i.e., comprehensive maps) if they see to it that nobody's children are too overmotivated or too frustrated. Only then can these children learn to look before and after, learn to see that there are often round-about and safer paths to their quite proper goals—learn, that is, to realize that the well-beings of White and of Negro, of Catholic and of Protestant, of Christian and of Jew, of American and of Russian (and even of males and females) are mutually interdependent.

We dare not let ourselves or others become so overemotional, so hungry, so ill-clad, so overmotivated that only narrow strip maps will be developed. All of us in Europe as well as in America, in the Orient as well as in the Occident, must be made calm enough and well-fed enough to be able to develop truly comprehensive maps, or, as Freud would have put it, to be able to learn to live according to the Reality Principle rather than according to the too narrow and too immediate Pleasure Principle.

We must, in short, subject our children and ourselves (as the kindly experimenter would his rats) to the optimal conditions of moderate motivation and of an absence of unnecessary frustrations, whenever we put them and ourselves before that great God-given maze which is our human world. I cannot predict whether or not we will be able, or be allowed, to do this; but I *can* say that only so far as we *are* able and *are* allowed, have we cause for hope.

20

BIBLIOGRAPHY OF THE PUBLISHED WORK OF EDWARD CHACE TOLMAN

More concerning the temporal relations of meaning and imagery. *Psychol. Rev.*, 24 (1917), 114–138.

Retroactive inhibition as affected by conditions of learning. Psychol. Monog., 25, no. 1 (1918), 50 pp.

(With I. Johnson) A note on association-time and feeling. *Amer. J. Psychol.*, 29 (1918), 187–195.

Nerve process and cognition. *Psychol. Rev.*, 25 (1918), 423–442.

English and mathematical abilities of a group of college students. *J. Educ. Psychol.*, 10 (1919), 95–103.

Instinct and purpose. *Psychol. Rev.*, 27 (1920), 217–233.

A new formula for behaviorism. *Psychol. Rev.*, 29 (1922), 44–53.

Concerning the sensation quality. A behavioristic account. *Psychol. Rev.*, 29 (1922), 140–145.

Can instincts be given up in psychology? *J. Abn. Psychol.*, 17 (1922), 139–152.

The nature of instinct. *Psychol. Bull.*, 20 (1923), 200–216.

A behavioristic account of the emotions. *Psychol. Rev.*, 30 (1923), 217–227.

Mr. Mursell's concept of sensation. *J. Phil.*, 20 (1923), 271–272.

(With A. E. White) A note on the elimination of long and short blind alleys. *J. Comp. Psychol.*, 3 (1923), 327–331.

The effects of underlearning upon short- and long-time retentions. *J. Exper. Psychol.*, 6 (1923), 466–474.

The inheritance of maze-learning ability in rats. *J. Comp. Psychol.*, 4 (1924), 1–18.

(With F. C. Davis) A note on the correlations between two mazes. *J. Comp. Psychol.*, 4 (1924), 125–135.

Behaviorism and purpose. *J. Phil.*, 22 (1925), 36–41.

(With C. F. Sams) Time discrimination in white rats. *J. Comp. Psychol.*, 5 (1925), 255–263.

Purpose and cognition: the determiners of animal learning. *Psychol. Rev.*, 32 (1925), 285–297.

The nature of fundamental drives. *J. Abn. & Soc. Psychol.*, 5 (1926), 349–358.

(With L. A. Jeffress) A self-recording maze. *J. Comp. Psychol.*, 6 (1925), 455–463.

A behavioristic theory of ideas. *Psychol. Rev.*, 33 (1926), 352–369.

Habit formation and higher mental processes in animals. *Psychol. Bull.*, 24 (1927), 1–35; 25 (1928), 24–53.

A behaviorist's definition of consciousness. *Psychol. Rev.*, 34 (1927), 433–439.

(With D. B. Nyswander) The reliability and validity of maze-measures for rats. *J. Comp. Psychol.*, 7 (1927), 425–460.

Purposive behavior. *Psychol. Rev.*, 35 (1928), 524–530.

(With R. C. Tryon and L. A. Jeffress) *A self-recording maze with an automatic delivery table.* Univ. Calif. Publ. Psychol., 4 (1929), 99–112.

(With C. H. Honzik and E. W. Robinson) *The effect of degrees of hunger upon the order of elimination of long and short blinds.* Univ. Calif. Publ. Psychol., 4 (1930), 189–202.

(With C. H. Honzik) *"Insight" in rats.* Univ. Calif. Publ. Psychol., 4 (1930), 215–232.

(With C. H. Honzik) *Degrees of hunger, reward and non-reward, and maze learning in rats.* Univ. Calif. Publ. Psychol., 4 (1930), 241–257.

(With C. H. Honzik) *Introduction and removal of reward, and maze performance in rats.* Univ. Calif. Publ. Psychol., 4 (1930), 257–275.

Maze performance a function of motivation and of reward as well as of knowledge of the maze paths. *J. Gen. Psychol.*, 4 (1930), 338–342.

Book Review: *The Great Apes*, by Robert M. Yerkes and Ada W. Yerkes, *Amer. Anthropologist*, 32 (1930), 313–316.

Purposive Behavior in Animals and Men. New York: Century, 1932, xiv + 463 pp.

Lewin's concept of vectors. *J. Gen. Psychol.*, 7 (1932), 3–15.

(With C. S. Hall and E. P. Bretnall) A disproof of the law of effect and a substitution of the laws of emphasis, motivation, and disruption. *J. Exper. Psychol.*, 15 (1932), 601–614.

(With I. Krechevsky) Means-end-readiness and hypothesis. A contribution to comparative psychology. *Psychol. Rev.*, 40 (1933), 60–70.

Sign-gestalt or conditioned reflex? *Psychol. Rev.*, 40 (1933), 391–411.

(With J. Horowitz) A reply to Mr. Koffka. *Psychol. Bull.*, 30 (1933), 455–459.

The law of effect. A reply to Dr. Goodenough. *J. Exper. Psychol.*, 6 (1923), 463–470.

Backward elimination of errors in two successive discrimination habits. Univ. Calif. Publ. Psychol., 6 (1934), 145–152.

Theories of learning, *in* F. A. Moss, *Comparative Psychology*. New York: Prentice-Hall, 1934, pp. 367–408.

(With E. Brunswik) The organism and the causal texture of the environment. *Psychol. Rev.*, 42 (1935), 43–77.

Psychology vs. immediate experience. *Philos. Sci.*, 2 (1935), 356–380.

Book Review: *Wahrnehmung und Gegenstandswelt-Grundlegung einer Psychologie vom Gegenstand her*, by Egon Brunswik. *Psychol. Bull.*, 32 (1935), 608–613.

Connectionism; wants, interests, and attitudes. *Character and Personality*, 4 (1936), 245–253.

Operational behaviorism and current trends in psychology. *Proc. 25th Anniv. Inauguration Graduate Studies*. Los Angeles: University of Southern California, 1936, pp. 89–103.

(With C. H. Honzik) The perception of spatial relations by the rat: a type of response not easily explained by conditioning. *J. Comp. Psychol.*, 22 (1936), 287–318.

Demands and conflicts. *Psychol. Rev.*, 44 (1937), 158–169.

The acquisition of string-pulling by rats—conditioned response or sign-gestalt? *Psychol. Rev.*, 44 (1937), 195–211.

An operational analysis of "Demands." *Erkenntnis*, 6 (1937), 383–390.

The determiners of behavior at a choice point. *Psychol. Rev.*, 45 (1938), 1–41.

A reply to Professor Guthrie. *Psychol. Rev.*, 45 (1938), 163–164.

The law of effect. *Psychol. Rev.*, 45 (1938), 200–203.

Physiology, psychology, and sociology. *Psychol. Rev.*, 45 (1938), 228–241.

(With C. H. Honzik) The action of punishment in accelerating learning. *J. Comp. Psychol.*, 26 (1938), 187–200.

Prediction of vicarious trial and error by means of the schematic sowbug. *Psychol. Rev.*, 46 (1939), 318–336.

(With R. S. Crutchfield) Multiple-variable design for experiments involving interaction of behavior. *Psychol. Rev.*, 47 (1940), 38–42.

Spatial angle and vicarious trial and error. *J. Comp. Psychol.* 30 (1940), 129–135.

Psychological man. *J. Soc. Psychol.*, 13 (1941), 205–218.

(With F. M. Geier and M. Levin) *Individual differences in emotionality, hypothesis formation, vicarious trial and error, and visual discrimination learning in rats.* Comp. Psycol. Monog., 17, no. 3 (1941), 20 pp.

Motivation, learning, and adjustment. *Proc. Amer. Philos. Soc.*, 84 (1941), 543–563.

Discrimination vs. learning and the schematic sowbug. *Psychol. Rev.*, 48 (1941), 367–382.

Drives Toward War. New York: Appleton-Century, 1942, xv + 118 pp.

(With E. Minium) VTE in rats: Overlearning and difficulty of discrimination. *J. Comp. Psychol.*, 34 (1942), 301–306.

Identification and the post-war world. *J. Abnorm. & Soc. Psychol.*, 38

(With F. M. Geier) Goal distance and restless activity. I: The goal gradient of restless activity. *J. Comp. Psychol.*, 35 (1943), 197–204.

A drive-conversion diagram. *Psychol. Rev.*, 50 (1943), 503–513.

(With B. F. Ritchie) Correlation between VTE's on a maze and on a visual discrimination apparatus. *J. Comp. Psychol.* 36 (1943), 91–98.

A stimulus-expectancy need-cathexis psychology. *Science,* 101 (1945), 160–166.

(With B. F. Ritchie and D. Kalish) Studies in spatial learning. I: Orientation and the short-cut. *J. Exp. Psychol.*, 36 (1946), 13–25.

(With B. F. Ritchie and D. Kalish) Studies in spatial learning. II: Place learning versus response learning. *J. Exp. Psychol.*, 36 (1946), 221–229.

(With B. F. Ritchie and D. Kalish) Studies in spatial learning. IV: The transfer of place learning to other starting paths. *J. Exp. Psychol.*, 37 (1947), 39–47.

(With B. F. Ritchie and D. Kalish) Studies in spatial learning. V: Response learning vs. place learning by the non-correction method. *J. Exp. Psychol.*, 37 (1947), 285–292.

Kurt Lewin. *Psychol. Rev.*, 55 (1948), 1–4.

Cognitive maps in rats and men. *Psychol. Rev.*, 55 (1948), 189–208.

There is more than one kind of learning. *Psychol. Rev.*, 56 (1949), 144–155

Interrelationships between perception and personality: A symposium. Part I. Discussion. *J. Personality,* 18 (1949), 48–50.

(With Henry Gleitman) Studies in spatial learning. VII: Place and response learning under different degrees of motivation. *J. Exp. Psychol.*, 39 (1949), 653–659.

The nature and functioning of wants. *Psychol. Rev.*, 56 (1949), 357–369.

The psychology of social learning. *J. Social Issues,* Special issue (December, 1949), 5–18.

(With Henry Gleitman) Studies in learning and motivation. I: Equal reinforcements in both end-boxes, followed by shock in one end-box. *J. Exp. Psychol.*, 39 (1949), 810–819.